Hidden Hands

Hidden Hands

Working-Class Women and Victorian Social-Problem Fiction

Patricia E. Johnson

Ohio University Press
Athens

Ohio University Press, Athens, Ohio 45701

Printed in the United States of America

Ohio University Press books are printed on acid-free paper ∞ ™

09 08 07 06 05 04 03 02 01 5 4 3 2 1

Library of Congress Cataloging-in-Publication Data

Johnson, Patricia E., 1951-
Hidden Hands : working-class women and Victorian social-problem fiction / Patricia E. Johnson.
p. cm.
Includes bibliographical references (p.) and index.
ISBN 0-8214-1388-0 (cloth : alk. paper) — ISBN 0-8214-1389-9 (pbk. : alk. paper)
1. English fiction—19th century—History and criticism. 2. Working class women in literature. 3. Literature and society—Great Britain—History—19th century. 4. Women and literature—Great Britain—History—19th century. 5. Working class writings, English—History and criticism. 6. Social problems in literature. I. Title.

PR878.L3 J64 2001
823'.809352042—dc21

00-054534

In memory of my father, E. Orville Johnson,

and my brother, Jimmy Johnson,

and, always, for Dennis and Thomas

Contents

Acknowledgments

I am grateful to the Capital College Research Fund at Penn State Harrisburg, the Institute for Arts and Humanistic Study at Pennsylvania State University in University Park, and the National Endowment for the Humanities for travel grants which supported the research for this project. An NEH summer seminar and summer institute were also important formative experiences.

A number of friends and colleagues read parts of the manuscript at earlier stages and made helpful comments or offered ongoing support and advice. I want to say thank-you to Matthew Wilson, Margaret Rose Jaster, Marjan van Schaik, Tace Hedrick, Troy Thomas, Gordon Hirsch, Louise Yelin, Matthew Brennan, and Glen Mazis—with an additional thanks to Glen for revealing some of the mysteries of Word. Several anonymous readers of my manuscript made important suggestions that I have tried to make good use of. I would also like to thank William Mahar, director of the School of Humanities, for his support of my research.

I am especially grateful to Jane Kromm for her friendship and intellectual comradeship across the years and across the miles. My family has been generous with their enthusiasm and support, particularly my mother, Mary Finch Johnson; my sister, Rita Pardieck; and my father-in-law, Charles Dougherty. Finally, I want to thank Dennis Dougherty for his confidence in my work and companionship in my life: you and Tommy make it all worthwhile.

Hidden Hands

Introduction

THIS STUDY began with the consideration of an anomaly. The mid-Victorian fictions that Raymond Williams famously classified as "the industrial novels" often focus on women characters, yet none of the women whose lives those novels use as templates for industrial transformation ever works in—or even enters—a factory.[1] Victorian statistics make this anomaly even more striking. Working-class women fueled the Industrial Revolution, making up as much as 60 percent to 80 percent of the workforce in light industries such as cotton manufacturing. Yet their labor, and sometimes very existence, seems hidden in the industrial novels as well as in later Victorian social-problem fiction. The absence of women factory workers—placed alongside the emphasis on women—is the contradiction that this study focuses on, a contradiction that has its roots in the complex role of working-class women in Victorian ideology. I have chosen to use Williams's "industrial novels" as my core group of fictions, first of all, because they have largely set the terms of debate about social-problem fiction and industrial questions, and, second, because it was the relative absence of factory women in these novels that roused my initial interest. I have, however, expanded on Williams's list by including works by key women writers—such as Charlotte Elizabeth Tonna, Charlotte Brontë, and Frances Hodgson Burnett—who address the issue of working women, as well as some examples of the treatment of working-class women in late-nineteenth-century social-problem fiction.

Women's industrial labor was an explosive issue in the 1840s, and yet, despite that fact, female factory labor goes almost unmentioned in "the industrial novels." In earlier Victorian novels about industrialism, such as Frances Trollope's *Michael Armstrong, the Factory Boy* (1839) and Elizabeth Stone's *William Langshawe, the Cotton Lord* (1842), factory girls play significant supporting roles. Charlotte Elizabeth Tonna's *Helen Fleetwood* (1839–41) even centers on the experiences of female factory workers. By 1845, however, when "the industrial novel" proper appears, the female factory worker is relegated to the margins.[2] Factory girls are minor characters in Benjamin Disraeli's *Sybil, or The Two Nations* (1845), but the title character, whose father is a factory overseer and Chartist leader and who refers to herself as "a daughter of the people," turns out to be a dispossessed aristocrat. Mill girls appear on the streets in Elizabeth Gaskell's *Mary Barton* (1848), but the heroine is apprenticed to a milliner, because her factory-worker father disapproves of mill work for women. In Charlotte Brontë's *Shirley* (1849), the girls who make up most of the workforce in Robert Moore's mill are never directly represented and are mentioned only twice in passing. Charles Kingsley's *Alton Locke, Tailor and Poet: An Autobiography* (1850) separates himself from his working-class mother and sister and is attracted only to upper-class women. In *Hard Times* (1854), Charles Dickens deleted the story of a factory girl who dies after being injured by a machine before he published the novel, and Elizabeth Gaskell's *North and South* (1854–55) presents Bessy Higgins, a former factory girl who is dying of lung disease. By the time of George Eliot's *Felix Holt, the Radical* (1866), not only has the female factory worker disappeared but working-class women themselves are rendered nearly invisible. The trajectory of these representations suggests a crisis in the early 1840s which made women's industrial labor at once a hot topic and yet almost impossible to address directly. The ambivalence about working-class women in these novels also lays the groundwork for their representation in later Victorian social-problem fiction with its continuing pattern of repression of and return to working-class women and their labor.

Critics, also, have been relatively silent about the ways in which female factory workers are represented in these novels. I argue that, because Victorian social-problem fiction has been read in relation to, on the one hand, a working-class history traditionally defined by male-dominated strikes and the movement for universal male suffrage, or, on the other hand, to a women's movement conceived primarily in middle-class terms, the crucial role of working-class women has remained obscure. Drawing on the recent work of feminist historians, as well as original historical research, I reframe the novels by describing the complex role of working-class women—as workers, political activists, and symbols—in factory reform legislation and working-class and feminist political movements. This new context provides the groundwork for a reinterpretation of social-problem fiction that examines its treatment of the issues that particularly affected working-class women. For what is remarkable in Victorian literature is not just the repression of working-class women and the labor they perform but also their return. Although the processes by which these women are marginalized or erased are important, equally revealing are the traces that they leave behind them and the corresponding displacement of the issues that affect them on to other, more manageable female characters. The novels do foreground women, often working-class women, and through them they indirectly struggle with the troubling issues that the female laborer raises. Therefore, it is not just the avoidance of working-class women that this study examines but also social-problem fiction's continual drive to come to grips with the forces that made them so dangerous. This leads them, although by a circuitous path, to take on a variety of charged issues—ranging from sexual harassment in the workplace and on public streets; to women's inevitable involvement in the politics of such movements as Luddism, Chartism, and unionism; and from a religious millenarian rhetoric that expressed desires for sexual—as well as class—equality; to the violence that shadowed the attempts to enforce working-class women's domesticity.

My starting point for understanding the contradictions at the base of representations of working-class women is the figure of the factory girl. Critics have often dismissed or overlooked this figure's importance. On the one hand, she is seen as merely sentimental, a pathetic victim, who becomes politically significant only if she inspires male action.[3] On the other hand, images of degraded factory women are part of a larger pattern that uses monstrous, sexualized working-class women as emblems of ultimate social chaos.[4] But, as Cora Kaplan points out, representations of working-class women are far from univocal; in fact, they are "peculiarly incoherent and contradictory."[5] It is that incoherence and the contradictions it exposes that this study aims to elucidate. The economic and sexual independence of the factory women made them doubly threatening. Politically, too, the image of working women was disruptive. As historian Sonya O. Rose argues, "Public oratory which made men central and women peripheral to the workplace portrayed working women as on the sidelines of working-class politics. But, ironically, the marginalization of women and its consequences were at the very heart of those politics."[6] In the 1840s, Tory paternalists, middle-class moralists, and working-class Chartists joined ranks in arguing that working-class women should be returned to the home. This return was imagined as a panacea for a variety of problems ranging from working-class gender conflict to economic hardship, which middle-class moralists claimed could be resolved by the working-class woman's skillful management of household resources. The middle class also envisioned a domesticated working-class woman as a way of pacifying working-class men, keeping them at home and away from drink and politics. The triumph of domestic ideology and the repression of working-class women's public roles in the 1850s are reflected in *Hard Times* which has chapter titles such as "Masters and Men" to describe the relations between mill owners and workers and "Men and Brothers" to describe the union movement. Similarly, Gaskell's *North and South* repeatedly uses the phrase "masters and men" to describe industrial class relations. How long this erasure of working-class women lasted is indicated by a 1981 historical study of the Preston Strike of 1853–54—a strike which influenced both Dickens and Gaskell. The study describes the all-male strike leadership in detail and frequently employs the phrase "masters and men" to describe class relations. Yet tucked into the study is this revealing statistic: of the 18,000 workers who struck in Preston, 11,800 were women and girls.[7]

My title—*Hidden Hands*—underlines the ways in which class and gender have combined to obscure the role of working-class women in the transformative processes that have produced the modern industrial state. The tendency of Victorian factory owners to refer to their workers as "hands" was often criticized by writers such as Dickens and Gaskell as dehumanizing. In the 1840s and 1850s, working-class men transformed themselves from disembodied hands into political and economic actors. But the designation "working men," of course, also repressed the actual gendered makeup of the factory workforce. Thus, women remained invisible and disembodied sources of cheap labor. Classic *laissez faire* economic theorists from Adam Smith onward have posited an "invisible hand," a godlike, abstract force that regulates markets and orders the distribution of wealth for the general good. My study focuses on the ignored underside of this image: the hidden hands of thousands of working-class women, whose forgotten, poorly paid labor created some of the surplus wealth which made the achievements of the Industrial Revolution possible.

Dangerous Figures

Although female factory workers are marginalized in Victorian novels, other figures associated with social disruption, notably prostitutes and male radicals, abound. There is often a blurring of the lines between prostitutes and working-class women involved in nondomestic kinds of labor. Any woman working outside the home, especially in a mixed-sex workplace, was in danger of being classified as a prostitute. Such studies as James Kay Shuttleworth's *The Moral and Physical Condition of the Working Class Employed in the Cotton Manufacture in Manchester* (1832) and Peter Gaskell's *The Manufacturing Population of England: Its Moral, Social, and Physical Conditions, and the Changes Which Have Arisen from the Use of Steam Machinery* (1833) are typical in their obsession with working-class women's sexual morality and in their claims that factory girls were sexually precocious and the factories hotbeds of promiscuity.[8] Prostitution is the famous "social evil" of the Victorian period; and, therefore, it is particularly striking that it becomes more acceptable for Victorian literature to present the working-class woman as a prostitute, as in the case of Esther Barton, than it is to represent a woman actively engaged in factory work. The reasons behind this substitution are manifold. The prostitute both stands in for the factory worker and avoids the contradictions that she makes so apparent. Although the figure of the prostitute can be used to represent the threats of social chaos and class conflict, it can also be managed through eroticization and sentimentalization.[9] In addition, the prostitute is symbolically cordoned off from other women, and she does not threaten male dominance. Female factory workers, by contrast, draw the reader's attention to the very problems that the prostitute obscures: class and gender conflict, systemic economic exploitation, and the irresolvable contradictions at the base of domestic ideology. And, to make her even more frightening, the factory worker still contains the threat of working-class female sexuality, made even more dangerous because it is associated with an unfeminine economic independence.

Similarly, although critics, following Raymond Williams, quite rightly stress that the industrial novels are fueled by a fear of revolution,[10] the novels can still represent and even sympathize with such working-class radicals as Walter Gerard, John Barton, Alton Locke, and Felix Holt. This, despite the fact that all these men not only engage in working-class politics but also in violence of some kind: each of them participates in a riot and/or actually kills someone as a result of his political beliefs. Their acts of violence are condemned or punished in some way, but these characters' concerns about their class are treated with respect. As men, they assert a right to political action, which the novels recognize as basic to masculinity, even if their actions are represented as misguided. Not incidentally, each of these radicals espouses conservative sexual politics. Walter Gerard is typical, opining that the most damaging aspect of industrialization is that "[t]he domestic principle waxes weaker and weaker every year in England" and, as a result, the working class live like animals.[11] Such statements suggest that the right of working-class men to be politically active is intertwined with their ability to domesticate their women.

Thus, the representation of working-class women engaged in factory labor becomes more subversive of mid-Victorian values and more dangerous to class and gender ideologies than either the representation of prostitution or working-class male radicalism. In *Nobody's Angels: Middle-Class Women and Domestic Ideology in Victorian Culture,* Elizabeth Langland points out that, during this same time period, the plot of the working-class heroine who marries her master also disappears from the novel, a disappearance that I see as directly related to the larger problems of representing working-class women that I am discussing. Langland postulates that certain plots become "non-narratable" at particular historical moments because plots are always "informed by a culture's ideologies, its assessment of value and meaning and possibility."[12] In the working-class woman the categories of gender and class, always in contention in Victorian England, take on a particularly charged relationship because she underscores the contradictions at the base of their formation. During the first half of the nineteenth century, the increasing dominance of men in working-class movements and the construction of the ideal of "the male breadwinner" meant that to be fully working class was to be male. At the same time, the rise of domestic ideology meant that a true woman adhered to a middle-class standard that was impossible for the working class to achieve. In a sense, the very concept of "the working-class woman" became an oxymoron, a contradiction in terms. What made the representation of working-class women so difficult was the ideological burden they came to bear. By the mid-1840s, the Tory reformer Lord Ashley, upper- and middle-class women, working-class men, and even many middle-class factory owners had come to agree that working-class women must be returned to the domestic sphere. This consensus was unusually powerful because it represented the common ground for so many important constituencies. On the other hand, it was also extremely fragile and rife with contradictions. To narrate the life of a working-class woman was to come dangerously close to destroying that consensus and exposing the contradictions that it hid. In fact, domestic ideology rested on the exploitation of the working-class woman, both working double shifts in working-class homes and working for low pay as domestic servants in middle- and upper-class homes. To represent her life was to confront the cost of enforced domesticity as well as the many exceptions to the ideal of the working-class male breadwinner who could support a separate sphere for his women: the men who did not make enough money or were seasonably employed or unemployed, the men who were sick or alcoholic or who deserted their families, the unmarried women, and the widows. Such "exceptions" were the rule, pointing out that the male breadwinner remained a fiction for most of the working class. To narrate the life of a working-class woman meant describing the hard labor she was made to perform, the money she earned in full-time or part-time labor, and the strength and independence that these tasks demanded, all elements which conflicted with the Victorian view of "the feminine."

Theorizing Gender and Class

On the surface, it would seem that, even if novelists wished to emphasize the importance of keeping working-class women confined to the domestic sphere, novels could still represent a girl or woman who worked in the factory to the detriment of herself and her family and then saw the error of her ways. What are readers to make of the disparity between a Victorian factory workforce that was heavily female and a Victorian industrial novel that cannot represent a female factory worker? What does it mean that such a story becomes non-narratable while women factory workers, if they appear at all, appear only in the margins? In *A Theory of Literary Production,* Pierre Macherey argues for the significance of what is not said and of what is placed in the margins, noting that "what begs to be explained in the work is not that false simplicity which derives from the apparent unity of its meaning, but the presence of a relation, or an opposition, between elements of the exposition or levels of the composition, those disparities which point to a conflict of meaning. This conflict is not the sign of an imperfection; it reveals the inscription of an *otherness* in the work, through which it maintains a relationship with that which it is not, that which happens at its margins." It is in a novel's margins that we read both the unconscious of the work and its relation to history: "Thus, it is not a question of introducing a historical explanation which is stuck on to the work from the outside. On the contrary, we must show a sort of splitting within the work: this division is *its* unconscious, in so far as it possesses one—the unconscious which is history, the play of history beyond its edges, encroaching on those edges: this is why it is possible to trace the path which leads from the haunted work to that which haunts it."[13] Applying Macherey's concepts to this literature, it becomes clear that the figure of the female factory worker haunts the industrial novels, just as the specter of her descendants troubles later Victorian social-problem fiction. Her constant repression and return are crucial to an understanding of their focus on women and their fascination with the interrelationships between gender and class.

Class relations and gender relations are each, in themselves, complex fields of study. When we try to understand them in relation to one another, the complications are more than doubled. Yet this is one place where representations of working-class women can be particularly revealing, because they make manifest the contradictions in and between class and gender ideologies. That is, they both demonstrate the masculine bias in the construct of the Victorian working class and the middle-class bias in its construct of femininity. Further, it is important to remember that class and gender positions are neither static nor isolated. Class and gender are composed dynamically and dialogically; they can only be understood in relation to one another: middle class is constructed in relation to working class, masculine in relation to feminine. In order to visualize such complex relationships, it might help to map them on to A. J. Greimas's semiotic rectangle:[14]

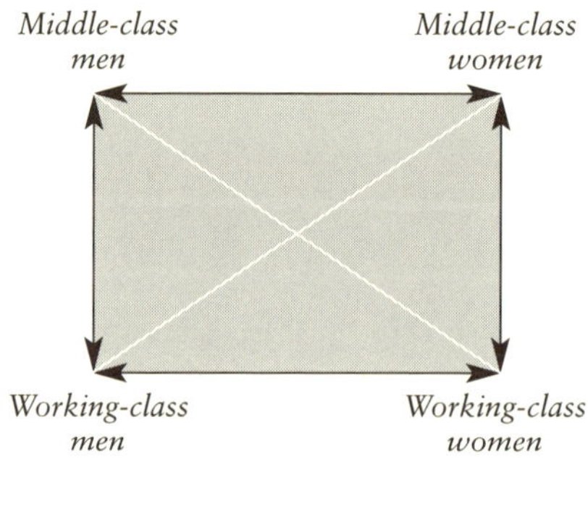

Here the rectangle represents the nodal points implicit in the Victorian ideological system of gender and class relations. The texts I will be examining play out every variation and combination of these positions. As Fredric Jameson argues in *The Political Unconscious: Narrative as a Socially Symbolic Act,* they seek "desperately to transcend" the inherent contradictions of the system, generating more contradictions of their own in the process of moving through "all the syntheses logically available," as well as repressions, sublimations, and displacements.[15] So, as we shall see, Victorian social-problem fiction works through a series of configurations —middle-class, working-class, men, women—playing with every possible combination of these terms in its attempt to come to terms with the dynamics of class and gender relations.

Working-Class Women and History

My readings of these literary representations would not be possible without the work of feminist historians. Their research not only describes the conditions of working-class women's lives but also argues for their importance even to issues that have traditionally seemed to exclude them, such as politics and economics. As Joan Wallach Scott claims, "The realization of the radical potential of women's history comes in the writing of histories that focus on women's experiences *and* analyze the ways in which politics construct gender and gender constructs politics. Feminist history then becomes not the recounting of great deeds performed by women but the exposure of the often silent and hidden operations of gender that are nonetheless present and defining forces in the organization of most societies."[16] The history of industrialization and of working-class politics alters significantly when viewed through a feminist lens. Sonya Rose comments, "Gender . . . was implicit in working men's struggles even when women were not directly involved."[17] Yet male dominance was not a foregone conclusion. Barbara Taylor's *Eve and the New Jerusalem: Socialism and Feminism in the Nineteenth Century,* which provides the foundation for my argument that religious rhetoric is particularly significant for working-class women, demonstrates that early-nineteenth-century movements such as Owenism were receptive to a radical rethinking of gender roles, while millenarian religious sects, such as Southcottianism, both featured women in prominent leadership roles and employed a language of aspiration that reflected hopes for gender equality. By the 1830s, however, the suffrage and union movements were becoming more and more male dominated. While in the 1830s Chartism debated the idea of "universal suffrage" and political equality for men and women, in 1842 the Chartists decided to exclude women and call for "universal manhood suffrage." As Scott argues, after "a moment of flux and experimentation," "[t]he version of class that Chartists espoused affirmed a working-class family structure resembling middle-class ideals and susceptible to middle-class pressures: a family organization that no later radical theories of economics managed entirely to displace."[18] Similarly, as its title suggests, Anna Clark's *The Struggle for the Breeches: Gender and the Making of the British Working Class* describes the struggles over the definitions of masculinity and femininity that were central to the political formation of the nineteenth-century working class. She demonstrates that working-class political and union movements made a series of choices to abandon gender equality for male dominance, and she uncovers evidence of ongoing gender conflict, as well as a significant strain of misogyny, in popular plebian culture.

In the 1830s and 1840s, the woman worker was also at the center of parliamentary debate. In 1842 the publication of a blue book by the Children's Employment Commission on Mines caused an uproar due to its revelations about the conditions of women's work. Following a debate that one minister remembered as the most emotional that had ever taken place in the House of Commons, Parliament voted to exclude women from underground work in the mines and to classify women with children as a protected group.[19] In 1847 Parliament passed further protective legislation, voting to limit the daily hours of factory work for women and children. These votes are significant in contradictory ways. On the one hand, they represent a crucial break with *laissez faire* economic doctrine, preparing the way for legislation that would address the working conditions of men as well as women. Such unlikely allies as Lord Ashley and the unions fanned the flames of gender anxiety and forced Parliament to pass legislation for working-class women that would, then, benefit working-class men, either because it eliminated women's competition for jobs or because such reforms as shortened work hours would automatically be extended to them.[20] On the other hand, by classifying women with children, Parliament and the unions effectively silenced working-class women, indicating that women were to be represented by men and "protected" as they saw fit, rather than allowed a political voice of their own.[21]

Dorothy Thompson states, "Working-class women seem to have retreated into the home at some time around, or a little before, the middle of the century."[22] This symbolic truth, however, is contradicted by statistics that demonstrate that women constituted a growing percentage of the factory workforce.[23] But, because of the triumph of domestic ideology, by the 1850s working-class women largely disappear as topics of political discourse, and there is a corresponding repression of their ongoing dominance in the factory workforce. Although one might see this silence as strictly a Victorian problem, it has had continuing effects. Until recently, historians erased women's contribution to industrialization, and working-class and socialist movements excluded women's issues from serious consideration. Barbara Taylor describes the resultant fracturing of radical politics:

> As the utopian imagination [of early working-class movements] faded, so also did the commitment to a new sexual order. As the older schemes for emancipating "all humanity at once" were displaced by the economic struggles of a single class, so issues central to that earlier dream—marriage, reproduction, family life—were transformed from political questions into "merely private" ones, while women who persisted in pressing such issues were frequently condemned as bourgeois "women's rightsers." Organized feminism was increasingly viewed not as an essential component of the socialist struggle, but as a disunifying, diversionary force, with no inherent connection to the socialist tradition. And thus the present disowns the past, severing connections and suppressing ambitions once so vital to those who forged them.[24]

This divorce of class and gender issues will affect working-class and women's movements not only in the nineteenth but also in the twentieth century. This study positions itself as part of a larger effort by literary scholars and historians to recover these obscured stories and interpret the ways in which gender and class relate to one another.

Uncovering Hidden Hands

I begin in Part One, "Industrial Fictions," with the social and literary ramifications of early Victorian debates over women's industrial work. Chapter 1, "The Death of the Factory Girl," traces this figure's troubled history. Before the mid-1840s, novels—most revealingly, Tonna's *Helen Fleetwood*—provided detailed descriptions of the lives of factory girls. After the early 1840s, however, factory girls almost disappear from "the industrial novels." I argue that the public uproar over the 1842 parliamentary blue book on the mines, which included woodprint illustrations of women at work, was the turning point in this development because it revealed the woman worker's threat to Victorian ideologies of gender and class and resulted in her repression: in response to the report, Parliament voted to forbid women's work in mines and, for the first time, to classify women with children as a protected group, incapable of self-determination. The impact of this political event is seen in Disraeli's *Sybil* and Gaskell's *Mary Barton* where the working-class heroine is recast as a nonworker or in a more feminine occupation such as millinery. Charles Kingsley's *Alton Locke* demonstrates the connection between the erasure of working-class women and the confirmation of working-class men as political subjects, the spokesmen for their class. In the 1850s and 1860s, Gaskell's *North and South,* Dickens's *Hard Times,* and Eliot's *Felix Holt* both resurrect factory girls and working women and kill them off or mutilate them, revealing the power of domestic ideology and the ways in which working-class women continue to disrupt its compromises.

Chapter 2, "Naming the Unnameable: Sexual Harassment and Working-Class Women in Novels of Industry," examines some key responses to the sexualized images of working women that emerged from parliamentary blue books and relates them to the issue of sexual harassment. Contradictory ideologies of class and gender made it particularly difficult for working-class women to articulate their experiences of sexual harassment. They were caught in a vise between a middle-class view of working-class women, especially those employed in certain kinds of work, as *de facto* prostitutes and the harassment of working-class men who sought to keep women in occupationally segregated jobs, if not eliminate them from the workplace altogether. Nevertheless, this chapter argues that sexual harassment and its relationship to the working-class heroine's right to self-determination become central features in three novels of the 1840s. It is most remarkable in *Helen Fleetwood* whose title character works in a factory where sexual harassment is a condition of employment, and Helen's articulated resistance to harassment exposes Victorian society's hypocritical attitudes toward working-class women. Later novels present images of harassment which are more occluded by class and gender ideologies. This is particularly true of Disraeli's *Sybil* which portrays harassment as widespread but resolves the problem by scapegoating working-class men and consigning its heroine to lifelong aristocratic protection. Gaskell's *Mary Barton* addresses the class and gender myths that obscure the issue by rewriting the popular working-class melodrama of working girl beset by upper-class seducer in order to create a heroine who is seen as the agent of her own rescue.

The book's second section, "Women, Class, and Politics," considers the complex interplay of gender and class issues in Disraeli's *Sybil* and Brontë's *Shirley,* two novels that both describe working-class political movements and take women's political involvement seriously. "Two Nations: Women and Politics in *Sybil*" examines all categories of women in the novel and relates their roles to the rhetoric of the factory debate of the 1840s in which Lord Ashley and other politicians used the concept of "Woman" as a transclass category, thus converting her into a political symbol. Through specifically classed characters such as factory girls and aristocratic political hostesses, Disraeli suggests that women are politically interested and influence the political process in significant ways. But what he gives with one hand, he takes with the other. Sybil, the central female character who describes herself as "a daughter of the people," mystifies that influence: she is the "Woman" of Ashley's rhetoric. Her otherworldliness removes her from political interest at the same time that it transforms her into a useful symbol of political authority which male politicians compete to possess and manipulate.

"Hidden Connections/Missing Links: Luddism and Feminism in *Shirley*" considers why *Shirley* is able to posit a potentially revolutionary connection between the position of women and the position of the working class but also looks at why it is unable to imagine a way to develop that connection. One of the novel's two middle-class heroines, Caroline Helstone, parallels herself to the Luddites who have just attacked a cotton mill. The second, Shirley Keeldar, has millenarian visions which link her to the Luddite assassin Michael Hartley. Although female factory workers are not directly represented, women's work in the form of housework is emphasized by the novel's continual references to servants. But, I argue, the novel's search for connections between the working class and women falters because, on the one hand, the male-dominated Luddite movement ignores the importance of women's issues and even directs its strikes against women's factory work while, on the other hand, unaddressed class issues trouble the novel's feminist visions.

Part Three, "Class Relations," focuses on how the industrial novels lay the basis for ongoing patterns in the representation of working-class women. Chapter 5, "Domesticating Violence: Hard Times for Working-Class Women," discusses the link forged between domestic violence and class in later Victorian literature. As working-class women largely disappear from political discussion after 1850, *Hard Times* reveals the cost of enforced domesticity—as well as the political and ideological reasons behind it—through its many subtle images of domestic violence. *Hard Times,* unlike other industrial novels, presents no strikes or riots; instead, it displaces violence on to the working-class household where women both receive and manage it. *Hard Times* thus suggests that the ultimate social task of the working-class woman is to contain violence within the home so that it will not infect the political or economic spheres. Later fictions—such as Frances Hodgson Burnett's *That Lass O' Lowries* (1877), George Gissing's *The Nether World* (1889), and Rudyard Kipling's "The Record of Badalia Herodsfoot" (1892)—seal the bond between domestic violence and working-class women by representing it as endemic to their lives and evaluating women by the variety of ways in which they adapt to such an environment.

My epilogue is both a conclusion and a beginning, looking back at Victorian social-problem fiction through the lens of the last industrial novel, Eliot's *Felix Holt,* and forward to the developing tradition of working-class women's writing in the twentieth century. Written on the eve of both the Second Reform Bill and the start of the women's movement in England, *Felix Holt* seems to lay disruptive working-class women to rest by subsuming them under the general category of "women." The troubling questions that they had once raised—work for women and rebellion against the traditional limits put on women's lives—are now represented by upper-class women such as Mrs. Transome. In the twentieth century, voices that had been largely silenced in the nineteenth begin to emerge, and working-class women speak for themselves. I examine the autobiographies of working-class women, such as Ellen Johnston, "the Factory Girl" poet; the suffragist Annie Kenney; and London dressmaker Kathleen Woodward, who discuss their working lives and, while doing so, appropriate images of working-class women from Victorian social-problem fiction and use them for their own purposes.

In *Uneven Developments: The Ideological Work of Gender in Mid-Victorian England,* Mary Poovey describes both the importance and instability of gender as an organizing force in Victorian society and concludes by calling on critics to examine the changing relations between class, race, and gender in order to construct "a history of ideological formulations that might help us understand the impetus behind and resistance to change in ways our old histories have failed to do."[25] Building on her work, and that of many other feminist and Marxist literary critics and historians, I intend here to contribute to that new history. Looking at Victorian social-problem fiction through its representations of working-class women effects a striking reversal. These hidden workers are revealed as centrally important: their factory labor enabled industrialism, their work as servants lay at the basis of domestic ideology, and their exclusion from politics underlay the construction of the male worker as respectable breadwinner and head of household. Not only did working-class women provide the foundation for these developments, but questions of women's right to self-determination, political involvement, and work outside the home gradually spread upward to affect all women, and only when middle-class women began to address these issues did the feminist movement start to exert force in England. Thus, representations of working-class women—and the contradictions in and between class and gender formulations that they expose—become openings through which history pours.

Examining the margins of this literature has helped me to understand more fully what is at its center. The texts avoid addressing the challenge of working women's lives directly, but they undergird the questions the novels pose about women and politics, women and work, and women and domestic ideology. Although these works put working-class women through a series of transformations, they always remain a crucial and disruptive factor, their very existence threatening to expose the dominant—and, in the case of the working class and middle-class feminism, still emergent—ideologies of class and gender. These works re-present and reinforce those ideologies, but what most fascinates me about them are their extraordinary moments of disruption and resistance. At the very least, they demonstrate the ongoing costs to working-class women of middle-class and male hegemony. At their most incisive, they bring together a confluence of factors—working class, middle class, male, female—in such ways as to reveal their problematic impact on social, economic, and political life—an impact that, at the beginning of the twenty-first century, we are still struggling to understand.

PART ONE

Industrial Fictions

Chapter 1

The Death of the Factory Girl

[A]ny sight more disgustingly indecent or revolting can scarcely be imagined than these girls at work. No brothel can beat it.

—Commissioner Symons, *Mining Report*, 1842

On May 7, 1842, 2,000 copies of the first report of the Children's Employment Commission on the conditions of work in collieries and mines appeared in print. The printing of this blue book set off a firestorm in both Parliament and the press, eventually resulting in the first break with *laissez faire* economic policy and the regulation of adult labor. It also formed a moment of crisis in the representation of working-class women, because, despite the fact that the commission was specifically delegated to investigate children's work in the mines, it was the work of women and girls that became its central topic. The report and the response that it evoked are the most extreme examples of the explosive debate that raged around women and industrial labor in the first half of the nineteenth century. Victorian ideas of what a woman's role should be came into direct conflict with the experience of working-class women, highlighting contradictions that the Victorians were not prepared to confront.

At the instigation of Lord Ashley, the Children's Employment Commission had been instituted in 1840 to investigate the conditions of children's work in a number of industries. But the twenty commissioners who entered the mines extended and redefined their investigation because they were so shocked by the discovery of the nature of women's work. To emphasize their responses, for the first time the parliamentary blue book they produced included pictorial illustrations in the form of wood engravings—illustrations particularly focused on the areas where women were employed in the greatest numbers.[1] The blue book documented brutal working conditions, describing children towing coal cars up steep declines and men working naked in tiny shafts. It pictured women, dressed in trousers and stripped to the waist, dragging coal cars with chains between their legs. The blue book's illustrations were quickly reproduced and exaggerated in the popular press, creating the first notable example of social reportage in which illustrations were emphasized.[2] And it was, in particular, the images of working-class women that attracted the most attention and provoked the most intense response. *Bell's Penny Sunday Chronicle,* like several of the new illustrated papers, ran a month-long series of front-page illustrations from May 15 to June 12, 1842. Under the banner headline "Murder of the Working Classes," its first edition featured the most controversial images of women and girls at work: one figure showed a young girl, stripped to the waist, hauling coal through a twenty-inch passage; another showed a woman drawing a boy and girl up from a mine while they were seated cross-lapped on an iron chain.

The interpretations of the parliamentary commissioners set the tone for much of the ensuing debate. Although poor wages and dangerous working conditions received concerned but measured commentary, the images of working-class women set the commissioners on fire. Commissioner Symons wrote: "One of the most disgusting sights I have ever seen was that of young females, dressed like boys in trousers, crawling on all fours, with belts around their waists, and chains passing between their legs. . . . The chain, passing high up between the legs of these girls, had worn large holes in their trousers, and any sight more disgustingly indecent or revolting can scarcely be imagined than these girls at work. No brothel can beat it."[3] Seeming at once to disgust and excite, contradictorily to erase the signs of femininity and yet to be sexually emphatic, representations of women at work were read as emblems of sexual license and gender anarchy. (See fig. 1.) The commissioners frequently asked the workmen about the women's morals and whether they made good wives or not, and numbers of workmen claimed that sex in the coal seams was a frequent occurrence and that the women lacked all proper domestic training. Foreseeing the spread of social chaos from such undisciplined women, Commissioner Kennedy lamented that the state of the women's morals and their lack of domestic skills would result in "the growth of an ignorant, depraved, and dangerous population."[4]

Fig. 1 Woman coalminer. Article on the *First Report of the Children's Employment Commissioners: Mines and Collieries. Westminster Review* 38 (1842), 123. Reprinted by permission of the Bodleian Library, University of Oxford.

As with the illustrations, these sentiments were echoed by and amplified in the popular press. Commenting on the illustrations, *Bell's Penny Sunday Chronicle* urged its readers to "look at figure 1, and ask yourself, how *you* would feel were *your* daughter made to toil for twelve hours daily, with a chain rubbing that particular part of her person? And we are English! And we are a gallant people! . . . And now turn to figure 2, a naked man and woman *cross-lapped!* Let the reader carefully study the *positions* of these two figures." (See fig. 2.) Like the commissioners, the *Chronicle* interpreted the women's work as a form of the most reprehensible sexual misconduct, promising to try to "rescue, in future times, myriads of English children from being tortured, and myriads of English women from being exposed, in a manner which, at present, makes a *MINE* several degrees less decent than a *BROTHEL!*"[5] The same notes were struck in a wide variety of other publications. *The Illustrated London News* described the women's work as "unholy prostitution."[6] The Chartist *Northern Star* attacked the "unsexing employment" and urged: "Keep [the women] at home to look after their families; decrease the pressure on the labour market and there is then some chance of a higher rate of wages being enforced."[7] The *Edinburgh Review* claimed that "[t]his general want of the qualifications of a housewife in the women of this class, is stated by clergymen, teachers, medical men, employers, witnesses, and all others, in all the districts, to be one great and universally prevailing cause of poverty and crime among the working classes."[8]

The intensity of the response to the publication of the blue book was followed by an equally intense repression. Rather than addressing the very real problems in the working conditions that the report revealed, there was merely an attempt to abolish the image of women at work. On June 7, 1842, Ashley introduced the Mines and Collieries Bill in an impassioned two-hour speech to the House of Commons. His first request was the total exclusion of female workers from the mines. The support was tremendous and cut across party lines. The coal owners in the House of Lords, led by Lord Londonderry, forced the age of boys allowed to work in the pits to be lowered from twelve to nine, but the exclusion of women emerged intact. Ashley admitted that he was "disposed to sacrifice the children in order to save the women."[9] Total exclusion of women from the pits became the first clause of the Mines and Collieries Bill; it passed on August 10, 1842; all females had to leave underground work in six months.

Again, public response was passionate, creating intense images of those involved. In *Bentley's Miscellany*, for example, Edward Kenealy's poem, "Lines on the Lord Ashley's Motion," celebrated Ashley's eloquence and his "god-like task" while lamenting English girlhood as "[w]ork'd to deformity, crippl'd, debased. . . . Those gentle feelings (jewels of the sex)/Corrupted all, and turn'd to criminal deeds/That blush to see the light" and English womanhood as "labour[ing] naked among naked men. . . . Rivalling man in blasphemy and crime."[10] The mining

"The sketch here given is intended to represent Ann Ambler and William Dyson, hurriers in Messrs Ditchforth and Clay's colliery at Elland, in the act of being drawn up cross-lapped upon the clatch-iron by a woman. As soon as they arrived at the top the handle was made fast by a bolt drawn from the upright post; the woman then grasped a hand of both at the same time, and by main force brought them to land. The corve on these occasions is detached from the hooks to render the load lighter."*

* S. S. Scriven, Esq., Report, § 26: App. pt. ii, p. 61.

Fig. 2. Drawing up from the mines. Article on the *First Report of the Children's Employment Commissioners: Mines and Collieries. Westminster Review* 38 (1842), 105. Reprinted by permission of the Bodleian Library, University of Oxford.

women had reported to the commissioners that their work was hard—many disliked it—but in the absence of other jobs, they had no choice. Many were widows or supporting disabled husbands and a family. The response was to exclude their labor with no compensation, no retraining, and no help in finding other employment. Those women who could not find other employment continued to work illegally in the mines for even poorer pay and under worse conditions. Thus, the problem of women at work was apparently disposed of, but the poverty and working conditions that led to it were perpetuated and even increased.[11] Although women in the mines constituted only a tiny fraction of working women and the conditions they worked under were extreme, what happened to them was simply the most intense instance of a wider pattern. The entire drama that unfolded—from the revelation of the nature of the women's work, to the sexualized responses to it, to the attempt to destroy the problem by simply forbidding female labor—has ongoing repercussions for the representation of working-class women in all areas.

Similar accusations had already been leveled against women and girls who worked in factories. There were, of course, significant differences between women's factory labor versus the conditions in the mines. Working conditions were not nearly as harsh, and the pay was good, relative to other jobs open to women. In fact, it could be—and was—argued that factory labor was better than most other jobs that were considered acceptable women's work, such as millinery or domestic service. Nonetheless, work outside the home in a mixed-sex workplace set off alarms and provoked the same kinds of fears and fantasies about working-class women that the images of mining women had. Peter Gaskell's 1833 study, *The Manufacturing Population of England: Its Moral, Social, and Physical Conditions, and the Changes Which Have Arisen from the Use of Steam Machinery*, imagined factories as hotbeds of vice, much in the same way that Symons had imagined the mines as brothels. Gaskell argued, "The crowding together members of the young of both sexes in factories, is a prolific source of moral delinquency. The stimulus of a heated atmosphere, the contact of opposite sexes, the example of lasciviousness upon the animal passions—all have conspired to produce a very early development of sexual appetencies. Indeed, in this respect, the female population engaged in manufactures approximates very closely to that found in tropical climates; puberty, or at least sexual propensities, being attained almost coeval with girlhood."[12] Throughout the century, parliamentary blue books repeatedly claimed that factory girls were immoral. The 1833 Royal Commission on the Employment of Children in Factories, for example, quotes one witness as stating that "it would be no strain on his conscience to say that three-quarters of the girls between fourteen and twenty years of age were unchaste." In an 1863 report a factory commissioner argued that "female labour in factories, even though it be necessary, is at variance with domestic teaching, and that, for the sake of the wages it brings, everything that is good and holy in the female character is often sacrificed."[13]

The 1842 Mining and Collieries Bill, having broken the bar of legislating the work of adult women, was followed by the Ten Hours Bill, also introduced by Lord Ashley, which shortened the working hours of women and children in the factories. In the 1844 debate over its passage, he continued his rhetorical attack on "the appalling progress of female labour," drawing a graphic picture of a world turned upside down where "the females not only perform the labour, but occupy the places of men; they are forming various clubs and associations, and gradually acquiring all those privileges which are held to be the proper portion of the male sex." He foresaw social chaos as the result of these developments, declaiming, "But every consideration sinks to nothing compared with that which springs from the contemplation of the moral mischiefs this system engenders and sustains. You are poisoning the very sources of order and happiness and virtue; you are tearing up root and branch, all the relations of families to each other; you are annulling, as it were, the institution of domestic life, decreed by Providence himself, the wisest and kindest of earthly ordinances, the mainstay of social peace and virtue, and therein of national security."[14] Ashley's rhetoric once again stirred Parliament to action: after his speech, the Ten Hours Bill was passed, only to be revoked two nights later. The bill was finally enacted in 1847. Even then Ashley pressed on, and following his lead, numerous politicians, both conservatives and Chartists, argued that it would be best to abolish women's factory work altogether, not merely limit their hours, although the sheer number of female factory workers made this impossible.

Not all Victorian commentators viewed the issue as divided between unimpeded *laissez faire* economics, on the one side, and the abolition of female labor, on the other, however. In an 1843 article in the *Athenaeum,* prominent essayist and art critic Anna Jameson curtly dismissed the celebrations of domestic ideology and focused, instead, on the actual position of working-class women. While politicians and press repeat truisms about woman's place and the glory of motherhood, Jameson points out that "the real state of things is utterly at variance with them. Our social system abounds with strange contradictions in law, morals, government, religion. But the greatest, the most absurd, the most cruel of all is the anomalous condition of the women in this Christian land of ours." Jameson is particularly perceptive in commenting on the image of working-class women that such an ideology produces: "These future mothers of our labourers and operatives are described as wretched, diseased, debased, haggard, enfeebled creatures, whose offspring must, of necessity, be physically degenerate. . . . Is she, therefore, a born monster?" Jameson asserts that, by refusing to acknowledge the necessity of women's work and to address the issues it raises, Victorian reformers like Ashley leave working-class women worse off than they were before. Jameson compares the "beautiful theory" of woman's existence presented by domestic ideology with the actual fate of working-class women: toiling from the age of five; unable to acquire domestic skills and, should they acquire them, unable to practice them; often victimized by men, their supposed "protectors." She points out that limiting or abolishing such women's jobs places them in an untenable position: "[B]y what right will you take the food out of the mother's mouth, procurable by no other means than through her own and her children's perpetual toil? What alternative do you leave her besides this course of unnatural cruelty and absolute starvation? These are questions to be asked and answered, or our merciful reforms are like to be only new forms of injustice and oppression."[15]

Jameson directly examines the painful, contradictory position that working women confront and challenges her society to do the same, but hers was an isolated voice. The degraded, monstrous images of working women that the blue books presented tended to replace any reasoned discussion of their contradictory roles. Thus, women working outside the home became almost impossible to represent, considered too hot a topic to handle, in a range of sources. After the mining blue book, government reports did not use illustrations again. *The Illustrated London News,* which had promised its readers a full examination of the topic of women in the mines in its inaugural issue, decided that it was too controversial a topic, unsuited for family reading, and abandoned it.[16] Such self-censorship is also reflected in novels on industrial topics. Before the 1842 blue book, prominent novels on industrial subjects contained important characters who were factory girls. Frances Trollope's *Michael Armstrong, the Factory*

Boy (1839) also tells the story of a factory girl, Fanny Fletcher, who, like Michael, is an orphan laboring in the Deep Valley Mill. Elizabeth Stone's *William Langshawe, the Cotton Lord* (1842) contains a significant subplot involving the seduction of a factory girl by her employer's son. Charlotte Elizabeth Tonna's *Helen Fleetwood* (1841–42) even focuses on women's factory work, its characters mirroring the fact that the majority of the cotton mill workforce was female. Therefore, unlike the post-1842 blue book "industrial novels," *Helen Fleetwood* can actually describe work inside the mill. The reader learns, for example, that older girls like Helen work in the carding room, "where the cotton is pulled out and prepared for the spinners," while younger girls like Mary Green work as piecers: "there are a great many cotton threads reaching from the bottom to the top of the frame; and while the machine moves about, the threads go running up, and twist round the little rollers above. Now the threads being thin and fine, they often break, and I have to keep a great watch, to get hold of the two ends when one breaks, and put them together, the same as in spinning." Even younger girls work as scavengers: "You see, bits of cotton wool will stick to the thread, and they mustn't go on the reels; so there is a little girl huddled up under the frame and she snatches off all the loose wool, and throws it down so fast! and when the machine runs back, if the little scavenger did not bob and duck, and get very low, she would have a fine knock on the head."[17] But such a story of factory work and factory girls becomes unnarratable after 1842; the issues raised by the factory and mining reports—working-class women's lack of proper femininity, domesticity, and chastity—continue to haunt and disrupt the industrial novels, but they are displaced on to less controversial figures.

> Whole lines carefully erased, page after page torn out, evidently long after the MSS. were written.—*Alton Locke*

Examining the ways in which female factory workers appear—and disappear—in the industrial novels reveals a great deal about the politics of women's industrial labor in the mid-Victorian period. *Sybil* (1845) and *Mary Barton* (1848) fully record the seismic shift of the early 1840s and the resulting crisis in the representation of working-class women. Factory girls are marginalized, and working-class women are represented by more properly "feminine" figures. In both novels the title characters are the daughters of factory workers, but their class markers are either erased, as in the case of Sybil, or deemphasized, as in the case of Mary Barton. It is almost as if the authors have to erect barriers around these putatively working-class heroines in order to separate them from the taint of the factory; yet, at the same time, each of them takes up and addresses at least part of the accusations leveled at working-class women. In fact, as I will argue in this and later chapters, while Disraeli and Gaskell avoid grappling with the overheated topic of women's labor directly, at the same time they strategically address some of the issues it raises indirectly. Three factory girls are minor characters in *Sybil,* but the eponymous heroine is constructed as a kind of anti-factory girl. Although she refers to herself as "a daughter of the people," she has no experience of actual working-class life. Compared to a madonna and dressed like a medieval nun, she was literally raised in a cloister, and she never worries about such mundane matters as making money or getting a job. What a contrast to actual working-class women, especially those "prostituted" by their work in mixed-sex settings. Yet, while Disraeli thus segregates his "daughter of the people" from the taint of factory labor, I will argue in the next two chapters that the saintly Sybil faces sexual threats and political questions that resonate with the problems of working-class women.

While *Sybil* is the earliest and most extreme case of the segregation between the industrial novels' working-class heroines and the factory girls, similar patterns of separation, repression, and erasure occur in all of them. Set in working-class Manchester where 60 percent of the factory workforce was female, *Mary Barton* provides one passing glimpse of these workers: "Groups of merry and somewhat loud-talking girls, whose ages might range from twelve to twenty, came by with a buoyant step. They were most of them factory girls, and wore the usual out-of-doors dress of that particular class of maidens; namely, a shawl, which at mid-day or in fine weather was allowed to be merely a shawl, but towards evening, or if the day were chilly, became a sort of Spanish mantilla or Scotch plaid, and was brought over the head and hung loosely down, or was pinned under the chin in no unpicturesque fashion."[18] Interestingly, this image contradicts the inflammatory accusations made in parliamentary debates and press coverage, indicating Gaskell's desire to, at least partially, refute them. The girls are somewhat boisterous, but, otherwise, just happy, modestly dressed "maidens." Several secondary characters who are former factory girls, however, illustrate the popular evil effects. Mary Barton's Aunt Esther, a former factory worker turned prostitute, represents the fears about work for women and what it might produce. Reported in retrospect, her life follows a stereotypical path: the money she earned through factory work increased her vanity about her looks and her defiance of proper supervision. She buys fine clothes and resists her brother-in-law John Barton's attempts to control her behavior. When she separates herself from the family by moving out of the Bartons' house and sets up on her own, ruin follows almost immediately: she runs off with a soldier and has an illegitimate child. Now, years later, having been abandoned by the soldier and lost her child, she haunts Manchester as a street prostitute. In *Tainted Souls and Painted Faces: The Rhetoric of Fallenness in Victorian Culture*, Amanda Anderson provocatively describes Esther's character as "a ghost from another genre,"[19] but one might question precisely what genre that is. At first glance an apparition out of a romantic melodrama who finds herself on the streets of an industrial novel, Esther also haunts the text like a ghost out of some parliamentary blue book. If Esther represents the dangers of too much independence and the resulting sexual immorality, another former factory girl, Mrs. Wilson, represents the lack of domestic skills. Having worked in the factory since the age of five, she knew nothing of housework when she married. Her trial and error approach to housekeeping is treated humorously, but the suggestion is that, if her husband had not been an unusually helpful and patient man, the results could have been disastrous for the marriage.

With factory work for women presented only in the margins or at a remove, the two working-class girls who play major roles in the novel—Mary Barton and Margaret Legh—work as seamstresses. Mary's father underlines the reasons for this and their basis in contemporary opinion: he opposes women's factory work as damaging to their morality and domestic skills. Therefore, at considerable financial sacrifice, he apprentices the sixteen-year-old Mary to a milliner: "Mary was to work for two years without any remuneration, on consideration of being taught the business; and where afterwards she was to dine and have tea, with a small quarterly salary (paid quarterly, because so much more genteel than by week), a *very* small one, divisible into a minute weekly pittance. In summer she was to be there by six, bringing her day's meals during the first two years; in winter she was not to come till after breakfast. Her time for returning home at night must always depend upon the quantity of work Miss Simmonds had to do" (63). Millinery, of course, is considered a feminine occupation, and, like Sybil's cloister, provides an all-female environment. Apparently, that is worth two years' salary. And, yet, ironically, the plot points out that this cloistered environment does not protect Mary's morals; in fact, the reverse is true. The narrator comments that Mary probably received her job because of her good looks, indicating that the establishment liked to put pretty seamstresses on display to sell its wares: thus, while assisting in the showroom, Mary meets Harry Carson and comes close to repeating Esther's fate. So the problems that the novel avoids by marginalizing factory girls reappear in a somewhat more manageable guise, displaced on to a working-class girl who can represent their experience without also being made to bear the particular taint of factory work—or, to put it more bluntly, being considered as already prostituted by it.

A more negative effect of the marginalization of working-class women becomes apparent in Charles Kingsley's *Alton Locke, Tailor and Poet: An Autobiography* (1850): the ways in which it serves to underpin the validation of working-class men as the sole voice of and political agents for their class. This fictional autobiography of a working-class man has little to say about working-class women. As an adult, Alton associates exclusively with working-class men, either fellow tailors like Mike Kelly or intellectuals like Sandy MacKaye. A lifelong bachelor, Alton will pursue careers as a tailor, a poet, and a Chartist activist. In none of these careers, apparently, does he meet a working-class woman worthy to be his friend, his sexual partner, or even a flirtation of passing interest. His only romantic attachments are to upper-class women such as Lillian Stanton and Lady Eleanor Lynedale. What the novel does reveal is the way that class and gender can combine forces to erase working-class women's experience and silence their voices. The tailors' workshops that Alton enters are versions of the aggressively male artisanal culture revealed in Anna Clark's *Struggle for the Breeches*. Clark describes the typical workshop as a place of male bonding and heavy drinking, and artisan culture is depicted as a bachelor culture in which an "artisan's status had rested on his place in the fraternity of skilled men rather than on his ability to keep a wife at home." Tailors were also one of many trades that drew "upon a long tradition of artisans combining into a trade union to restrict the unapprenticed—especially women—from working in their craft." In bitter strikes during the 1820s and 1830s, tailors went out of their way to attack tailoresses, calling them whores and even physically assaulting them.[20] As David Vincent's *Bread, Knowledge, and Freedom: A Study of Nineteenth-Century Working-Class Autobiography* reveals, Alton's fictional life story also has much in common with the actual biographies of working-class male intellectuals, who seldom mention women, apparently separating their mental life from association with them. Instead, like Alton, many such working-class autobiographers emphasize their relationship with a male mentor.[21] So working-class women are eclipsed in every aspect of Alton's experience. In the marketplace they are perceived by all-male tailor shops as competitors; in the political atmosphere of Chartism, they have become a nontopic; to male working-class intellectuals, they are unnecessary distractions. And Kingsley takes this erasure of working-class women one step further: if they do not represent their class, neither do they represent women. *Alton Locke* presents them as unattractive and unfeminine, made ugly by poverty and narrowness. According to Alton's "poetic" philosophy, only upper-class women are gifted with beauty, sexual attractiveness, and true femininity. Yet, as in all texts, the story that is apparently not told resurfaces in interesting ways that reveal both repression and guilt.

Alton's adult separation from working-class women is made all the more striking by the fact that he is raised by a mother and sister. His life as working-class poet, intellectual, and Chartist is made contingent on his permanent break with them. The novel's first plot line is the story of how this separation came about. With a mixture of self-justification and guilt, Alton describes the conflict between "my duty to my mother and my duty to myself."[22] His duty to himself wins the day. His mother is presented as a good woman whose life is controlled by a narrow religious fanaticism; his sister grows up to become a less sympathetic version of that stereotype. This is one of a number of places where the relationship between working-class women and religion becomes important, a connection that is especially significant because working-class religious movements were one of the few places where they could voice their concerns; the novel, it seems, has a particular investment in replacing this religion and these voices with that of Christian Socialism as presented by Lady Eleanor Lynedale. Conflict arises when Alton's poetic vocation asserts itself and he begins to read the secular literature that his mother has forbidden him. Thus, his "inward thirst for mental self-improvement" (53) and his self-selected poetic vocation make the break inevitable. It is interesting to compare his abandonment of home with that of fictional factory girls like Esther in *Mary Barton*. The factory girl is condemned while Alton's break is read as a necessary step into masculine independence. At their final confrontation, Alton openly rebels against his mother's way of life, asking, "[H]ave I not slaved for you, stinted myself of clothes to pay your rent? Have I not run to and fro for you like a slave, while I knew all the time you did not respect me or trust me?" His rebellion asserts itself in gendered terms: he claims his present course of life is doing "my father's works" and rejects his mother's religion as "fit only for women and children" (55–56). Then, Alton claims his freedom: "I'm old enough to think for myself, and a free-thinker I will be, and believe nothing but what I know and understand" (56). His mother then orders him out of the house, and Alton states, "That room—that mother I never saw again" (57).

After that moment, Alton's mother and sister, his closest family as well as his only working-class female connections, resurface only once in an important context. Alton seldom mentions them until one day he receives notification that his mother has died. In a curious chapter entitled "Short and Sad," Alton attends her funeral and sees his sister for the last time, "now a tall handsome woman, but become all rigid, sour, with coarse grim lips, and that crushed, self-conscious, reserved, almost dishonest look about the eyes, common to fanatics of every creed" (185–86). After the funeral, his sister gives him his only inheritance from his mother, what might be thought of as *her* autobiography: "certain notes and diaries of my mother's, which she had bequeathed to me on her death-bed" (186). But his mother's story, as well as that of his relationship to her, will not be revealed here; it is suppressed on multiple levels. First, Alton refuses to describe his own emotions: "I shall pass over the agonies of the next few days. There is self-exenteration enough and to spare in my story, without dilating on them. They are too sacred to publish, and too painful, alas! even to recal. I write my story, too, as a working man. Of those emotions which are common to humanity, I shall say but little" (185). This is an interesting excuse, especially given Alton's detailed descriptions of his feelings about upper-class women. Second, he refuses to share what he finds in her diary: "Let the words I read there be as secret as the misery which dictated them. I had broken my mother's heart!—no! I had not!—The infernal superstition which taught her to fancy that Heaven's love was narrower than her own . . . that, that had killed her!" And, most remarkably, his mother's diary has already been mutilated when it reaches him: "whole lines carefully erased, page after page torn out, evidently long after the MSS. were written. I believe, to this day, that either my poor sister or her father-confessor was the perpetrator of that act" (186). So his mother's life story has been censored and her voice silenced, not by Alton or by the novelist, but by her religious beliefs, which they condemn. Abandoned, repressed, erased—working-class women are relegated to the margins of Alton's personal and professional life.

Yet other glimpses of working-class women in the novel use them and their sexuality, in blue book fashion, as ultimate symbols of working-class degradation and a diseased civilization. Thus, paradoxically, the abandoned working-class woman becomes the foundation for understanding working-class life. For example, after the success of Alton's first book of poetry, a Byronic fantasy about life in the South Pacific, Alton's intellectual father, Sandy Mackaye, hopes to inspire him to be a true poet of the people. To that end, he takes him on a tour of London's lower depths. Also a lifelong bachelor, Mackaye launches into a jeremiad that turns obsessively on working-class women's corrupt and corrupting sexuality: "Look at thae bare-footed, bare-backed hizzies, with their arms roun' the men's necks, and their mouths full o' vitriol and beastly words! Look at that Irishwoman pouring the gin down the babbie's throat! . . . Drunkards frae the breast!—harlots frae the cradle!—damned before they're born!" When Alton responds, "Well—but—Mr. Mackaye, I know nothing about these poor creatures," Mackaye continues, "Then ye ought. What do you ken anent the Pacific? Which is maist to your business?—thae bare-backed hizzies that play the harlot o' the other side o' the warld, or these—these thousands o' bare-backed hizzies that play the harlot o' your ain side—made out o' your ain flesh and blude?" (88). Then, he takes Alton to visit the room of some seamstresses. There, for the first and only time, Alton is put in brief proximity to three working-class girls of his own age who might become his friends or sexual partners. But the girls are disqualified from those roles by the wages of poverty. The one "pure" girl, dying of tuberculosis, is "ugly, small-pox-marked, hollow-eyed, emaciated" (89). As she coughs and expectorates, Alton describes her fit as "painful, apparently, to the sufferer as it was, I confess, disgusting even to me" (90). The two other girls, still attractive, have been forced into part-time prostitution in order to supplement their meager wages. Desperately lamenting her lost purity and her need to sell herself, one of them "burst[s] out into that peculiar wild, ringing, fiendish laugh—has my reader never heard it?"

(93). The first girl is made ugly and disgusting by physical suffering, the second two by moral corruption.

Alton remains steadfastly in ignorance of "these poor creatures" (88). His only sexual and emotional attachments are to the upper-class Lillian Stanton and Lady Eleanor Lynedale. There is the suggestion that a man of Alton's poetic temperament could never be attracted to a working-class woman because she, by definition, lacks true femininity, which is embodied only in such aristocrats. As he writes of Lady Eleanor,

> Her dress was as plain as that of any quaker; but the grace of its arrangement, of every line and fold, was enough, without the help of the heavy gold bracelet on her wrist, to proclaim her a fine lady; by which term, I wish to express the result of that perfect education in taste and manner, down to every gesture, which Heaven forbid that I, professing to be a poet, should undervalue. It is beautiful; and therefore I welcome it, in the name of the Author of all beauty. I value it so highly, that I would fain see it extend, not merely from Belgravia to the tradesman's villa, but thence, as I believe it one day will, to the labourer's hovel, and the needlewoman's garret. (148).

Femininity, grace, and beauty are redefined as class distinctions and class property here—only a fine lady can possess them—although there is the distant hope that some day these attributes may trickle down even to working-class women.

Alton Locke's awareness that working-class women are somehow the foundation of its problems, yet its unwillingness to represent their experience is also apparent in the career of Lady Eleanor. The beautiful Eleanor becomes Alton's savior and Kingsley's mouthpiece for Christian Socialism. Revealingly, her first step into that role comes when she abandons aristocratic life to set up a commune of seamstresses. She goes to live among working-class women, but her sole description of that experiment focuses exclusively on her role:

> To become the teacher, the minister, the slave of those whom I was trying to rescue, was now my one idea; to lead them on, not by machinery, but by precept, by example, by the influence of every gift and talent which God had bestowed upon me; to devote to them my enthusiasm, my eloquence, my poetry, my art, my science; to

> tell them who had bestowed these gifts on me, and would bestow, to each according to her measure, the same on them. (376)

In this commune, the influence is strictly top-down. The erasure of working-class women becomes complete when Eleanor turns her missionary zeal toward Alton, confessing, "I have saved many a woman already; and this one thing remained—the highest of all my hopes and longings—that God would allow me, ere I died, to save a man" (383–84). Using working-class women as a shorthand for all the evils of poverty and yet never addressing their position, *Alton Locke* puts all its hopes for change in an upper-class woman and a working-class man who repeatedly silence their voices and erase their experience.

> "But when you've been used to doing things, and they've been taken away from you, it's as if your hands had been cut off, and you felt the fingers as are of no use to you."—*Felix Holt*

In the 1850s, as working-class women symbolically retreat into domesticity, portraits of female factory workers reappear and become both more complex and more violent. The later industrial novels, in fact, often reveal a desire to disable and kill off the factory girl. In *Hard Times* (1854) and *North and South* (1854–55), the dead or dying factory girl appears right at the juncture of crucial political negotiations. In each novel, too, there is a struggle to come to terms with her, to write her out of the novel or to rewrite her, but her story remains a stubborn shadow that haunts and disrupts their resolutions. In the last industrial novel, *Felix Holt* (1866), such ambivalence is extended to all working-class women. Eliot's artisan hero orders his mother to stop making the drugs she has sold to support them. In the midst of her housework, Mrs. Holt complains that her hands feel as if they have been amputated, an image that might speak to the situation of a number of working-class women in the 1860s.

Although readings of *North and South* tend to focus almost exclusively on the triangulated relationship between its middle-class heroine, Margaret Hale; the mill owner, John Thornton; and the unionist, Nicholas Higgins, Bessy Higgins is the most extensive portrait of a factory girl in the mainstream industrial novels; and, as such, she reveals the political and economic tensions surrounding working-class women. Gaskell remains committed to the negotiations she sets up between her three central representatives, but her treatment of the factory girl—allowing her her own voice and a significantly different viewpoint—suggests some awareness of what middle-class men and women and working-class men may leave out of their calculations. Even here factory work and the factory girl are at a remove—Bessy enters the novel dying. After years of work in a carding room, she has developed lung disease, and she dies halfway through the novel. Before she dies, however, a contradictory set of issues is filtered through her conversations with Margaret Hale. Margaret is introduced to working-class life by Bessy, but perhaps it is not surprising that critics have tended to overlook her in favor of her father's blunt unionism.[23] For Bessy's comments address the specific problems of working-class women, problems that both the unions and the middle class have an interest in ignoring. Although she embraces the domestic ideal that her culture presents to her, Bessy cannot reconcile it with the facts of her existence. She continually laments that her mother died before teaching her domestic skills and that she has none to pass on to her younger sister, Mary. She lives the contradictions between the feminine role her society demands of her and the economic realities of working-class women's lives. It might also be said that she dies of them.

Once again, religion becomes the central vehicle through which Bessy attempts to come to terms with the contradictions of her life. Her millenarian beliefs are another reason that Bessy's role tends to be downplayed. In his influential *The Making of the British Working Class,* E. P. Thompson criticizes working-class millenarian movements, suggesting that they appear only when effective politics stop; he calls them "the Chiliasm of despair."[24] His sense of millenarianism as the language of working-class desperation matches Nicholas's and Margaret's disturbed rejections of Bessy's obsessive religious rhetoric. But in *Eve and the New Jerusalem,* Barbara Taylor interprets such millenarian movements as providing radicals with an ultimate language of social transformation. Not only that, but she stresses their particular significance for working-class women because the mystical religious imagery they employed allowed debate about sexual equality.[25]

So Bessy's religious beliefs are two-sided: on the one hand, despairing, on the other, voicing working-class women's aspirations—and even her despair contains a violent anger against the present social order that her father's unionism entirely represses. Bessy explains, "If yo'd led the life I have, and getten as weary of it as I have, and thought at times, 'maybe it'll last for fifty or sixty years—it does wi' some'—and got dizzy, and dazed, and sick, as each of them sixty years seemed to spin about me, and mock me with its length of hours and minutes, and endless bits o' time—oh, wench! I tell thee thou'd been glad enough when th' doctor said he feared thou'd never see another winter."[26] Her father confirms her words when he speaks her epitaph over her corpse, "What wi' hard work first, and sickness at last, hoo's led the life of a dog. And to die without knowing one good piece o' rejoicing in all her days!" (283). Her story is told in retrospect, and she has now given up on this life. Her mind is filled with images from the Book of Revelations, what her father dismisses as "her dreams and her methodee fancies, and her visions of cities with goulden gates and precious stones" (133). Unlike the radicals in Taylor's *Eve and the Jerusalem,* however, who had earlier dreamed of transforming life on this earth, when Bessy asks Margaret to "[r]ead about the New Heavens, and the New Earth" it is to "forget this" life on earth, not to envision transforming it (261). Her despairing comment on life in the 1850s is that "[o]ne can bear pain and sorrow better if one thinks it has been prophesied long before for one: somehow, then it seems as if my pain was needed for the fulfilment, otherways it seems all sent for nothing" (187). As her father puts it, "Hoo's so full of th' life to come, hoo cannot think of th' present" (181). Bessy's views, therefore, apparently disconnect her from working-class politics, even while they serve a number of political functions. Tired of struggle, she is set against the strike which she views through her religious fatalism. She explains to Margaret, "th' Union says they'll not be doing their duty if they don't make the masters give 'em their share. But masters has getten th' upper hand somehow; and I'm feared they'll keep it now and evermore. It's like th' great battle o' Armageddon, the way they keep on, grinning and fighting at each other, till even while they fight, they are picked off into the pit" (202).

But, while Bessy criticizes unionism, she has a politics of her own which both reveals her sense of disenfranchisement from the ongoing struggles between "masters and men" and presents the most telling evidence in the novel of the inequities of the class system. The contrast between the healthy Margaret and the dying Bessy, both nineteen years old when they meet, makes inequity plain. Bessy confronts injustice in its most naked form, telling Margaret,

> "And I think, if this should be th' end of all, and if all I've been born for is just to work my heart and my life away, and to sicken i' this dree place, wi' them mill-noises in my ears for ever, until I could scream out for them to stop, and let me have a little piece o' quiet—and wi' the fluff filling my lungs, until I thirst to death for one long deep breath o' the clear air yo' speak on . . . I think if this life is th' end, and there's no God to wipe away all tears from all eyes—yo', wench, yo'!" said she, sitting up, and clutching violently, almost fiercely, at Margaret's hand, "I could go mad and kill yo', I could." (145)

Bessy's clutching hand and momentary desire to kill Margaret are the most ferocious expressions of class antagonism that *North and South* contains.

At another point, Bessy explains to Margaret that she became ill from inhaling cotton fluff, a problem that might be prevented: "Some folk have a great wheel at one end o' their carding-rooms to make a draught, and carry off th' dust; but that wheel costs a deal of money—five or six hundred pound, maybe, and brings in no profit: so it's but a few of th' masters as will put 'em up; and I've heerd tell o' men who didn't like working in places where there was a wheel, because they said as how it made 'em hungry, at after they'd been long used to swallowing fluff, to go without it, and that their wage ought to raised if they were to work in such places. So between masters and men th' wheels fall through. I know I wish there'd been a wheel in our place, though" (146). For a moment here, a gap opens and we glimpse the possibility of another politics—"between masters and men," the problems of the factory girl "fall through." That is just a moment, however. Within this context the death of the factory girl is necessary. *North and South* is about unionization and negotiations between masters and men, and, as a part of the negotiation, the old image of the factory girl will die, and a new one will be born which "gives her a domestic turn."[27]

Bessy prepares the way for the new domesticated image through her relations with her father, the role she passes on to her younger sister Mary, and, most of all, the connection she establishes between her father and the properly domestic middle-class woman, Margaret. Although Bessy is unable to do housework both because of her illness and because she was never properly instructed in it, her love and sympathy create a haven for her father. Her worry throughout the novel is that he will turn to drink because of his troubles. She wants to prepare Mary to take her place and to do even better at housework. To this end, she tells Margaret, "I wanted to ask yo' to be a friend to her . . . I don't want her to go to th' mill." When Margaret admits that they need a servant but that Mary is too untrained, Bessy responds, "No, I see. I reckon yo're right. Our Mary's a good wench: but who has she had to teach her what to do about a house? No mother, and me at the mill till I were good for nothing but scolding her for doing badly what I didn't know how to do a bit. But I wish she could ha' lived wi' yo', for all that" (147). After Bessy's death, her wish will come true as the Hales briefly employ Mary as a servant. Bessy's main function in the plot, however, is to bring Margaret and her father together, a function she performs so well that most readers discount her significance altogether. Margaret first talks to and visits the Higginses because of Bessy, and her death seals the relationship of Margaret and Higgins. When Margaret learns of Bessy's death, she and Higgins go to look at her corpse together. Afterwards, Margaret invites Higgins to her home, and they begin their political discussions. When Margaret attacks the union's policy of forced compliance, she is afraid Higgins will be angry, but he replies, "Nay, . . . yo' may say what yo' like! The dead stand between yo' and every angry word o' mine. D'ye think I forget who's lying *there*, and how hoo loved yo'?" (296). Thus the middle-class woman and the working-class man strike up an alliance literally over the corpse of the factory girl.

After the death of Bessy, *North and South* will try to use this alliance to produce different relations between masters and men. The concrete images of those new relations are, not incidentally, related to domestic responsibilities. Thornton and Higgins combine forces to care for the mill worker Boucher's orphaned children. At the novel's conclusion, the major innovation in Thornton's reformed mill is a dining hall that the men run cooperatively. But the problematic factory girl is not quite laid to rest. She returns in the figure of Bessy's younger sister Mary in a final attempt to reconcile domestic ideology with economic reality. Mary's work history—which combines work for pay with domestic responsibilities—proves to be an instructive one. She goes from fustian cutting to support herself and her father when he cannot get work after a strike, to working in the Hale household as a servant, then she returns to fustian cutting while also looking after Boucher's children, and finally she goes to work in Thornton's mill. Thornton's innovation provides a last glimpse of the factory girl. Now removed to London, Margaret learns from her servant Dixon "that Mary had gone to work at Mr. Thornton's mill, because her father wished her to know how to cook; but what nonsense that could mean she didn't know. Margaret rather agreed with her that the story was incoherent enough to be like a dream" (492). Attempting to combine a satisfactory domesticity with factory work, obedient to her father's wishes, the incoherent dreamlike image of Mary cooking in the mill uncovers the contradictions in the factory girl's life, just as Bessy had. While the other parties to the novel's negotiations—middle-class Margaret, mill owner Thornton, working-class Higgins—seem to make satisfactory contracts, the factory girl continues to trouble Gaskell, outside the bounds of the compromises she works to impose.

While Gaskell kills off her factory girl and then tries to resurrect her in a more acceptable form, *Hard Times* and *Felix Holt* take still more aggressive approaches to the threats she poses, both literally and metaphorically attacking the hidden hands. At significant moments in *Hard Times* female factory workers are made invisible: the factory workers' conflicts with the mill owners are described as between masters and men while the union organizer Slackbridge addresses a crowd of "men and brothers" in which no women are present. There is, however, a trinity of factory girls/women who function in important ways for Stephen Blackpool, the novel's representative working man, both condemning him and saving him. Their dramatic roles suggest that working-class men's life and happiness depends, not on their economic or political situation but on the behavior of their women. The first of Stephen's trinity is the saintly Rachael, his beloved and savior. She is a lifelong factory worker, yet, perhaps because she is an older unmarried woman, seemingly removed from sexuality, she is not only unthreatening but, in fact, is used to control any disruption of the social order. Her primary function in the novel is to safeguard Stephen from taking violent action, and she is presented as ideally domestic, performing housework in his room. The second woman is Stephen's wife, the unnamed former factory girl who is now an alcoholic prostitute. Mrs. Blackpool is the factory blue book nightmare—undomestic, unchaste, and violent—who ruined Stephen's life and haunts his imagination.

And there is yet a third factory girl, who appears as some kind of apparition: Rachael's dead little sister. In drafts of *Hard Times*, Blackpool describes this little sister as dying as a result of unfenced machinery in the factory, "wi' her child arm tore off afore [Rachael's] face." This description made it into the final draft of the novel before Dickens excised it in the proofs.[28] Thus, it seems, disabling and killing this factory girl was not enough. The novel, however, still contains a handful of vague references to her which occur at crucial moments in Stephen's life, suggesting through their very incoherence how ideologically disruptive the female factory worker might be.

These three extreme images of the factory girl/woman—saint, whore, victim—come together in the nightmarish scene in which Stephen is tempted to murder his wife. The scene is a crucial one for Stephen's character, not least because it concludes with his promise to Rachael that he will avoid anything that angers him. Yet the sequence of events that leads up to this promise of political passivity is convoluted and, at times, incoherent. In part this is because Stephen's sleep, as well as his waking life, is haunted by the image of his drunken wife. In fact, when looked at from the perspective of its representations of working-class women, it becomes clear that they are the sources of the scene's strange illogic. Tormented by his hatred of his wife and his desire for Rachael, Stephen longs to kill the debauched factory woman so that he can marry the domesticated one. But the novel entraps him, just as Victorian society itself was trapped by its own ideologies: how can they get rid of the debauched factory woman without guilt or violence, on the one hand, or without getting rid of the factory system itself, on the other?

When Rachael prevents the murder and Stephen gives her his fateful promise, a further layer of obscurity and incoherence is added when they both refer to the dead little sister whose story Dickens had erased. In these references the threatening factory girl is neither a mutilated victim nor a potential Mrs. Blackpool. She is now simply transformed into an angel in heaven. Stephen promises: "I nevermore will see or think o' anything that angers me, but thou, so much better than me, shalt be by th' side on't. And so I will try t' look t' th' time, and so I will try t' trust t' th' time, when thou and me at last shall walk together far awa', beyond the deep gulf, in th' country where thy little sister is" (126).[29] Because of this obscure promise, Stephen seals his fate by refusing to join the union and becoming isolated from Coketown's working-class community. This incoherent reference to a dead factory girl occurs at a telling juncture. Placed between a moment of averted domestic violence in a working-class home and Stephen's promise to avoid political violence or even protest, the factory girl is linked to ideas of gender conflict and political change. The dead factory girl in heaven becomes the image through which all conflict—both domestic and political—will be magically resolved.

At the novel's end, as he himself is dying after falling into an abandoned mine shaft, Stephen once more refers to Rachael's little sister in heaven. These confused references are all that remains of the factory girl; but, by entangling her fate with the muddled relationship that Dickens sets up between Stephen and the union, by involving her in scenes about anger, politics, domestic violence, and death, they indicate why she has to be suppressed: to describe directly what had happened to her would mean that Stephen's passivity would be unacceptable; he would be called upon to take action against the system that brought about her mutilation and death. Thus, on one level, the imperfect erasure of the factory girl is bound up with the imperfect erasure of political protest. On a second level, her erasure points to the problem of working-class gender conflict. The story of the little sister is replaced by those of Rachael, the factory worker who is only shown doing domestic work in Stephen's room, and of Sissy Jupe, the lower-class girl who ministers to her father and then to the middle-class Gradgrind household. The political implications of their housework and the way in which it is shadowed by domestic violence will be discussed in chapter 5.

The image of the mutilated hands of a working woman recurs in the last industrial novel, *Felix Holt*. Although the novel is putatively about the working class, by the 1860s working-class women of any type have nearly disappeared. For example, Eliot's appendix, "Felix Holt's Address to the Working *Men*" (emphasis mine) includes only one minor mention of working-class women—Felix emphasizes the care and education of children as the most important duty of the working class and aims to "rouse to the utmost the feeling of responsibility in fathers and mothers."[30] Felix's political oratory both here and in the novel proper is directed specifically and exclusively to working-class men. Like the misogynistic artisans that Anna Clark describes in *The Struggle for the Breeches*, and in the tradition of such fictional predecessors as Alton Locke, Felix holds his political discussions in the all-male setting of the pub, and his schoolhouse is devoted exclusively to boys. The derisive comment is made that "there was nothing better than a dame school in the hamlet" (219), but, that, apparently, is good enough for the girls. One of the few glimpses the novel provides of a specific working-class woman's life is the miner Dredge's account of how he beats his wife: "I've been aforced to give my wife a black eye to hinder her from going to the preachin'. Lors-a-massy, she thinks she knows better nor me, and I can't make head nor tail of her talk" (224). This image of a woman determined to speak her opinion despite her husband's control indicates that religion is one area where women still feel empowered to express themselves, but her actual voice is not heard.

The image of working-class women being violently put in their places is again evident in Mrs. Holt, the novel's most extensive portrait of a working woman of the lower classes. She has raised a son while running a successful business mixing and selling Holt's Elixir, the drug invented by her husband. Although her description of her labors is unintentionally comic—

> And when everybody gets their due, and people's doings are spoke of on the house-tops, as the Bible says they will be, it'll be known what I've gone through with those medicines—the pounding, and the pouring, and the letting stand, and the weighing—up early and down late—there's nobody knows yet but One that's worthy to know; and the pasting o' the printed labels right side upwards. (138)

—still, as she points out, she has supported herself by it while her son Felix was apprenticed to a country apothecary. But Felix's first action on returning home is to attack Holt's Elixir as a fake, and a dangerous one at that, and to forbid his mother to sell it in future. He boasts, "I shall keep my mother as well—nay, better—than she has kept herself" (144). So Mrs. Holt dwindles from an independent laborer with a home business to cooking and cleaning for Felix and his pupils. As she tells Esther Lyon, "there were the dumplings to see to, and what little I've got left on my hands now, I like to do well. Not but what I've more cleaning to do than ever I had in my life before, as you may tell soon enough if you look at this floor. But when you've been used to doing things, and they've been taken away from you, it's as if your hands had been cut off, and you felt the fingers as are of no use to you" (323). Even Felix, who usually ignores his mother's words and "who often amused himself and kept good-humoured by giving his mother answers that were unintelligible to her" (321), is struck by her "great image" of her feeling like her hands have been cut off. This "great image" resonates for working-class women generally, suggesting some of the costs of society's determination to return them to domesticity.

Thus, the later industrial novels kill off old representations of the factory girl and try to replace them with newer ones that will more easily support domestic ideology and enable negotiations between working-class men and middle-class men and women. But the factory girl, and the larger class of working women that she represents, troubles these moves. The novels reveal a desire to make her a party to their terms, but she remains stubbornly outside them. Struggling to control her, they uncover the very ideological contradictions that they are trying to escape. The incoherence present in Bessy Higgins's contradictory life story and beliefs, in the image of Mary Higgins learning how to cook in a mill, and in *Hard Times*'s fragmentary allusions to Rachael's sister paired with the violent repression found in images of mutilated hands and death indicate the factory girl's, and all working women's, ongoing disruptive potential and what makes her so dangerously difficult to represent.

Chapter 2

Naming the Unnameable

Sexual Harassment and Working-Class Women in Novels of Industry

> Woman's consciousness erupts through fissures in the socially knowable.
>
> —MacKinnon, *Sexual Harassment of Working Women: A Case of Sex Discrimination*

MOST DISCUSSIONS of sexual harassment in Victorian England focus on the experience of middle-class women. Deborah Epstein Nord's *Walking the Victorian Streets: Women, Representation, and the City* describes the difficulties middle-class women faced when negotiating the city streets and contrasts their feelings of exposure and vulnerability with the privileged position of the male *flaneur,* who, as wanderer and spectator, experiences the city as an ultimate freedom. She points out that when women attempt to take on the role of *flaneur,* the result is disruptive, and that "a woman's occupation of public space does more than unsettle her domestic and private identity; it threatens her respectability, her chastity, her very femininity."[1] In *City of Dreadful Delight: Narratives of Sexual Danger in Late-Victorian London,* Judith R. Walkowitz documents the social changes that brought middle-class women into the London streets in the 1880s—changes such as the opening of department stores and the entry of women into the professions. In the late nineteenth century, various magazines carried letters from such women complaining about the "male pests" who accosted them as they attempted to take advantage of these new opportunities.[2] As Nord notes, however, "[t]he question of the presence of working women on the streets has to be addressed in a slightly different manner,"[3] and it is working-class women's different experience of sexual harassment that is the subject of this chapter.

In the workplace itself, as well as going to and from work, working-class women were vulnerable to various forms of sexual harassment. While middle-class women struggled to achieve access to public spaces, working-class women were already there, unshielded by the rank of class or by socially accepted claims to respectability. Working-class women faced many other problems as well, such as low pay and harsh working conditions. They shared many of these problems with working-class men. But the Industrial Revolution provoked gender conflict in the working class: sexually mixed workplaces like factories introduced the possibility that women might work as equals alongside men. That is one reason that sexual harassment of working-class women becomes a crucial factor to consider during this period. On this issue the interests of working-class men and women are separate from and often in conflict with one another. Although the working-class press regularly used images of working-class women attacked by upper-class rakes as a symbol of class exploitation, most working-class women were harassed by men of their own class. Even more crucially, harassment functions to subordinate women, economically and socially. Given the tensions between men and women at a time when many working-class men felt their jobs and their control of the family threatened by changing economic conditions, sexual harassment played an important role in securing male dominance.

Even without a shared, social definition, it becomes apparent that nineteenth-century England witnessed a confluence of forces that hinged upon sexual harassment. In fact, Victorian representations of what today would be called sexual harassment provide a critic with the opportunity to examine the ideologies of the period in an attempt to reveal how class and gender interact to produce power relations and to define the issues in social debate. It may seem anachronistic to apply the term to nineteenth-century workplaces or literary representations, but there is ample evidence that it existed. At the same time, the issue itself remained hidden or distorted by different combinations of class and gender interests. In *Sexual Harassment of Working Women,* Catherine MacKinnon cites the first use of the term by the Working Women's United Institute in 1975. She argues that, although the lack of a term may have silenced women about the experience, this does not mean that it did not exist earlier: "It is not surprising either that women would not complain of an experience for which there has been no name. Until 1976, lacking a term to express it, sexual harassment was literally unspeakable, which made a generalized, shared, and social definition of it inaccessible." In the Victorian period ideas about prostitution and working-class women's sexual purity, debates about women's right to work outside the home, and competing class alignments all shaped the ways in which such incidents could be interpreted. Sexual harassment was used to harry working-class women back home or, if they remained in the workplace, to justify their exclusion from higher paying jobs claimed by men and to secure their position in sex-segregated, lower-paying jobs. As MacKinnon argues, sexual harassment is "neither incidental nor tangential to women's inequality, but a crucial expression of it, a central dynamic in it." MacKinnon defines two specific ways that harassment functions to place women at an economic disadvantage: first, it can be used to insure sex-segregated jobs, and, second, it enforces a hierarchy where women act as men's subordinates.[4] Both elements were present in the nineteenth-century factory where male unions repeatedly fought to exclude women from jobs and where the factory hierarchy used gender as a central organizing principle. Women might have children working for them, but teenaged and adult female workers were supervised exclusively by men, and women were assigned more supervisors than men were. Overseers were male; head carders were male; the workers who fixed machinery, and whose favor, therefore, could affect a worker's productivity, were male.

Even without a term for it, an awareness of sexual harassment as a serious problem for working-class women emerges in a variety of sources. In Charles Booth's *Life and Labour of the People of London* (1902), Clara Collett, one of the first female factory inspectors, reports what factory workers told her about their problems with male supervisors: "The factory girls make very little complaint about their work or their wages. . . . But they repeatedly complain about their treatment by foremen. 'The masters are kind, but the foremen treat us like animals.'" Collett goes on to assess the girls' vulnerability to abuse, especially sexual abuse, and to analyze the ways in which the structure of the factory system enables it:

> It is very difficult to decide in any particular case whether the foreman is in the right or whether the girl is telling the truth. But if in a factory the foremen are habitually tyrannical and subject the girls to rough treatment, the employers must be regarded as represented by the foremen, and many of them deserve the severest censure for their indifference in this respect. . . . A very little reflection on the

> darker side of life in the East End will show to what insult a girl may be exposed by her employer's indifference to the moral character of the man to whom he intrusts the management of young girls. The system of payment adopted by some employers, who pay their foreman by the piece and leave him to engage and dismiss the girls in his department, confers on him a power which the average foreman will be strongly tempted to abuse. . . . [The foremen] may be tempted to increase their incomes, or indulge themselves at the expense of the girls, who must find favour in their eyes if they wish to be left unmolested in other ways.[5]

In *The Wrongs of Women* (1842), Charlotte Elizabeth Tonna pays particular attention to the sexual exploitation and harassment that working women are often exposed to. The story, "The Forsaken Home," for example, provides an instance of harassment that parallels what Collett describes. Its heroine, Alice Smith, takes a job in a screw factory when her husband is unemployed. There the man who repairs tools begins to address her "in language exceedingly revolting to her feelings as a modest woman and a virtuous wife." When she repels his advances, he takes revenge by keeping her waiting whenever she comes to him for assistance: "[T]hus she is kept waiting, not only to have her ears wounded by his disgusting discourse with others less scrupulous than herself, but also to the great hindrance of her day's work, so that she is made to appear deficient in industry." Alice then begins to be reprimanded for her laziness and is in danger of losing her job. When she complains of her treatment to her employer, he ignores her, arguing that she is lying because no other women have dared to complain before her. Tonna's story is grimly effective because, while Alice resists the harassment and complains about it, the system is unresponsive. "The Forsaken Home" concludes with Alice still at work, her problem unresolved.[6]

Historians have also uncovered official complaints of sexual harassment in nineteenth-century factories, despite no definition of harassment or ongoing union concern with it. In the 1833 factory report, girls complained about the "practical jokes" that the boys played on them, ranging from spying on them while they changed their clothes, to pulling up their clothes during rest periods, to shouting obscenities. One seventeen-year-old girl claimed, "a lass stands no chance with so many boys."[7] In her study of sexual assault during the period of 1770 to 1845, Anna Clark describes several cases of overseers who were accused of raping the girls who worked for them. Even in these extreme cases, however, the prosecution was either unsuccessful or the punishment was a small fine for the guilty party. One overseer, for example, was fined five pounds when found guilty of sexually assaulting a girl in the cotton mill where they worked. Another, who impregnated a fourteen-year-old girl, was nearly mauled by a crowd when the magistrates dismissed the case against him.[8] In another case in 1887 operatives at the Henshaw-Street Spinning Company in Oldham went on strike to demand an investigation of a head carder who was accused of, first, sexually pressuring and, then, assaulting twelve girls who worked under his authority. The case was taken to court where the defense discredited the female complainants who were fifteen or sixteen years of age "by calling them sexually *precocious,* and insisting they acted as willing partners." The defense also cited the unwillingness of the victims to complain and the time lapse between the alleged incidents and the charges of assault. The outcome was that the carder was fined five pounds plus court costs. The mill apparently discharged him, but it also refused to rehire the workers who had struck.[9]

Sexual harassment can be defined only when women are recognized as having the right of choice and the right to occupy public spaces and workplaces. It is just that definition of women as responsible, self-determining agents which was so elusive for working-class women. The official response to reports that girls were sexually harassed, or even raped, in factories was not to pass legislation to make factories safe to work in but, instead, to claim that factory work "corrupted" women. While working-class men struggled for the vote and to achieve a family wage, parliamentary legislation placed working-class women in the same category as children, classifying them as "unfree agents," unable to contract their own labor. In addition, unlike middle-class women, working-class women in public spaces and employed in certain types of jobs were liable to be classed as prostitutes. Parliamentary blue books claimed that women working in factories and mines were sexually immoral.[10] Based on such reports, newspapers trumpeted the "wholesale prostitution" of women working in such places.[11] This ongoing elision of working-class women and prostitutes reached its height in the Contagious Diseases Acts of 1864 and 1866, which legislated that any suspicious-looking woman on the streets of certain towns could be seized and examined for venereal disease. Such definitions produce large repercussions. As Amanda Anderson argues in *Tainted Souls and Painted Faces,* prostitutes were defined as unfree and lacking character; they are, therefore, determined by their environment and seen as unable to act as self-determining agents.[12] The stereotypical view of the prostitute, of course, is that she cannot be sexually harassed because she is inviting sexual approach and has forfeited the right of free choice. Thus, the general charge of sexual immorality directed at working-class women and the tendency to represent them as prostitutes often stood in for and obscured the realities of sexual harassment, assault, and rape. Consequently, women were blamed for their own victimization. If they were subjected to harassment or even rape in the factory or the mine, it was they who were corrupt, not the men who attacked them or the system that permitted it to happen.[13] Yet at the same time that they were held responsible, they were denied the right to choose for themselves.

The working class, on the other side, constructed an image of sexual harassment in which the harasser was always upper class. In this way it erased working-class men's stake in harassment. In "The Politics of Seduction in English Popular Culture, 1748–1848," Anna Clark describes the ways in which the melodramatic image of "the poor maiden victimized by the aristocratic libertine provided a very specific symbol of class exploitation" during the first century of industrialization. The popular melodramas she analyzes were structured in such a way as to convert the sexual exploitation of women into a battle between working- and upper-class men, and, further, working-class women are displaced even as victims. So the melodramas focus on the suffering not of the women but of their fathers and lovers, who, then, actively take on the role of avengers. As Clark demonstrates, like middle-class beliefs, such images distorted or ignored working-class women's real problems. Similarly, they also tended to trap women within a male-defined ideal of passive chastity.[14] Indeed, parliamentary blue books reveal a kind of collusion between middle-class and working-class men as they find common ground on working-class women's sexual immorality and employ it as a reason to exclude or control women's labor. The parliamentary commissioners often asked the men about the women's morals and whether they made good wives or not. And working-class men often provided images of the women that fed the commissioners' most intense fears and fantasies about working-class women's sexuality.[15]

Examining three early Victorian novels of industry from this perspective uncovers a revealing congruence. Despite the lack of a term, and in the midst of conflicting ideologies of class and gender, sexual harassment is a key aspect in the lives of such heroines as Tonna's *Helen Fleetwood,* Disraeli's *Sybil,* and Gaskell's *Mary Barton.* For Helen Fleetwood, sexual harassment is the most painful part of her work in the factory. Sybil Gerard rejects the sexual blackmail of working-class radical, Stephen Morley, and risks being seized as a prostitute when she ventures into the slums of Seven Dials in search of her father. Mary Barton is sexually harassed by the mill owner's son, Harry Carson, after she rejects him as a suitor. In each instance, the heroine's response to harassment forms the turning point of her life. In response to it, she makes the choices that will either define her or allow her to define herself. Although the authors structure harassment in different ways and offer contrasting responses to the situation, the sexual threat in the heroines' lives and their handling of it reveal how each author negotiates the problem of sexual harassment and its interconnections with class and gender conflicts.

"The poor harassed girl."—*Helen Fleetwood*

In *Helen Fleetwood,* the narrator describes the effects of factory work on the sixteen-year-old title character:

> Helen Fleetwood was . . . not a girl of robust make, or rude strength; but no tendency to a sickly habit had ever appeared in her constitution. The rapid effect of mill-labour upon it had led her to suspect some lurking unsoundness; but a little more experience and observation would have proved to her how short a resistance the stoutest frame could offer to the debilitating effects of the atmosphere and other evils to which she was exposed throughout the live-long day. Neither could it be questioned that the mental sufferings which could not but await any modest, right-minded female in such society, had a very large share in undermining her bodily health. This is one of the worst features of mill-labour. . . . There is no protection for the ear of female modesty, against all that can outrage it. . . . This had been the great ordeal to Helen. . . . She felt herself in a manner degraded, from being the unwilling but helpless witness to so much infamous language, accompanied as it will always be by conduct no less abandoned. . . . She longed to escape it; she pined for deliverance: and this grief of heart preyed on her life to an extent that soon defied all human skill. (627–28)

Thus Tonna's narrator describes the experience of sexual harassment long before the term was invented.

Charlotte Elizabeth Tonna's fiction is unique in Victorian literature for its emphasis on working-class women and its detailed examinations of the nature of their work. *Helen Fleetwood* provides an unusually detailed picture of the workplace as well as its effect on Helen and other factory girls.[16] This emphasis presents the contradiction between the Victorian belief that society protected women and the reality of a brutal factory system that exploited them so graphically that the reader is faced with the choice of a reformation so total that it amounts to abolishing the factory system itself.[17] And at the center of its depiction of factory work is the issue of sexual harassment. Tonna's description is remarkable on several levels: for its specificity in naming the unnameable, for its identification with its working-class heroine, and for its criticism of the system itself as the responsible party. The narrator even uses the specific word "harassed" several times to describe the experience Helen undergoes (549, 554, 629). Helen describes herself, for example, as being "unceasingly harassed" in the factory (554). While part of the harassment stems from Helen's orphaned state and intense religiosity, much of it is sexual in nature. Although girls her own age "seemingly hardened past all fear or shame" join in, "[h]er greatest annoyance however by far, was from the boys, who were often set on to insult her in ways more trying than the rest" (538). Eventually, harassment envelops her, even affecting her love for her fiancé: "[E]ven as she looked on Richard's honest countenance, beaming with integrity, with manly sincerity, and godly simplicity, the thought arose to repel the yearnings of innocent affection towards the dear playmate of her infancy" (629). Tonna's approach does not entirely avoid the class and gender stereotypes of the period. The novel sometimes blames the victims of the system for the system's effects, seeing some of the factory workers as inherently corrupt. Its patriarchal Evangelicalism turns continually to men for a resolution to the problem, even though men are shown as either complicit with the system's evils or ineffectual in their responses to it. But Tonna's protofeminism is the novel's energizing force, although it is a feminism that finally fails to win the day. Two women—Helen Fleetwood and her guardian, the Widow Green—face the system, describe and try to combat its evils, and suffer the consequences.

Helen Fleetwood tells the story of a country family tricked by the parish poor-law commissioners into relocating to a factory town. While the oldest boy, seventeen-year-old Richard, is left behind as a useful laborer for the local squire, his grandmother, the Widow Green, takes her three younger grandchildren—two boys, James and Willy, and one girl, Mary—and an adopted orphan, Helen Fleetwood, to find work in the factories. When the family arrives in the factory town of M., it immediately becomes clear that the fate of the girls will be the significant measure of the factory system. At first, the Widow Green lodges with her married daughter, Mrs. Wright. The Wright family provides a diagram of what factory work produces. One son works in the factory and has been made cynical by it. The effects on the two daughters, however, are extreme. One of them, Sarah, represents the physical outcome: missing an arm through a machinery accident, her spine bent from her years of labor, she is dying of consumption. The other daughter, Phoebe, is morally deformed. It is she who instigates the harassment of Helen, apparently out of an instinctive hatred of Helen's goodness. Eventually, Phoebe becomes a prostitute. The emphasis on the girls continues when only Helen and Mary begin factory work, because the two boys are too young. Still another factory girl is drawn into the family when Mary takes up the cause of her little Irish scavenger, Katy.

The novel details the destruction of this family group as a whole; however, it is named for the orphan Helen because it is she who not only experiences factory work but also struggles against it. Critics have tended to find Helen an uninteresting character: Catherine Gallagher judges her to be "a submissive and largely nonanalytical consciousness," while Susan Zlotnick claims that Tonna has merely "substitute[d] one stereotype for another, replacing the aggressive, independent, and fallen factory girl of the popular imagination with one borrowed from the factory reform discourse, which figures her as the unwitting victim of a brutal industrial regime."[18] But the narrator sees Helen differently, representing her both as a representative working girl and as particularly reserved and sensitive: "There was nothing in her character unusually elevated above the class to which she belonged," although she has "a delicate mind" and her orphaned state has given her "a more contemplative, and perhaps a more imaginative turn of thought than most of her young companions, while a modest reluctance to make her own concerns more prominent than was suitable for so humble a person habituated her to . . . keeping her own counsel" (517).

The novel stresses Helen's habitual reserve, describing her as a girl "whose thoughts had never learned to clothe themselves in language worthy of the occasions that called them into existence" and as one who "had little to say" and whose "lips had hitherto been mute" (503). Helen's habitual silence underlines the significance of her ultimately speaking out: factory work leads her to "testify" in every sense of the word. She testifies to her experience there, to her religious faith, and even in a courtroom trial. Helen first speaks about her experiences when she describes the sexual harassment to the Widow Green. In analyzing her situation, Helen points an accusing finger not so much at her fellow workers as at the overseers and employers. When the widow says she will complain to the managers about the conditions Helen is working in, Helen tells her: "You are greatly mistaken if you think the men who overlook our work care for our morals—they themselves are often among the worst of the bad" (550). Of her employer, Mr. Z., Helen speaks even more strongly:

> Mr. Z I know, has daughters growing up: would he send them among us for an hour every day? Not he. He knows too well that their health would be destroyed by staying even so long in the heat, the steam, the stench, and the dust of rooms where we are pent up from early morning to late night; and he knows that they would never again be let into respectable society if they were supposed to hear the vile, filthy talk that his poor labourers use, and the men he sets over them encourage; and which he never dreams of checking, either by his own presence, or by setting any moral, not to say religious person, to watch them.

Her religious conviction that Mr. Z. is ultimately responsible for the abuses around her leads her to "bless God that I [am] a poor despised factory-girl, and not an employer" (552).

Helen has a firm conviction that there is no earthly redress for what she suffers. The Widow Green, however, cannot believe that such things can happen in England and goes to the male authorities to ask for help. Her search is thorough and entirely fruitless. In the course of it, she meets with the mill owner's agent, the mill owner himself, the mill owner's elder brother who lives on the profits and has a reputation of being a respectable and caring family man, and finally the local clergyman. The agent's response to her concerns is to abuse her: "What the deuce, woman, do you think I sit here to be pestered with long saws from an old fool like you, because a couple of mawkish parish girls are not treated like countesses in the mill!" (556). The owner dismisses her with "Learn, Mrs. What's-your-name, to know your place; and remember too, that my private residence is not an office" (558). But the novel makes its strongest case for broad societal hypocrisy when it indicts the people who are not directly involved in running the factory. The mill owner's brother angrily reprimands the widow for describing Helen's situation in front of one of his daughters, "a young lady, whose ears ought not to have been assailed by discourse so unfit for a delicate mind" (560). The widow responds that "though of very humble rank, my poor Helen is modest and delicate as you yourself can desire a female to be; and she is obliged to hear and to see in their worst forms, all the evil things that I spoke of, and others that I could not even mention before the young lady." This only provokes Mr. Z. further: "'Really, woman, your assurance is matchless! Not content with insulting my daughter by your low conversation, you must now place some dirty factory girl on the same level with her, and thence argue that I am to go, in person of course, and rescue your distressed damsel from the mill!' and he laughed in bitter scorn, as he spoke" (560). Obviously, all the responses stress the separation between upper-class women and the respect with which they are to be treated and dirty working-class factory girls. When the widow finally turns to the clergyman, she begins to despair because, although he alone listens to her with patience, all he can recommend is acquiescence to the system.

The family's conflict with the factory system reaches its climax when the Widow Green, Helen, and the granddaughter, Mary, complain to the factory inspector and take an overseer to trial. The trial, however, is not about sexual harassment, which, of course, has no legal existence. By this time events have escalated into acts of physical abuse, when, first, an overseer hits Helen with a rod. The trial itself brings a charge of "ill usage" against another overseer who is accused of "various acts of unnecessary severity to Mary Green . . . particularly with having, on a certain day kicked her on the shins, so as to hurt and bruise her considerably" (586). Sexual harassment lays a foundation for the events of the trial in several ways, however. First, the emphasis laid on it suggests the ways in which an atmosphere of harassment lays the groundwork for physical assault. Second, the trial demonstrates that such harassment is only one of the abuses that factory workers face. Finally, the Greens lose their case and the overseer is acquitted because the defense attorney calls the girls' characters into question. The trial is the culmination of the family's search for earthly justice, and, as Helen had predicted, it is not to be found.

In the end it is consumption, not harassment, that kills Helen. By the novel's conclusion, the protesting, testifying women have been swept away: Sarah and Helen are dead (as James is, as well: he dies of consumption without ever being exposed to factory work); the Widow Green is consigned to the parish workhouse; Mary has been sent off to some humble country job which, it is hoped, will wash away the taint of the factory; and the orphaned Katy has been abandoned to her fate in the factory town. The final comments in the novel are given to men who ineffectually debate the nature of the system and the fate of Helen. A doctor who had befriended the Greens in the country comes to town and, after hearing their history, goes to the mill owner to complain about Helen's harassment. When he learns Helen's history, however, Mr. Z. merely repeats his distinction between working-class women and ladies, saying, "We are not to judge of the conversation kept up in a mill by the standard of drawing-room propriety; nor to suppose that what would wound the delicacy of a young lady causes any trouble to a bobbin-filler" (641). Of the original family group, only two boys, Richard and Willy, remain together, reunited in their old country parish: "It was on a bright day in Spring, after labouring together in their master's park, that Richard and Willy seated themselves to eat their frugal meal beneath an ash, just putting forth its tender leaves to the fostering ray" (643). Despite this Edenic setting, their thoughts are grim as they argue about whether it was the harassment or the physical harshness of factory work that was responsible for Helen's death. Willy takes the former view: "I am sure it was the wickedness of the place, more than the work, that killed Helen," while Richard maintains, "But the work was enough to do it" (643).

Tonna's novel ends in failure with Helen dead and the factory system intact, but its depiction of a girl's resistance to workplace harassment is still a victory. Helen defies the attacks made on her and asserts the right to her own integrity. Despite her constitutional reserve, she does not suffer in silence but actively contests what is done to her. In fact, Helen becomes a spokeswoman for her class, first, because she dares to describe her experience to people outside the factory, second, because she finally assigns responsibility, not just to her fellow workers, but also to the system and its beneficiaries, and, third, because she defines this as a women's issue, rather than simply a class issue. Tonna succeeds in describing the hostile atmosphere created by sexual harassment and in allowing her working-class heroine to both articulate and resist it. And, what is most distinctive, Tonna stresses a cross-class identification of women with women, but it is an identification that is rooted in the working-class woman's experience, not one that requires her to masquerade as a middle-class woman.

"Heaven will guard over you! . . .
for you are a celestial charge."—*Sybil*

As one moves from *Helen Fleetwood* to the industrial novel proper, represented by Disraeli and Gaskell, it becomes clear what is lost when the factory girl is marginalized. The whole issue of sexual harassment in the workplace disappears and, along with it, a concrete sense of the economic forces that enable it. Sexual harassment had provided Tonna with a specific issue from which to critique the factory system. That connection and the systematic critique that it fuels disappear, and harassment becomes both more diffuse and more obscured by class and gender ideologies in Disraeli and Gaskell, although each writer struggles to reinterpret those ideologies. What they lose in specificity about working-class women, however, they partially regain by creating heroines who, not trapped within an unresponsive factory system as Helen Fleetwood was, potentially have more freedom to define their lives. For one thing, in the later novels, harassment takes place on the public streets; thus, class issues are partially effaced in what becomes a problem that women of all classes encounter. So the class-morphing Sybil Gerard, working-class Mary Barton—and, later in Gaskell's *North and South,* even middle-class Margaret Hale—all encounter reactions to their presence on the streets ranging from passing comments to physical threats.[19] In each case, too, such encounters have the power to call the heroine's reputation into question. This, in itself, is an important move because it suggests the ways in which the prostitute or fallen woman haunts all women, middle-class as well as working-class, policing their behavior and limiting their freedom of movement.

By looking at Disraeli and Gaskell, too, one can judge the differences and limits of a male observer versus a female middle-class one on this issue. Both novelists rewrite the popular class-based melodrama of the poor maiden assaulted by a rich libertine but do so from different perspectives and with contrasting results. Here, as well as elsewhere, Disraeli provides a perceptive and interestingly ambivalent examination of the role of women. On the one hand, he is sympathetic, providing women with a degree of freedom and influence. On the other hand, his Young England political stance tends to short-circuit his analysis, locking him into a traditional chivalric response that finally fails to come to terms with either the gender or the class issues he represents. Disraeli explicitly recognizes harassment as a general problem that women of all classes face, and his narrator presents a London rife with it. At the same time, however, gender and class prejudices hover around his specific example—only the angelic, convent-bred Sybil is harassed, not the factory girls, who are represented as freely roaming the streets and drinking in a pub. The implication is that only the properly cloistered, respectable woman can be harassed; factory girls, who work in mixed-sex settings, are immune. Thus, while *Sybil* suggests how harassment entraps all women, its specific example is exceptional, rather than typical. Further, although many male characters claim to view Sybil with an awed chivalry, the novel demonstrates how quickly such chivalry evaporates the moment that she ventures outside her protected space. But, while the male aristocrats who see Sybil all betray a sexual interest in her, the specific cases of harassment involve only working-class men. Rewriting the melodrama of the poor maiden, Disraeli effects a role reversal where the woman is assaulted, not by the upper class but by members of her own class, and even more specifically, by men associated with radical politics. The upshot is not a consideration of how the system could be altered to provide more freedom for women but the provision of an upper-class protector for Sybil and her permanent removal from the threat of working-class men and working-class politics.

Although her father is a factory overseer, Sybil Gerard does not work outside the home; in fact, so protected has she been from the outside world that she has spent most of her life in a convent. Once she emerges from that convent, whenever she ventures out alone—first, in the countryside near the home she shares with her father and, later, on the streets of London—she is in danger of harassment. Even in the comparatively idyllic setting of the country, there is a need for protection, and, when Sybil goes out there, she is always accompanied by her faithful guard dog, Harold.[20] The hovering threat of harassment does not become a reality, however, until Sybil and her father move to London where he is a delegate at the Chartist convention. There, as she tries to negotiate the streets, Sybil finds herself in increasing danger of misinterpretation—in that any woman seen on the streets can have her reputation questioned—and attack. In London the aristocratic hero Egremont encounters Sybil, first of all, in the sacred precincts of Westminster Abbey. As they emerge on to the streets, he chivalrously raises the question of Sybil's safety, insisting, "Let me walk home with you. . . . You must indeed let me attend you!" Sybil admits that there is reason for his concern, confessing how much harassment shapes the way she navigates the city: "The nearest way to [home] is straight along this street, but that is too bustling for me. I have discovered . . . a more tranquil path." She then tells Egremont that her two weeks in London have revealed it to be "a great prison. How strange it is that, in a vast city like this, one can scarcely walk alone." Egremont comments, "You want Harold" (285), the faithful dog who has been left back in the country. On another occasion, he encounters her in St. James Park, and, when she refuses his escort, says, "Heaven will guard over you! . . . for you are a celestial charge" (355). These exchanges provide the pattern that the novel will follow on the issue of harassment. They demonstrate how radically it limits women's freedom, turning a city into a prison. The narrator says of London, "There is no European city where our fair sisters are so little independent as in our metropolis; to our shame" (344). But such a description of harassment is so generalized and unlocatable that the result is not a questioning of the systemic forces that create it. Instead, the novel's resolution to the problem is that pure women such as Sybil need protection, a Harold to accompany them wherever they go. Sybil will never be able to "walk alone"; she will always be accompanied, by either a harasser or a protector.

Generalized harassment is the shape of Sybil's experience of London; specific harassment comes from working-class men and radical politics. What Sybil needs to be guarded against soon becomes apparent. When the peaceful presentation of the Charter fails and her father is drawn into a plot of armed rebellion, Sybil is exposed to sexual attacks, first from her father's political ally, Stephen Morley, and then from the slum dwellers of Seven Dials. This is where the novel's reversal of the poor maiden/rich libertine plot becomes apparent. Morley has been presented as an old family friend and a trusted political ally. He has devoted his life to the cause of the people, and it is he who delivers the novel's famous "Two Nations" speech. But, when Sybil turns to this longtime family friend for help, he suddenly reveals himself to be a wolf in sheep's clothing, transformed from a principled working-class radical to a sexual predator: Morley tells her that he knows both where her father is and how to save him from being arrested for armed conspiracy, but the price he demands for this knowledge is Sybil herself.

The scene that unfolds between Morley and Sybil self-consciously reverses the melodrama of the poor maiden and the rich libertine. Attempting to appeal to Morley's better nature, Sybil pleads with him to "be generous" and to "save [her father] from death and me from despair" (367). But Morley is determined to use his power over her to attain his end: " I am ready to do this great service; to save the father from death and the daughter from despair,—if she would but only say to me, 'I have but one reward, and it is yours.'" Sybil's response to the terms of Morley's demand makes explicit both the melodramatic sources of this scene and the way in which the novel has reversed the class roles in it: "I have read of something of this sort . . . this bargaining of blood, and shall I call it love? But that was ever between the oppressors and the oppressed. This is the first time that a child of the people has been so assailed by one of her own class, and who exercises his power from the confidence which the sympathy of their sorrows alone caused. It is bitter; bitter for me and mine—but for you, pollution" (368).

The revelation that Morley, previously represented as an intelligent, hard-working, self-sacrificing political radical, is really only a hypocritical sexual blackmailer comes as a shock, both to Sybil and to the reader. The only way this transformation makes sense is to look at it as an attack on his politics, which are aligned with radical Owenism, a working-class movement that competed with Chartism in the 1830s and 1840s. In direct contrast to Sybil's Chartist father, who exalts the domestic principle, Morley argues that "the Home" is a failed institution and that the working class must turn to new concepts of community for answers. As Barbara Taylor demonstrates in *Eve and the New Jerusalem,* Owenism rejected the patriarchal family and hoped that communities organized around voluntary cooperation would provide both new property relations and equality between the sexes. Periodicals like *The New Moral World,* which the factory worker Dandy Mick proudly names as one of the London papers his working-man's Institute subscribes to, contained articles by Owenite feminists, as well as working-class intellectuals like Morley, who argued the benefits of different familial and sexual relations. But Taylor also points out that many working-class women distrusted the new ideals of sexual liberty, seeing them as merely a cover for male libertinism.[21] Disraeli's handling of Morley plays on such fears. While Egremont, as representative of Young England, treats Sybil with exaggerated chivalry, Morley resorts to sexual blackmail the moment the opportunity presents itself. Morley's behavior thus carries political implications: a restructuring of the family and increased sexual freedom will not profit women; traditional aristocratic protection is needed, not a rethinking of women's roles and political radicalism.

Left alone after her rejection of Morley, Sybil prays and gathers strength to attempt to rescue her father herself. Her descent into the slums of London is Sybil's most striking independent action in the novel. It is also as close as she ever gets to actual working-class life and to being treated as a working-class woman. The narrator portentously announces, "[T]hen alone and without a guide, the shades of evening already descending, this child of innocence and divine thoughts, born in a cottage and bred in a cloister, she went forth, on a great enterprise of duty and devotion, into the busiest and the wildest haunts of the greatest of modern cities" (371). As she winds deeper and deeper into the city, traveling, first, to a Chartist coffeehouse where she learns the conspirators are meeting in a printshop, and, then, to the "ugly neighborhood" of Seven Dials (375), she is greeted by rude stares, insulting treatment, and, finally, physical threats. When her cab loses its wheel, Sybil finds herself surrounded by cockney slum dwellers, "a knot of young thieves, almost young enough for infant schools, a dustman, a woman nearly naked and very drunk, and two unshorn ruffians with brutality stamped on every feature." Although one of the thieves makes an unsuccessful "dash at [her] purse," the real threat is not robbery but rape—which is pictured here as being seized into prostitution. One of the ruffians makes this clear when he orders, "No wiolence . . . we'll take the young lady to Mother Poppy's, and there we'll make a night of it." At this moment a policeman fortuitously appears, coming to the rescue, ironically, not of Sybil but of her cab: "seeing one of her Majesty's carriages in trouble [he] thought he must interfere." Only when the cabman swears to Sybil's character does the policeman free her from the crowd, commenting, "Oh, that's it . . . the lady's respectable is she?" (377). As she travels on, the threat of rape/prostitution comes ever closer. Following a friendly stranger who offers to lead her to the printshop, Sybil is nearly tricked into entering a brothel: "'Here we are,' said the man; and he pushed the door open, inviting Sybil to enter. She hesitated . . . but while she faltered, an inner door was violently thrown open, and Sybil moving aside, two girls, still beautiful in spite of gin and paint, stepped into the street" (378–79). These scenes draw on yet another melodramatic scenario—the pure maiden seized into prostitution. Disraeli's use of it has something in common with Judith Walkowitz's description of W. T. Stead's successful exploitation of prostitution to sell newspapers in 1885. In a series called the "Maiden Tribute of Modern Babylon," Stead, editor of the *Pall Mall Gazette,* "documented in lurid detail how poor 'daughters of the people' were snared, trapped, and outraged, either when under the influence of drugs or after a prolonged struggle in a locked room." As Walkowitz demonstrates, such melodramatic coverage often serves the purpose of frightening women, rather than freeing them.[22]

Throughout her journey, Sybil's cloistered innocence and ladylike behavior serve a double function, both putting her at risk and inviting male rescue from the chivalrous. In the all-male setting of the Chartist coffeehouse, Sybil finds herself ignored and afraid to ask for directions: "All her feminine reserve and modesty came over her; alone in this room among men, she felt overpowered" (372). By the time she reaches Seven Dials, she is disoriented and largely unaware of her surroundings: "Absorbed in her great mission Sybil was almost insensible to the scenes through which she passed, and her innocence was thus spared many a sight and sound that might have startled her vision or alarmed her ear" (376). While her "innocence" is spared the sight of the slums, however, her ignorance leaves her more vulnerable to attack. As she hesitates at the door of a brothel, unsure of whether to enter or not, the narrator comments that "it did not agree with the description that had been given her by the coffee-house keeper, but she had seen so much since, and felt so much, and gone through so much, that she had not at the moment that clear command of her memory for which she was otherwise remarkable" (379). Seeing and yet not seeing, about to mistake a brothel for a printshop, Sybil only draws back when she comes face to face with the two young prostitutes.

Along the way, Sybil is guided by men, some of whom prove to be protectors like Egremont and some of whom prove to be villains like Morley, who take advantage of her moment of crisis. The cabman is a faithful guide, who only deserts her when his cab is disabled and even then speaks a good word for her to the policeman. All this only underlines how dependent she is on men for the fulfillment of her mission. When she realizes she is on the verge of entering a brothel, she responds with shock: "'This cannot be the house,' exclaimed Sybil starting back, overwhelmed with shame and terror. 'O! holy Virgin aid me!'" Fortunately, her exclamation attracts the attention of an Irish man who responds to her appeal for aid and her Catholic prayer with "And will I not? . . . I should like to see the arm that would hurt you" (379). He then guides her to the printshop where her father's meeting is being held. But her innocent helplessness and resulting dependence on men form a dilemma: how can she tell the true guides from the false ones? Unable to find her own way, Sybil relies on men. Ironically, the man who leads her to the brothel, who is "of a very superior appearance to the people of this quarter, good-looking, though with a dissolute air" (378), also goes out of his way for her and treats her with apparent chivalry.

Sybil reaches her father—but not in time to save him from arrest and imprisonment. The failure of her rescue mission matches her larger failure to face down harassment and define a field of action for her own. When she finally reaches the printshop, she rallies long enough to advise the conspirators to "fly" and, then, incapable of uttering another word, she faints (389–90). When a police sergeant follows on her heels, her father and his co-conspirators defend her, rather than vice versa, from being classed with the rest of them. Housed separately from the men in prison, Sybil sends a letter of appeal to Egremont who rescues her from prison and restores her to the convent. There is no evidence that she testifies at her father's trial. Her aura of saintliness and ladylike manners are not enough to protect her in a world of bestial poverty and political disorder. At the end of the novel these last two elements come together to pose a final threat to Sybil's innocence. When the Wodgate Hell-cats attack Mowbray Castle, even Harold cannot protect Sybil. Surrounded by a "band of drunken ruffians," a reminder of Seven Dials, Sybil is on the verge of being raped—"One ruffian had grasped the arm of Sybil, another had clenched her garments"—when her ultimate protector, the aristocrat Egremont, arrives, "sabre in hand," just in the nick of time, and "hurried to the rescue" (491).

"[S]ome dispute about a factory girl."—*Mary Barton*

When Mary Barton takes the train from Manchester to Liverpool on her way to provide an alibi for Jem Wilson, she overhears two men discussing Jem's upcoming trial and describing the murder of Harry Carson as arising out of "some dispute about a factory girl" (344). The two men represent the public discourse about women who step outside their proper place. As a result of the publicity surrounding the trial, Mary has become a notorious woman. It is notable, too, that this inappropriate working-class woman is characterized as "a factory girl," although, in fact, Mary works as a seamstress. The public discourse also reenacts the popular melodrama: the only story of Carson's murder that the public will hear is the story of a working-class man killing an upper-class one as they fight over the possession of a woman. Yet in contrast to the public discourse is Mary's action, independently taking the train on her mission to rescue Jem.

The issue of womanly innocence and its relationship to self-determining action is at the heart of Elizabeth Gaskell's handling of sexual harassment and women's public appearances in *Mary Barton.* In her provocative article, "Why Political Novels Have Heroines: *Sybil, Mary Barton,* and *Felix Holt,*" Ruth Bernard Yeazell argues that "the innocent heroine" provides a cover story for each novel's politics: "Each of these novels entertains the possibility of violence, even half-sympathizes with it, only to take refuge at critical moments in the representation of female innocence, exchanging a politically dangerous man for a sexually unaggressive young woman, and a narrative that threatens drastic change for one that proves reassuringly static."[23] Within the context of sexual harassment, however, the issue of a working-class heroine's "innocence" becomes political, since, according to Victorian ideology, only an absolutely pure heroine can be harassed; the others are asking for it. In fact, it is just that problematic that Gaskell tries to address in *Mary Barton* by creating a more complex working-class heroine, one who is flawed, yet not corrupt, innocent, although far from saintly.

As a heroine, Mary shares elements with both Helen Fleetwood and Sybil Gerard. Like Helen, Mary works outside the home, resists her harassment firmly and courageously, and testifies at a trial. Like Sybil, Mary faces sexual harassment on the city streets and sexual pressuring from a man she knows well. Like Sybil, too, Mary's most striking independent action is a journey of rescue into an unknown city. But Gaskell's handling of these issues is to rewrite them from still a different perspective by creating a heroine who is both more flawed and more free. Certainly, Mary Barton is a pure woman, but the quality of her innocence is different from that of Helen Fleetwood and Sybil Gerard. She is more open to her environment.[24] The ways in which her public behavior is canvassed by those who witness it demonstrates the control of women, especially working-class women, that society exercises; and, on the other hand, her braving of society's censure demonstrates her desire to exercise greater freedom, both in what she is allowed to do and in her ability to define her actions and what they mean for herself.

As Catherine Gallagher has demonstrated, *Mary Barton* is unusually self-conscious about narrative conventions and the implications of plot, at various moments drawing upon tragedy, melodrama, farce, sentimental romance, domestic fiction, and religious homily.[25] One instance of this is the careful way in which, especially in contrast to *Sybil, Mary Barton* rewrites the melodrama of the poor maiden attacked by the rich libertine. That melodrama is re-created in Mary's relationship with Harry Carson in such a way as to emphasize the working-class woman's central role and freedom of choice. Mary Barton at first meets Carson of her own free will. She finds him amusing and attractive, and she imagines marriage to him as a way out of a life of poverty. When she discovers that she loves her old friend, the mill worker Jem Wilson, however, she rejects Carson. It is at this point that Carson, not believing in her decision, begins a campaign of sexual harassment.

Here Anna Clark's analysis of how the radical melodrama erased the role of the working-class girl and emphasized instead the pain and the desire for revenge of her working-class lover or father is particularly relevant. In contrast, Gaskell emphasizes Mary's role, and Mary is no poor passive maiden: she is the one who at first enjoys Carson's attentions and, then, makes the decision to reject them. The vanity and faulty judgment that lead her to encourage Carson's attentions might be viewed by censors as inviting or deserving harassment. But the issue here is Mary's freedom, her right of choice, which must include the right to make mistakes. And, while emphasizing Mary's role, Gaskell deemphasizes the traditional leads in the working-class melodrama, those of the lover and father. Jem Wilson tries to defend Mary from Carson but only succeeds in drawing suspicion on himself after Carson is murdered. Mary's father, John, assassinates Carson, but he does so at the union's behest: perhaps Gaskell's effort to rewrite the working-class melodrama in such a way as to stress the woman's agency is one reason for the rather odd fact that Barton is completely unaware of his daughter's relationship with Carson. In any event, the focus is taken off of Barton and Wilson and placed firmly on Mary. In a final reversal, it is

Mary who protects them, rather than vice versa, destroying the evidence that links her father to the murder and traveling to Liverpool to provide an alibi for Wilson.

Some critics have argued that Mary's relationship with Carson is divorced from her role as worker and that, therefore, Gaskell misses making a crucial point about working-class oppression.[26] It is true that the class and gender power dynamics so apparent in Helen Fleetwood's life disappear here. Mary is one of Miss Simmond's "young ladies," learning the respectable trade of millinery, not a "dirty factory girl" like Helen. On the other hand, this is a strategic shift in Gaskell's rewriting of the factory girl plot, displacing the sexual melodrama on to Mary, who has not already been "prostituted" by factory work. And class elements are at the base of the Mary/Carson relationship on both sides. She sees him as glamorous wealth; he sees her as a working-class plaything which he is determined to purchase "as cheaply as he could" (180). Although he is not her employer and the workplace as a specific location has been removed, nonetheless, it is still crucial: the opportunities for Carson and Mary to meet are all related to her work as a seamstress. He first sees her in the showroom of the millinery shop, having accompanied his sisters there, and he takes advantage of "her daily walks" to and from work to pursue her (121). Later, when Mary comes to dread Carson, she thinks, "Oh! how she loathed the recollection of the hot summer evening, when, worn out by stitching, and sewing, she had loitered homewards with weary languor, and first listened to the voice of the tempter" (205). Thus, the way in which the relationship begins and develops points to the particular vulnerability of working women.

The dynamics of the Mary Barton/Harry Carson relationship provide an almost textbook example of a type of harassment. Despite her attraction to Carson, from a very early point in the relationship, Mary puts limits on it. But, as she tries to withdraw, Carson escalates his pursuit, moving from unwanted attentions to threats and finally to force. Even while she still fancies herself in love with him, she asks that he not contact her while her father is attending the Chartist convention in London. Instead, Carson sends her letters begging her to see him. When Mary realizes that she loves Jem and tries to break off her relationship with Carson, he responds by stalking her. He finds that "unless he detained her by force, he had no chance of obtaining a word as she passed him on the street on her rapid walk home" (178). After she rejects him, Mary never willingly speaks with him again, but he pursues her with unwanted attentions, sending her letters at work, "[b]ut far worse than this, was the being so constantly waylaid as she went home by her persevering lover; who had been so long acquainted with all her habits, that she found it difficult to evade him. Late or early, she was never certain of being free of him. Go this way or that, he might come up some cross street when she had just congratulated herself on evading him for that day. He could not have taken a surer mode of making himself odious to her" (187). When this tactic does not produce the desired result, Carson turns to insults and force: he "made himself almost hateful, by the unmanly force which he had used to detain her to listen to him, and the indifference with which he exposed her to the remarks of the passers-by" (205).

Finally, Carson threatens her with rape: "[H]e beset Mary more than ever. She was weary of her life for him. From blandishments he had even gone to threats—threats that whether she would or not she should be his; he showed an indifference that was almost insulting to every thing that might attract attention and injure her character" (224). These descriptions demonstrate how exposed working-class women are to the threat of sexual harassment as they must use the same streets going to and from work. The idea of Carson deliberately injuring her reputation is another issue, especially threatening when working-class women were so elided with prostitutes. Yet, even within a narrative that gives considerable weight to working women's insecure position, economically and socially, Mary is no helpless victim, no cipherlike symbol of the working class raped by the upper classes. She speaks her mind with decision and declares her right to judge and choose. At this moment, she becomes the subject of the novel, not its object, and any agency she exerts in the novel flows from this moment. This retiming of Mary's assumption of agency may seem insignificant, as many critics comment on her central role in the novel after Carson's murder. I think, however, that her coming to the foreground in relation to the sexual harassment of working-class women is important.

Her rejection of Carson and resistance of his harassment form a turning point for Mary's character. Because of her fantasies and desire to escape poverty, Mary had drifted into the habit of meeting Carson. Now, in defiance of Carson, and without the support of her father or Jem Wilson, who know nothing about her dilemma, Mary firmly resists Carson's pressure and sticks to the course she has chosen for herself. Wisely, Mary resists every attempt to communicate, even to repeat her rejection. When fellow worker Sally Leadbetter delivers Carson's letters to Mary at work, "Mary could not all at once return it, without making some sensation among the work-women. She was even forced to take several home with her. But after reading one, she determined on her plan. She made no great resistance to receiving them from Sally, but kept them unopened, and occasionally returned them in a blank half-sheet of paper" (186–87). Mary's lonely battle against harassment is the first of several crucial choices she will make for herself.

The specific issue of harassment disappears from the novel after Carson's murder, but other interconnected issues remain central to Mary's development as a heroine. Her journey to Liverpool to track down Jem's cousin Will, who can provide him with an alibi, and her testimony at Jem's murder trial bring together her self-determining actions with women's entry into public spaces. Several elements are notable here, especially in relation to the similar journey taken by Sybil. The first is that Mary makes the decision not only to make the trip but also to make it alone, over the objections of Job Legh who tries to insist that he should go: "She could not bear the idea of deputing to any one the active measures necessary to be taken in order to save Jem. She felt as if they were her duty, her right. She durst not trust to any one the completion of her plan" (340–41). Second, Mary's forays into strange streets and docks and into the courtroom repeatedly place her in situations where she is interpreted as being a fallen woman. When Mary goes to Will's lodging house in search of him, his landlady suspects "some love affair, and, perhaps, one of not the most creditable kind" (346). When, at the climax of her search, she hails Will's ship, the irritated captain responds by swearing "a dreadful oath" and calling Mary "a disgraceful name" (358). When Mary, lost on the docks, is taken home by an old boatman, his wife thinks aloud, "Perhaps . . . thou'rt a bad one" (377). The gradual erasure here of Mary's identity as a respectable working girl elides her with the prostitute even in the mind of the boatman's kind-hearted wife. There is the clear suggestion here, present in Gaskell's later fiction as well, that women must inevitably brave sexual taint in order to take effective action in the public sphere.

This erasure and reinterpretation of Mary's identity are made official, middle class, and male at the trial. On the train to Liverpool, men are gossiping about the trial as "some dispute about a factory girl" (344). At the trial itself, Mary is reimagined as notorious women from myth and history—for old Mr. Carson she becomes "the fatal Helen" (388), and a spectator at the trial reports to the narrator that on the stand Mary reminded him of a portrait of "Beatrice Cenci" (389). All of these descriptions are misinterpretations, coming from people who know nothing of Mary, and all of them suggest levels of culpability and guilt on Mary's part. And, in fact, for most of Victorian society, Mary is guilty—of making choices, and mistakes, for herself, and of choosing to place herself in the public eye by insisting on testifying at the trial. It is almost as if Carson's guilty harassment, Jem's suspected guilt, and her father's real guilt are all projected on to Mary at this point. Unlike Helen Fleetwood, however, whose witness is unsuccessful when her character comes under attack, and, unlike Sybil Gerard, who is unsuccessful in her rescue mission, Mary Barton does succeed in saving Jem. Not only that, but her testimony that she loves Jem, given at the trial, clarifies her relationship with him. For Mary Barton, public action seems to bring vindication, not only in the public sphere but also in the private.

The problem of harassment and the question of women's right to self-determination are not so easily resolvable, however, and the conclusion to *Mary Barton* is not as positive as this sequence of events might suggest. Mary collapses after her testimony and falls ill. As with Helen Fleetwood and Sybil Gerard, the confrontation with harassment and the attempt to find a way for working-class women to work and to move freely in public spaces take their toll. Gaskell will continue to struggle with this issue throughout her career in such diverse works as *Ruth, North and South,* and *Wives and Daughters*. But, if they cannot finally resolve these issues, all the novels discussed here at least recognize their importance to their heroines' lives. In many ways, their concerns about harassment and its effect on women's work and right to public places point forward to the beginnings of the women's movement in England and, in particular, to the long campaign waged against the Contagious Diseases Acts. By taking up the interconnected issues of sexual harassment and prostitution in the 1860s, middle-class feminists like Josephine Butler brought deeply buried problems out into the open and confronted the problem of the sexual double standard codified into law.[27] Thus, significantly, the middle-class-dominated feminist movement in England began when it addressed what might be termed the legalized street harassment of working-class women. With reference to the ultimate failure of such working-class heroines as Helen Fleetwood—and, to a lesser extent, Mary Barton—it should be noted, too, that it took a community of middle-class women some twenty years to get the Contagious Diseases Acts revoked. The political activity of middle-class women, particularly on sexual issues, provoked outrage. Perhaps it is not accidental that Josephine Butler's best known words describe these campaigners' willingness to confront sexual harassment: "It was not personal violence we feared so much as the mental pain inflicted by the rage, profanity and obscenity of the men, of their words and their threats. Their language was hideous. They shook their fists in our faces, with volleys of oaths. . . . The new teaching and revolt of women had stirred up the very depths of hell. We simply stood shoulder to shoulder."[28]

PART TWO

Women, Class, and Politics

Chapter 3

Two Nations
Women and Politics in *Sybil*

The estimation of the sex has ever been held a test of the civilization of a people.

—Commissioner Scriven, *Mining Report*, 1842

To read Benjamin Disraeli's *Sybil, or The Two Nations* in light of its treatment of women is to uncover a fascinating aspect of its politics.[1] Disraeli is credited by some critics with the invention of the political novel; if he did not wholly originate it, he certainly created some of its most important examples. As biographer Robert Blake comments, "Disraeli conveys the drama and excitement of parliamentary life—not to mention the comedy—in a way that no one else has quite achieved."[2] In addition to being an important political novel, *Sybil* is, of course, the inaugural "industrial novel." Its counterpointed scenes of the lives of the aristocracy and the working class, its handling of Chartism, and its blue book-inspired set pieces of poverty provide a sweeping picture of life in the early Victorian period. Unique among the usually grim industrial novels, *Sybil* has a bouncy energy that suggests that everything is up for grabs: in the course of its pages, Chartist leaders are revealed to be dispossessed aristocrats, working-class unionists are transformed into successful capitalists—and even women claim the right to involve themselves in politics.

In fact, an important theme in the novel is the possible political agency of women. With a queen on the throne and the position of working-class women a topic of impassioned debate, the political, economic, and social roles of women in general were thrown into relief. *Sybil* fully registers that fact for, although its stated focus is the two nations of the rich and the poor, its political action, as its title implies, is negotiated through women.[3] Charles Egremont becomes a member of Parliament, but the reader never sees him on the floor of the House of Commons, in committee, or even discussing his ideas with his parliamentary colleagues.[4] Instead, the reader learns of his political beliefs through his relations with women.

By the time *Sybil* was published in 1845, the use of "Woman" as a charged political symbol in relation to industrial subjects was well established. Lord Ashley's passionate oratory had forced Parliament to pass the mining bill by arguing that Woman, the fountain of life, must be returned to her proper sphere. While such language might be expected from a Tory paternalist, the same rhetoric is used by a wide variety of political thinkers: Chartists, unionists, and, eventually, even resistant Liberals join the chorus. Thus a consensus developed among politicians of very differing stripes that women were to be excluded from political life because of their domestic role. At the same time, there was a recognition of the power that could be tapped into through the use of women as political symbols. Ashley demonstrated the power of gender in the passage of the mining and factory bills in 1842 and 1847, and working-class politicians were quick to capitalize on the rhetoric of gender when pressing for further legislation to restrict women's work. In his own political life, Disraeli is well known for his particular sensitivity to women as political actors and symbols. Throughout his career, he had many female confidantes, and he was one of the first major Victorian politicians to favor women's suffrage—in theory, at least. Disraeli's election to Parliament coincided with Queen Victoria's accession to the throne—as does his hero Charles Egremont's. The Young Englandism he professed in the 1840s positioned its youthful Tory politicians as the queen's chivalrous champions. When, years later, Disraeli finally achieved his ambitions and became prime minister, his personal courting of the queen, as well as his skillful deployment of her as a symbol of Empire, are renown. Always a dramatic politician, Disraeli wrote that he "recognized imagination in government as a quality not less important than reason."[5] What better way to tap into the Victorian imagination than by images of women?

In *Sybil* every class of female character represented has marked political opinions and active involvements in political movements, from Queen Victoria; to aristocratic political hostesses such as Egremont's mother, Lady Marney; and from a trio of factory girls who support Chartism; to

Sybil herself, whose passionate commitment to the cause of the people structures her life. In fact, when one examines all the women in the novel, it is surprising how much political involvement it allows them. Clearly, Disraeli believes women are inevitably imbricated in political questions and political power. Although *Sybil* often embraces women's involvement enthusiastically, the novel also marks out two problematically slippery roles for them. On one level, there are "women," specifically classed subjects who act—like men do—out of local concerns and problems. The political commitments of the aristocratic hostesses and the factory girls best represent these classed women. On another level, there is "Woman," a class-transcendent, generalized term, used as an idealized symbol of civilization. This is the "Woman" who haunts the political rhetoric of the 1840s and appears in the pages of the novel as the inhumanly perfect Sybil. Just as later in his political career Disraeli would both feel sympathy for the cause of women's suffrage and charm Queen Victoria into allowing him to use her as political capital, so in *Sybil* women are both political subjects with agendas of their own and political objects that male politicians compete to possess.

It is revealing that, in the cases of both the politicians of the 1840s and of Disraeli's *Sybil,* this politically symbolic, idealized "Woman" emerges specifically to counter images of savage, degraded working-class women. In the factory and mining debates of the 1840s, outraged descriptions of working-class women that focused on their sexuality and their supposed lack of maternal feeling and housekeeping skills are constantly paired with invocations of "Woman" as the fountain of life and the measure of civilization. Obviously, these bifurcated images are intimately connected, two sides of one coin. The degraded images call forth the ideal in a hysterical effort to calm fears of gender anarchy. The two read together also suggest a deeply rooted dichotomous attitude toward women as virgin/whore. Thus, women are either doormats, or they are placed on pedestals.[6] In either view, they are removed from everyday life and politics, the first, because they are too far below it, the second, because they are too far above.

Sybil repeats this pattern, using working-class women as a kind of shorthand for the horrors of poverty and reproducing the most inflammatory blue book images: cursing girls, "clad in male attire" (178); "unnatural mothers," who neglect and murder their children (131); girls working in mines "[n]aked to the waist" while "an iron chain fastened to a belt of leather runs between their legs" (178). Chartist leader Walter Gerard describes working-class women as "slaves, and the slaves of slaves" (172–73), the most degraded members of a degraded class. And, just as such images provoked Lord Ashley and other politicians to counteract them by eliminating women's work and invoking images of an ideal "Woman," so both Gerard and the Tory clergyman Aubrey St. Lys see the cure for working-class degradation in an idealized feminine domesticity.

While general, theoretical discussions of working-class women and the domestic principle fall neatly in line with the rhetoric of the 1840s, however, other aspects of *Sybil* suggest a more active, although still ambiguous, political role for women. In fact, one might see the novel debating what the precise political influence of women is or should be as they alternate between, on the one hand, a slippery sort of political agency and, on the other, a symbolic role that facilitates and confirms male power. This ambiguity is reflected in every class of women that the novel represents. It appears in its depictions of three aristocratic political hostesses (Lady Marney, Lady St. Julians, and Lady Firebrace) as well as, at the other end of the social scale, the trio of factory girls (Julia, Caroline, and Harriet) who, although marginalized in the novel, always remain politically involved. It is present in the novel's invocations of Queen Victoria. Most importantly, this ambiguity culminates in the central symbol of Sybil Gerard, who is described as "a daughter of the people." But, while she supposedly represents both women and the working class, the novel constructs Sybil in such a way that, at one and the same time, she seems to represent its political philosophy and yet to be empty of political content.

"The delicate and profitable authority of woman."—*Sybil*

Book 1 of *Sybil* concretely presents the dichotomy between male political power and female political influence that the rest of the novel plays out. The first two chapters establish the aristocratic hero, Charles Egremont, as a promising younger son who has yet to find a more profitable venue for his energies than the racetrack—where he bets on a loser. In the third chapter, the narrator encapsulates a political history of England since the Stuarts—a losing history which he indicts as being a betrayal of the English people to "the triple blessings of Venetian politics, Dutch finance, and French wars" (46). It is also a history in which heroes and villains alike are male. As the narrator assesses the political roles of major players like Pitt the Younger and the Duke of Wellington as well as minor figures like Major Wildman and Lord Shelburne, no woman is mentioned, with the exception of a passing reference to Queen Victoria. Then, the male worlds of the racetrack and the history books are abandoned, and the political action of the novel is launched—by a woman.

Charles Egremont's career as a member of Parliament is arranged, of course, by his mother, Lady Marney, as is illustrated in a comic scene between the two. Having invited her son to breakfast, Lady Marney interrupts his description of the Derby: "'My dear Charles . . . we must forget your naughty horse. I sent you a little note this morning, because I wished to see you most particularly before you went out. Affairs,' continued Lady Marney, first looking around the chamber to see whether there were any fairy listening to her state secrets, 'affairs are critical'" (51). Through her political connections Lady Marney has learned that King William IV is dying and that a general election is in the offing. She tells Egremont, "It is the greatest of secrets; known at this moment only to four individuals, and I communicate it to you, my dear Charles, in that absolute confidence which I hope will always subsist between us, because it is an event that may greatly affect your career" (51–52). Charles replies, rather blankly considering the general direction of the conversation, "How so, my dear mother?" Then, she announces triumphantly, "Marbury! I have settled with Mr. Tadpole that you shall stand for the old borough" (52).

Egremont's slowness off the mark is underlined by the fact that, while he agrees that he would "like very much to be in Parliament, and particularly to sit for the old borough," he fears it would be too expensive. His mother assures him that she will canvass for him, but, while Egremont responds, "I have great faith in your canvassing" (52), he still cannot imagine how he would pay the election expenses. His mother takes care of this problem, too, agreeing to write to Egremont's estranged older brother on his behalf. As it turns out, due to his brother's stinginess, the only money Egremont receives for his election comes out of his mother's jointure. I do not want to overstate Lady Marney's political influence and acumen, especially since Disraeli treats it humorously, but he does allow her to "interfere" in male politics in a beneficial way. One might contrast the happy result of Lady Marney's political machinations with what happens to Lady Glencora Palliser in Anthony Trollope's *The Prime Minister.* When Lady Glen dabbles in politics and arranges the election of the interloper Ferdinand Lopez, the results are catastrophic: the resulting scandal brings down her husband's government, and Lopez commits suicide.[7]

At this point, not only the practical details of Egremont's start in politics but also his whole political promise lies in his close relationship to his mother and in his general susceptibility to women's influence. Women are described as being responsible for the most successful part of his education. After an undistinguished university career at Oxford, Egremont gains his real education by "yield[ing] himself to the delicate and profitable authority of woman, and, as ever happens, it softened his manners and brightened his wit. He was fortunate in having a clever mother, and he appreciated this inestimable possession" (58). So, during the crisis leading up to the passage of the 1832 Reform Bill, Egremont "took his political cue from his mother, who was his constant correspondent" (57). His openness to women stands in direct contrast to the behavior of his reactionary brother, Lord Marney. As a political spokesman, Marney condemns himself when he declares, "I don't care what women say, high or low, they always exaggerate" (190). Thus, a man's relationship to women comes to signify in shorthand his fitness for power. Lord Marney abuses every power he has—in relation to his wife, his mother, his brother, and the working people on his estate. Under the influence of women, on the other hand, Egremont will become an exemplary member of Parliament and an ideal aristocrat.

Egremont's campaign placards urge "Vote for our young Queen and Egremont" (74), and it is more than a happy accident that Egremont's election to Parliament coincides with Queen Victoria's accession to the throne. Lady Marney launches Egremont's political career, and Queen Victoria opens a new age which heightens the themes of women's political influence and symbolism. Victoria is both a specific woman acting in a specific role in a way parallel to Lady Marney and a figurehead whose symbolic function holds multiple dimensions and contradictions. One of the tenets of Young Englandism as presented in *Sybil* is the desire to restore the power and prestige of the crown. This desire already points to fading royal authority and the contradictory role of a constitutional monarch in a country where the constitution is unwritten. One may wonder, however, how enthusiastic *Sybil* would be about the power of the crown were the throne occupied by a man, instead of a woman. King William IV enters the novel dying. He is a mere mortal who is assessed as having filled his role as best he could for all his faults: "He was a good man: with feelings and sympathies; deficient in culture rather than ability; with a sense of duty; and with something of the conception of what should be the character of an English monarch. Peace to his manes!" (66). Victoria, however, is young and female, and the novel finds her a rich store of political capital.

Sybil's first book concludes with six paragraphs of purple prose celebrating the accession of Victoria to the throne. The description creates Victoria as a female symbol of the state, the Anglican Church, and the aspirations of her people. In this way, it sets up the themes that will be more fully embodied in the character of Sybil. The queen and Sybil are similar in their physical attributes and in the religious aura with which they are surrounded. Victoria is described as having "a sweet and thrilling voice" and "the blood and beauty of the Saxon" (67). Her youth and virginity connect her to Mary, the Queen of Heaven. In fact, the announcement of her elevation to the throne is described as an Annunciation with a disembodied voice calling her to difficult new duties: "in a palace in a garden, meet scene for youth, and innocence, and beauty—came the voice that told the maiden she must ascend her throne!" (66). Here, as later in his actual political life, Disraeli draws on the special symbolic power of a queen. As Adrienne Munich argues in *Queen Victoria's Secrets,* the particular successes of Victoria's monarchy were directly related to her gender: the "age's notions about woman's mysterious powers add a special aura to Victoria's monarchy . . . Victoria and her image makers could depend on the power that made a social problem and a psychological mystery of the Victorian woman. Victoria's success in permeating the cultural imagination suggests a mysterious womanly formula, made all the more secret because possessed by a queen."[8]

But, although her symbolic role draws on images of women as inspiring and hopeful and might be read, therefore, as empowering to women generally, the investiture scene separates Victoria from other women and places her in relation to the men who chivalrously serve her: "Hush! the portals open; She comes! The silence is as deep as that of a noontide forest. Attended for a moment by her royal mother and the ladies of her court, who bow and then retire, *Victoria* ascends her throne; a girl, alone, and for the first time, amid an assemblage of men." It is these men who exercise the specific active power of England. They kneel before Victoria, "pledge their troth, and take the sacred oaths of allegiance and supremacy." The final sentence of book I is a question that places Victoria in relation to *Sybil's* central political problem: "Will it be her proud destiny at length to bear relief to suffering millions, and with that soft hand which might inspire troubadours and guerdon knights, break the last links in the chain of Saxon thralldom?" (67). The ambiguity of Victoria as a symbol is emphasized by the lack of clarity as to whether it will be her active role to relieve and free her people or whether she is merely a figurehead to be served by her chivalrous ministers.

"This is a lesson for you fine ladies."—*Sybil*

The follow-up to these opening suggestions of women's practical and symbolic political influence emphasizes their negative undersides. This is particularly true and disappointing in the case of Lady Marney, who had arranged her son's election to Parliament with such aplomb. From the novel's beginning, there is a satiric tone toward the aristocratic political hostesses who believe so much depends upon them. But there is also a satiric tone toward the political agents, Tadpole and Taper, Sir Robert Peel, and the M.P.'s in general. None of these male politicians, however, gets the direct comeuppance that the women do. At first, too, most of the satire is directed at Lady Marney's competitors, Lady St. Julians and Lady Firebrace, who seem always to guess wrong when Lady Marney guesses right. But, once Egremont takes his seat in Parliament, his relations with his mother subtly change. He is still personally close to her and visits her "almost daily" (256), but "that absolute confidence" which she hoped would "always subsist" between them has disappeared (51–52). She is no longer his political confidante; in fact, she is entirely unaware of the new views he is developing. The balance of power has shifted: he is in the know; she is not. "Serious" political action takes place in the House, where speeches are given and votes are taken that are reported to women at second- or thirdhand; compared with the direct power of male politicians, women's political gossip suddenly seems trivial and pointless.

Lady Marney's disenfranchisement from her son's career is dramatized when Young England makes its first parliamentary splash by speaking against its own party, the Tories, and voting with the Whig government. When the crucial vote is about to be taken, the House rings with the orders: "'Strangers must withdraw.' 'Division: clear the gallery. Withdraw.'" Only the elect remain for the vote: "The mysteries of the Lobby are only for the initiated. Three quarters of an hour after the division was called, the result was known to the exoteric world. Majority for the Ministers thirty-seven!" (259). Primary among "the exoteric" are the aristocratic women who fancy themselves at the center of the political world.[9] This is made clear when Charles's mother and Lady St. Julians discuss their mystification at the vote and especially at the fact that a Tory M. P., Mr. Trenchard, made a speech against his own party and voted with the Whigs. As they discuss the outcome the next morning, their outsider status is underlined: Lady St. Julians asks, "[B]ut this affair of this Mr. Trenchard . . . what does it mean? Do you know the man?" Charles's mother responds, "I have heard Charles speak of him, and I think much in his favour . . . if he were here, he would tell us more about it. I wonder he does not come: he never misses looking in after a great division and giving me all the news" (260). The ladies then plot to bring Mr. Trenchard under their influence by inviting him, and especially his wife, to their houses. Lady St. Julians asserts the credo of the aristocratic political hostess:

> People get into Parliament to get on; their aims are indefinite. If they have indulged in hallucinations about place before they enter the House, they are soon freed from such distempered fancies; they find they have no more talent than other people, and if they had, they learn that power, patronage and pay are reserved for us and our friends. . . . Well then, of course such people are entirely in one's power, if one only had time and inclination to notice them. You can do anything with them. Ask them to a ball, and they will give you their votes; invite them to dinner and if necessary they will rescind them; but cultivate them, remember their wives at assemblies and call their daughters, if possible, by their right names; and they will not only change their principles or desert their party for you; but subscribe their fortunes if necessary and lay down their lives in your service (261).

But, when Egremont finally appears, he puts paid to these ideas of aristocratic female political power. To his mother's surprise, he reveals that the traitorous Mr. Trenchard is "one of my intimate acquaintance" (262). In fact, he has just breakfasted with him, instead of with her. Egremont does not bother to explain his or Trenchard's political motivations; he simply makes clear that Trenchard is impervious to women's influence. He is not married, he has refused Egremont's invitations to visit his mother's house, and "[h]e has a horror of fine ladies; and there is nothing in the world he more avoids than what you call society" (263). Almost as if he had just overheard Lady St. Julians boasting about her power, Egremont concludes with the independent male politician's rejection of it: "This is a lesson for you fine ladies, who think you can govern the world by what you call your social influences: asking people once or twice a-year to an inconvenient crowd in your house; now haughtily smirking, and now impertinently staring, at them; and flattering yourselves all this time, that to have the occasional privilege of entering your saloons and the periodical experience of your insolent recognition, is to be a reward for great exertions, or if necessary an inducement to infamous tergiversation" (263–64). Having made his political allies within the House, Egremont rejects the female influence that got him there.

The power of Queen Victoria as constitutional monarch and female symbol of the nation is not disposed of so summarily as is the reign of the aristocratic political hostesses. But, after the paean of praise at her accession, Victoria is nearly invisible. She is occasionally invoked by the poor as their traditional protectress. The narrator suggests in passing that her heart is with her people, rather than with the greedy oligarchy, by having two minor M. P.'s gossip about the fact that "[t]he Queen is not over partial to making more peers" (249) and "[t]hey say her Majesty is more touched about these affairs of the Chartists than anything else" (250). It is suggested, too, that this is a politically propitious moment for her to assert herself because "when parties are in the present state of equality, the Sovereign is no longer a mere pageant" (250). But the central political event that Victoria provokes in *Sybil* is the minor, almost laughable, constitutional crisis, that has been nicknamed "the Bedchamber Plot." In May 1839, the Whig ministry of Lord Melbourne resigned and Sir Robert Peel was invited to form a Tory government. Victoria, however, refused to dismiss her Whig Ladies of the Bedchamber, and Peel, in turn, refused to take office unless she allowed him to appoint new court ladies. This stalemate returned the Whigs to power.

The novel handles this one concrete instance of Victoria's political power in a contradictory way. First, when it emerges that it is women who are keeping the Whigs in office and the Tories out of it, the narrator jokes about petticoat government: "It seemed, though of course no one could for a moment credit it, that these wrong-headed, rebellious ministers who would not go out, wore—petticoats! Was Conservatism, that mighty mystery of the nineteenth century—was it after all to be brained by a fan!" (327–28). Politicians at the time (including Disraeli), and historians since, have faulted Victoria's behavior, accusing her of acting unconstitutionally and of being motivated by a narrow-minded favoritism. Certainly, Victoria's emphasis on the social prerogatives of the crown aligns her with the triviality of which the aristocratic hostesses were accused, rather than the supposedly high-minded politics of the Young Englanders. The timing of the plot was such that it also distracted Parliament from serious consideration of the Charter, thus hinting that the queen was not so concerned with Chartism as to ignore the importance of patronage.

Although the narrator must assess the political outcome as negative because it kept the Whigs in power, he diplomatically chooses to emphasize the queen's untapped political potential rather than her actions: "A youthful princess on the throne, whose appearance touched the imagination, and to whom her people were generally inclined to ascribe something of that decision of character which becomes those born to command, offered a favourable opportunity to restore the exercise of that regal authority, the usurpation of whose functions has entailed on the people of England so much suffering and so much degradation." Then, he uses the occasion to criticize Sir Robert Peel's leadership of the Tory Party. The first of Peel's faults is his inability to handle the queen, or to put it another way, his lack of chivalry: "It was unfortunate that one who, if any, should have occupied the proud and national position of the leader of the tory party, chief of the people and champion of the throne, should have commenced his career as minister under Victoria by an unseemly contrariety to the personal wishes of the Queen" (329). The suggestion is that a Tory Party which took Young Englandism as its credo would return to its roots by strengthening the monarchy and, by the by, itself.

"The daughter of the people."—*Sybil*

Thus the female political influence that is celebrated in book 1 is later rejected by Egremont as a serious male politician, as in the case of the political hostesses, or is shown as being caught up in contradictions of which it is unaware, as in the case of the queen. One might argue that these problems are resolved in Sybil herself, who becomes the central female political influence on Egremont. Indeed, Sybil inherits the power of both Egremont's mother and the queen and seems to carry their influence to a higher level. For example, in an exchange that symbolizes Egremont's shift of political allegiance from his mother to Sybil, his mother invites him to choose a birthday gift, and he selects a painting from her apartment which is the image of Sybil, "the portrait of a saint by Allori: the face of a beautiful young girl, radiant and yet solemn, with rich tresses of golden brown hair, and large eyes dark as night, fringed with ebon lashes that hung upon the glowing cheek" (257). Sybil also has the thrilling voice, the sacred presence, the Mariological resonances, and the spiritual link with the people that the novel connects with the queen. Lest the reader somehow miss these parallels, when Sybil visits the Trafford's factory village, the children greet her with the cry, "the queen, the queen," and Sybil replies, "'My subjects" (226).[10] But, as I will argue, Sybil, the apparent heiress of women's political authority, is removed to a symbolic sphere that erases female power, even as it seems to celebrate it, and turns her into a political prize for men.

The role of Sybil and her eventual marriage to Egremont have been central interpretive cruxes for the novel. Two problems enter into any attempt at interpretation. The first is the characterization of Sybil. Thom Braun calls her "rather inhuman, even spectral," while Ruth Yeazell argues that she "resembles an icon rather than a woman."[11] Emphasizing Sybil as a symbol rather than a character, Catherine Gallagher argues that her marriage to Egremont "represents the Coleridgean union of the sacred with its rightful representative, the state," while for Robert O'Kell the marriage is part of the novel's political allegory: "the wedding of sensitive but secular leadership to the spirit of piety and devotion."[12]

The second, interrelated problem is Sybil's ambiguous class status. Why is she introduced as "the daughter of the people" and revealed to be an aristocrat at the novel's end? Some critics have felt cheated by that sleight of hand. For example, John Lucas criticizes the transformation as "a piece of creaking plot mechanism" that reveals the novel's hollowness, while Patrick Brantlinger emphasizes that, although one might be tempted to reject the transformation and marriage as "tommyrot," in fact it points to the very paradoxical nature of the novel's treatment of the Two Nations theme.[13] On the other hand, Gallagher argues that Sybil "does not represent first one class and then another, but neither," and O'Kell points out that Sybil's aristocratic heritage is suggested from the very beginning.[14] Actually, I find all these contradictory interpretations valid on some level. The mystical association of Sybil with the working class is repeated several times: Sybil refers to herself as "a daughter of the people" on three occasions (160, 336, 364). Egremont, and the unwary reader, are mislead into thinking of her as such as well: Egremont muses: "Who was this girl, unlike all women whom he had yet encountered, who spoke with such sweet seriousness of things of such vast import, but which had never crossed his mind, and with a kind of mournful majesty bewailed the degradation of her race? The daughter of the lowly, yet proud of her birth" (168–69). How can Sybil be both the representative of the working class and of aristocratic pedigree and yet also be seen as somehow sacred and classless? How can she be seen as eternally above politics and yet married to the state or to secular leadership? The answers lie in the political symbolism of "Woman," for "Woman" is a transclass or class-transcendent category. Thus as the ideal female character, Sybil functions as both the moral representative of the people and a born aristocrat, as both above politics and yet crucial to its development.

As the novel's title—*Sybil, or The Two Nations*—suggests, Sybil becomes a pivotal symbol for understanding its politics. The title implies some kind of equivalence between Sybil and the two nations of the rich and the poor whose political conflict the novel represents and attempts to resolve. This appears to make her political effect much more important than that of the aristocratic hostesses or even the queen, with whom she is paralleled. But, in fact, by separating Sybil from class and creating her as "Woman," the novel empties Sybil of any real political content. Gallagher quite rightly comments that Sybil "has no real political involvement," but that is not to say that she has no political uses.[15] Although she seems to represent a creed, Sybil is a political cipher, but at the same time she is the pivot that the novel's political plot turns around. At first she reflects the political beliefs of her Chartist father, Walter Gerard, as later she will reflect the Young England beliefs of her future husband, Egremont. That is her function in the novel: not to stand for political content herself but to serve as a sign, to confer political authority on the man who possesses her. And that is also the significance of her movement in the plot and its use of her as an object of exchange. Walter Gerard thinks of returning her to the convent, suggesting that no man is worthy of such authority. Three politically ambitious men—Charles Egremont, Stephen Morley, and Baptist Hatton—maneuver to win her hand in marriage because, again, the man who possesses her possesses the sign of political authority. It is at this point that it becomes clear that, however imbricated Sybil seems to be with class, she actually stands for her gender, for "Woman," an object of political exchange and a category that is seen as detached from class, and, therefore, from which all specific political content has been emptied. Like Queen Victoria, she seems to transcend class; like the queen, too, she has the symbolic role of conferring authority on men. And yet in this apparently exalted position, she possesses no political power of her own; instead, she clarifies the ways in which male politicians can use the category of "Woman" as a mirror that reflects back to them their own ideology and power.

Sybil's function as a political cipher is marked in many of the key elements of her character's presentation. One is the special significance of her name, which her suitors note. When Egremont first visits the Gerards' cottage, he examines a religious book inscribed with her name and exclaims, "Sybil Gerard! What a beautiful name is Sybil!" Sybil's father then explains the name's family history: "My mother's name . . . and my grandame's name, and a name I believe has been about our hearth as long as our race; and that's a very long time indeed" (215). Later, Baptist Hatton muses, "Her name is Sybil. Curious how, even when peasants, the good blood keeps the good old family names! The Valences were ever Sybils" (309). These repeated generations of Sybils connect themselves with the classical prophetesses, and, like Sybil herself, the ancient sibyls contradictorily suggest innate and special female powers at the same time that they continuously confirm male power.[16] In Virgil's *Aeneid* the famous Cumaean Sibyl was Aeneas's guide for his descent into the Underworld as Sybil might be seen as Egremont's guide as he descends into the underworld of the nineteenth-century working class. Aeneas later goes on to found Rome as Egremont will become a leader of a new generation of aristocrats. When the sibyl speaks, what she says is wrapped in darkness, so an interpreter is needed to decode her words. The fragmentary "Sibylline books" were kept in Rome to be consulted by the male leaders in times of crisis, again, just as Sybil's mysterious utterances about the people supposedly help Egremont to develop a politically coherent Young Englandism that will rescue the country from Chartism and political anarchy. My point is that the sibyls' gifts are used in the service of men who go on to found nations or steer them through political turmoil.

Sybil's virginity is also emphasized in the novel. She is first heard singing the evening hymn to the Blessed Virgin, and her every appearance emphasizes her otherworldly purity (96). She has lived most of her life in a convent and is considering taking vows as a nun. This excess of virginity makes her a blank page on which her husband will eventually write.[17] Her virginity is symbolic of her lack of experience—not only of sexual difference but also of class difference. As her father puts it: "She has passed a still sweet life in the convent . . . and Sybil knows nothing of the real world except its sufferings" (172). Even the sufferings she witnesses at a remove, rather than experiences for herself. When she visits the Trafford's factory village, she is received as a queen. When she goes to the poverty-stricken home of the unemployed weaver, Warner, she comes as a Lady Bountiful with a basket of food from the convent. Her sweet angelic behavior contrasts with the complainings of Warner's sickly wife: "[T]he querulous spirit of the wife was subdued by the tone of Sybil" (157). But Sybil's protected upbringing has given her little to complain of.[18] She may call herself "a daughter of the people," but "[i]t was impossible that one so rarely gifted and educated with so much daintiness, could ever make a wife of the people" (433). As her father tells Egremont, the convent may be the best place for her: "I would not have her take the veil rashly, but if I lose her it may be for the best. For the married life of a woman of our class in the present condition of our country is a lease of woe . . . slaves, and the slaves of slaves? Even woman's spirit cannot stand against it; and it can bear against more than we can, master" (172–73). A woman's experience of working-class life is represented here both as sexual and as a form of degradation; Sybil's convent background is the sign of her complete separation from its pollution. Thus the novel arrives at the contradiction that the "Woman" who represents "the people" is a woman who has no working-class experiences.

"An ambition that you shall govern."—*Sybil*

Sybil also functions symbolically in the novel's plot to the point where her placement is like the possession of the staff of office or the queen sending for the party leader. As she moves from the convent to her father's house and back again, from the courtship of three men to marriage to Egremont, so moves symbolic political authority. As the novel opens, Sybil has just left the convent to make a home with her father. Thus begins a contest for the future leadership of England. At this point, it seems that Gerard is best suited to that leadership: he is both an aristocrat of blood and a moral leader of the people. On the other hand, there is some doubt:

Sybil is his daughter, not his wife, and it is likely that she will leave him eventually, either to marry or to enter the convent. Gerard's relationship with his daughter is the novel's shorthand for his position of authority, and eventually he will lose both her and it. For the first half of the novel, her belief in his ability to lead the people is unshakeable. "What a leader of the people you would make!," she tells him (211). When she accompanies him to the Chartist Convention in London, she declares to Egremont, "All I desire, all I live for, is to soothe and support him in his great struggle; and I should die content if the People were only free, and a Gerard had freed them" (285). After hearing her father address the convention, she tells Morley, "When I heard my father speak the other night, my heart glowed with emotion; my eyes were suffused with tears; I was proud to be his daughter; and I gloried in a race of forefathers who belonged to the oppressed and not to the oppressors" (304). Significantly, as is usually the case in the novel, the reader does not hear the speech itself but, instead, is offered a woman's reaction to it. Sybil's emotional vote of confidence will later be transferred from her father's speeches to Egremont's.

There is, however, one point on which Gerard and his daughter disagree—the use of physical force—and that will eventually separate them. When Gerard discusses his attraction to armed struggle with her, Sybil warns that "there is ever your fatal specific of physical force" (210) and urges, "Oh! my father, I will believe that moral power is irresistible, or where are we to look for hope?" (211). In London, as he becomes more and more deeply involved in plotting armed resistance to the government, Gerard also sees less and less of his daughter and does not confide his plans to her. The crucial break between father and daughter occurs when Sybil confronts him about the conspiracy. Attempting to dissuade him from violence, she warns that "these are riots in which you are involved, not revolutions; and you will be a victim, and not a sacrifice" (357). When Gerard stubbornly defends his involvement, Sybil predicts his loss of leadership: "You have let this great moral power, this pearl of price, . . .—we cannot conceal it from ourselves, my father,—you have let it escape from your hands" (359). This disagreement provokes their only argument, but it is an argument with long-lasting results. Gerard dismisses Sybil's fears as "womanish weakness" (358), and when she urges him to return to their country home with her, he responds, "almost in a voice of harshness," "'I have no home, . . . but if the people will struggle, I will struggle with them; and die, if need be, in the front. Nor will I be deterred from my purpose by the tears of a girl,' and he released himself from the hand of his daughter with abruptness" (359–60). Gerard's rejection of womanly counsel as weak and emotional and his separation from Sybil signal his loss of authority. Father and daughter will never again share a home. First, they are separated by his prison term of a year and a half while she returns to the convent. When released, although, remarkably, he manages to get another job, he does not make enough money to provide a home for his daughter. They meet when they can, but such meetings are "comparatively rare": "the cheerful hearth and welcome home were no longer for Gerard" (433). Not only has he lost his daughter and his home, but he has also lost his claim to political authority.

The strange machinations of the courtship plot in *Sybil* take on new meaning if one equates the ownership of Sybil with the legitimation of political authority. At various points, Sybil declares that she will take the veil, implying that no man is worthy of being entrusted with England's political future. After the failure of the Charter, in her disillusionment with politics, Sybil tells Egremont that "my content at least . . . has never rested I hope too much on this world" (353). As Gerard ponders his daughter's future, he considers possible suitors but often agrees that the convent might be the best place for her: "But, to my mind, Sybil is right. She cannot look to marriage: no man that she could marry would be worthy of her" (347). The three men who compete for Sybil's hand in marriage—Egremont, Morley, and Hatton—represent three opposing political viewpoints, and each man sees Sybil in explicit relation to his ambitions. Thus, as they secretly jockey for position, they are competing not for mere marriage but also for political power. Notably, none of them is open about his desire to marry Sybil, each of them cozies up to her father, and each of them misrepresents himself—or, to put it less elegantly, lies—during his pursuit of her. In other words, political intrigue—including tactical alliances, secret rivalries, betrayals, and conspiracies—surrounds the courtship of Sybil.

Baptist Hatton makes the equation of Sybil with political legitimation the most obvious because he is cold-bloodedly rational about his pursuit of power and, thus, about his desire to marry Sybil, which are the same thing. He betrayed the Gerards long ago by selling the evidence of their aristocratic right to Mowbray Castle to its present occupant. Out of that betrayal, he has made an immense fortune, and he now hankers to rid himself of the blot on his conscience while at the same time founding a family. Sybil, a Catholic like himself, and, as he alone can prove, an aristocrat of blood, is merely the route to fulfilling those aspirations. Through her, he could legitimate his money and connect his lineage to that of an old aristocratic house. Hatton muses, "And for what object all this wealth and power? What memory shall I leave? What family shall I found? . . . Ah! had I a child—a child like the beautiful daughter of Gerard! . . . Could I restore her to the rank she would honour, assuage these sharp pangs of conscience, and achieve the secret ambition of my life? What if my son were to be Lord Valence? . . . To build up a great Catholic house again; of the old blood, and the old names, and the old faith,—by holy Mary it is a glorious vision!" (309–10).

As he assesses his chances of winning her, Hatton compares himself to another master politician: "I'm not a crook-backed Richard" (309). He may not be a hunchback, but he is a liar and a manipulator, like Shakespeare's Richard III, and, like that Richard, he is willing to marry for political gain. His desire has nothing to do with any passion for Sybil herself. The narrator explains that "Hatton was not, what is commonly understood by the phrase, in love with Sybil. . . . He wished still to marry Sybil for the great object that we have stated [founding a house]; he had a mind quite equal to appreciate her admirable qualities, but sense enough to wish that she were a less dazzling creature, because then he would have a better chance of accomplishing his end" (346). Hatton is a rationalist whose plots await the main chance. This suggests that his restoration of an aristocratic house would not involve any care for the people but would, instead, again like Shakespeare's Richard, be a usurpation of true authority.

Stephen Morley's case is more complex, and, for a while, he seems a worthy suitor for Sybil's hand. As Gerard contemplates Sybil's future, he assesses Morley favorably as a possible husband: "There was of all the men of his own order but one, who from his years, his great qualities, his sympathy, and the nature of his toil and means, seemed not unfitted to be the husband of his daughter; and often had Gerard mused over the possibility of these intimate ties with Morley. Sybil had been, as it were, bred up under his eye; an affection had always subsisted between them; and he knew well that in former days Sybil had appreciated and admired the great talent and acquirements of their friend" (433–34). Morley, too, at first seems to represent the people, as Sybil does. He presents the Two Nations idea to Egremont, and he has devoted his life to the people. His closeness to Sybil is based on these shared political sympathies. At times Sybil trusts his judgment more than her father's, as when she insists on Moral Power rather than physical force.

But Disraeli destroys Morley's character in such a way as to ruin both his marital and political hopes. It seems inexplicable that the same man who espouses Moral Force and serves the people with seeming selflessness could act as despicably as he does. As discussed in the previous chapter, Morley's working-class politics are presented as a front for sexual predation, and his role as a political leader is further undercut by what Rosemarie Bodenheimer calls "the contradiction between political theory and political action."[19] Theoretically, Morley's solution to the problems of the people is to replace the family with community, but this solution cannot finally coexist with his drive to possess both Sybil and political power. And, unlike Hatton, Morley's desire for Sybil is overriding and intense, suggesting an unscrupulous, irrational lust for power. Morley's politics are at odds with his emotions, an opposition which demonstrates that his beliefs not only deny abstract human nature but, more concretely, deny his own nature. Thus, he becomes a double-dyed hypocrite and betrays both Sybil and his political beliefs in ways which are intertwined. Morley's every action regarding Sybil is underhanded. He politically allies himself with her father, not because he agrees with his politics but in order to stay close to her. Similarly, he attends the Chartist Convention, not because he shares its goals but, as he explains to Sybil, because "[t]he fact is, in active life one cannot afford to refine. I could have wished the movement to have taken a different shape and to have worked for a different end; but it has not done this. But it is still a movement and a great one, and I must work it for my end and try to shape it to my form. If I had refused to be a leader, I should not have prevented the movement; I should only have secured my own insignificance" (304).

Morley supposedly believes in Moral Power, not physical force, but, again, his actions toward Sybil reveal the opposite. When he recognizes Egremont as a rival for Sybil's affections, he attacks him in the dark and attempts to kill him. He is similarly ruthless, grasping at every foothold, when he reveals his passion to Sybil. His declaration intertwines his secret pursuit of Sybil with each step in his political career: "And love of you, Sybil, has been to me for years the hoarded treasure of my life. For this I have haunted your hearth and hovered around your home; for this I have served your father like a slave, and embarked in a cause with which I have little sympathy, and which can meet with no success. It is your image that has stimulated my ambition, developed my powers, sustained me in the hour of humiliation, and secured me that material prosperity which I can now command" (365–66). By the end of the novel, Morley has sunk so low that he betrays the people by conspiring with Hatton, using his political influence to provoke a mob attack on Mowbray Castle in order to steal the document that proves Sybil an aristocrat. In his increasingly desperate attempts to win Sybil, Morley is like a politician who will stop at nothing in order to retain his grasp on power.

The true marriage of politician and symbol, of course, is that of Egremont and Sybil. The marriage, however, might not be quite as ideal as the novel claims it is. Like Hatton and Morley, Egremont lies so that he can be near Sybil when he takes on the disguise of the journalist, Mr. Franklin. Like them, he directly relates Sybil to his political ambitions. But, unlike them, his courtship of her is chivalrous and presented as gradually meshing with his political convictions, rather than conflicting with them. A large part of the courtship and marriage between politician and symbol has to do with the balance of power between them, a balance that, at first, seems to work in Sybil's favor but eventually rewards Egremont. Like Egremont's mother, Lady Marney, Sybil begins as a powerful influence because she, too, performs the important function of securing his vocation to him. Lady Marney hands Egremont a seat in Parliament; Sybil links him to a cause—improving the lives of the poor. But, again, as with his mother, once Egremont has been introduced to the cause, he will reject Sybil's guidance. Even so, Sybil crucially differs from Lady Marney in that her influence is strictly spiritual and emotional, never practical and concrete. In other words, she provides a general inspiration for Egremont, not a specific direction for his talents. Egremont's first encounter with Sybil in the grounds of Marney Abbey encapsulates her inspirational function and her separation from specific politics. When Egremont visits the abbey, he is already brooding about the reasons behind a rickburning on his brother's estate. With these thoughts troubling him, he meets Gerard and Morley, and their comments provide a political context for his musings. Gerard argues that the monks had been defenders of the poor, and that the despoliation of the Church had resulted in the degradation of the poor and, then, Morley makes the "Two Nations" speech. It is not until this moment that Sybil is introduced as a beautiful image, "a female form" with a countenance that "was impressed with a character of almost divine majesty" (97). The specific political content of the scene is provided by the men; Sybil does not even speak to Egremont. Her image, however, connects itself to Morley's speech about "The Rich and the Poor" and gives it an added emotional charge for Egremont. His consideration of and solution to the political problem will be connected to his discovery of the mystery of Sybil and his eventual possession of her as his wife.

The opening pattern is repeated a second time when Egremont meets the clergyman, Aubrey St. Lys, whose political arguments mirror Gerard's. Egremont accompanies St. Lys on a visit to the destitute Warner family, and there he sees Sybil again. As they talk, Sybil shocks Egremont's aristocratic pride when she attacks his family: "What people they must be—that family of sacrilege who hold these lands! . . . the people were most wretched round the Abbey; nor do I think there is any other cause for their misery, than the hard hearts of the family that have got the lands" (159). Egremont responds to her emotional intensity: "You feel deeply for the people!," and she responds, "I may well feel for them, even if I were not the daughter of their blood" (160). As in their first meeting, Egremont begins by being interested in the question of the rich and the poor on his own account. Further, it is again a man—this time St. Lys, instead of Gerard and Morley—who presents him with background information and who interprets the present political situation for him. Finally, Sybil enters and intensifies Egremont's emotional connection to the issues; his attraction to her combines with his already established interest in the people, and is heightened even more when she tells him that she is one of them.

Sybil's emotional influence over Egremont *is* important. Without her attractions, Egremont may well have forgotten about the problems of the poor and become a stereotypical Tory M.P. He takes a different developmental route when, in order to be near her, he abandons his aristocratic name and life and lives as Mr. Franklin in a humble cottage. But, however one might rate this on a political scale, once Egremont takes his seat in Parliament, Sybil's influence, like Lady Marney's, is at an end. This is made clear as their political arguments are counterpointed with his marriage proposals. In London at the Chartist Convention, Gerard learns that Egremont is not only an aristocrat but also a member of the hated Marney family. When this is revealed to Sybil, Egremont excuses his masquerade as Mr. Franklin by explaining that "I was told . . . that an impassable gulf divided the Rich from the Poor . . . I possessed a station which entailed on me some portion of its responsibility; to obtain that knowledge which could alone qualify me for beneficial action, I resolved to live without suspicion among my fellow-subjects who were estranged from me" (299). But Sybil rejects his efforts to cross the gulf: "I am one of those who believe the gulf is impassable . . . utterly impassable" (300).

Despite Sybil's declaration, the next day Egremont seeks her out in a scene that opens with a political debate and climaxes in a marriage proposal. Egremont's proposal emphasizes the influence that Sybil has exerted over his political life and promises her more. He says that "from the moment I first beheld you in the starlit arch of Marney has your spirit ruled my being and softened every spring of my affections. I followed you to your home, and lived for a time content in the silent worship of your nature. Since then for a moment your image has never been absent from my consciousness; your picture consecrates my hearth and your approval has been the spur of my career . . . I cannot offer you wealth, splendour, or power; but I can offer you the devotion of an entranced being—aspirations you shall guide—an ambition that you shall govern!" Sybil's response is "These words are mystical and wild" (335). They might strike a reader the same way, but for different reasons. Sybil is amazed that Egremont proposes a "union between the child and brother of nobles and a daughter of the people!" (336). But the real mysticism lies in Egremont's claim that Sybil will guide his aspirations and govern his ambition.

The political argument that leads up to his proposal completely rejects Sybil's guidance and governance. Egremont begins by telling her that she is "prejudiced" and "in error." The source of her flawed politics, Egremont argues, is that "you have formed your opinions upon tradition, not upon experience" (333). Here, he points to the essence of Sybil's contradiction, as well as all women who fall into the category of ideal Womanhood: the very lack of experience that makes her an influential political symbol at the same time makes her specific political convictions dismissible. He lectures her: "The world that exists is not the world of which you have read; the class that calls itself your superior is not the same class as ruled in the time of your fathers. There is a change in them as in all other things, and I participate in that change" (333–34). When Sybil tries to defend her position, arguing that "[i]f there be a change, . . . it is because in some degree the People have learnt their strength," Egremont sweeps her objections aside: "Ah! dismiss from your mind those fallacious fancies." Now Egremont is the expert on the people: "The People are not strong; the People never can be strong. Their attempts at self-vindication will end only in their suffering and confusion." Now he prophesies: "The new generation of the aristocracy of England are not tyrants, not oppressors, Sybil, as you persist in believing. . . . They are the natural leaders of the People, Sybil; believe me they are the only ones" (334). He then proves his claim by revealing the specific inside knowledge that her father is about to be betrayed by his associates.

Although the scene ends with Sybil rejecting both Egremont's marriage proposal and his politics, his ideas quickly become hers, and it soon becomes clear that the power in the relationship now belongs to him. At their next meeting, Sybil is ready to transfer her political loyalties to him. Egremont had predicted both the failure of the Charter and the betrayal of her father. In the wake of his predictions, seemingly overnight, Sybil discovers their truth for herself: "The People she found was not that pure embodiment of unity of feeling, of interest, and of purpose, which she had pictured in her abstractions" (349). Her belief in the perfection of the people damaged, Sybil finds another truth in Egremont. In a scene that emphasizes women's exclusion from active politics at the same time that it confirms Egremont's right to lead, Sybil reads a journal report of his speech to the House of Commons on the presentation of the Charter and finds comfort there:

> Yes! there was one voice that had sounded in that proud Parliament, that free from the slang of faction, had dared to express immortal truths: the voice of a noble, who without being a demagogue, had upheld the popular cause; had pronounced his conviction that the rights of labour were as sacred as those of property; that if a difference were to be established, the interests of the living wealth ought to be preferred; who had declared that the social happiness of the millions should be the first object of a statesman, and that if that were not achieved, thrones and dominions, the pomp and power of courts and empires, were alike worthless. (350)

This is the fullest expression of Egremont's politics provided by the novel, and it is presented at secondhand and by a woman. In assenting to it, Sybil does not react with questions, argument, or even discussion. Instead, her vote of confidence in Egremont is intuitive and emotional: "With a heart not without emotion; with a kindling cheek, and eyes suffused with tears, Sybil read the speech of Egremont. She ceased; still holding the paper with one hand, she laid on it the other with tenderness, and looked up to breathe as it were for relief" (350–51). Significantly, Sybil is reading the speech, not in the house of Chartist intrigue that she shares with her father in London, but in a fair garden, recalling the scene in which Queen Victoria learns of her accession. Like Victoria, Sybil listens to a disembodied voice: it calls her, however, not to political duties of her own but to belief in a male politician.

As if to underline that fact, Egremont suddenly appears before her in the flesh. Sybil looks up from the speech and "smiled through a gushing vision; and with a flushed cheek, impelled perhaps by her native frankness, perhaps by some softer and irresistible feeling of gratitude, respect, regard, she said in a low voice, 'I was reading your beautiful speech.'" Although Egremont calls her response "an honour,—a pleasure,—a reward, I never could have even hoped to have attained" (352), the transfer of political power has been ratified. Sybil no longer has the right to speak for the people as their daughter. Her faith in her cause and in herself has been shattered. When Egremont points out how quickly this change has occurred—"But when we spoke last, . . . you were full of confidence—in your cause, and in your means"—Sybil admits, "Alas! . . . I was but a dreamer of dreams" (352–53). She has even lost confidence in her ability to influence her father. When Egremont urges her to advise him to leave London, she asks: "Can I give counsel? . . . I who have been wrong in all my judgments? I came up to this city with him, to be his guide, his guardian. What arrogance! What short-sighted pride!" (353). Still, while she admires Egremont's beautiful speech, she doubts his political potency, his ability to influence others to follow him. Their discussion concludes with another lecture from Egremont on the readiness of the aristocracy to follow Young England.

Sybil and Egremont meet two more times, the second time never to be parted again. As if to answer Sybil's one doubt, each occasion confirms Egremont's power. When he first met Sybil, Egremont posed as a humble Mr. Franklin; then, he appeared before her as a member of the despised Marney family and as a suppliant for her hand in marriage. Now, Egremont appears, not so much in a personal role, but backed by the full power of the aristocracy. Each time, Sybil is the suppliant, Egremont, the savior. The first time they meet again, Sybil and her father have been arrested for conspiracy against the government. Sybil sends a note from prison to "The Hon. Charles Egremont M. P." which concludes: "You are powerful; you know all; you know what I say is truth. None else will credit it. Save me!" (394). Egremont saves Sybil by speaking directly to Lord John Russell who is attending a party at his mother's, thus securing a warrant for Sybil's release from the secretary of state (385). As the prison warden's wife comments: "There is nothing like a friend at court" (398). They meet the second time during the attack on Mowbray Castle when, leading a regiment of troops, Egremont rescues her from the mob. Egremont's persuasive oratory, knowledge of politics, hands turning the wheels of power—whether the power to influence the law or the power to command troops—win Sybil's heart and, perhaps more significantly for the themes of the novel, her political allegiance. As Sybil remembers his words of advice about her father, she thinks: "His voice even now lingered in her ear. She recalled without an effort those tones of the morning, tones of tenderness and yet of wisdom and considerate thought, that had sounded only for her welfare. Never had Egremont appeared to her in a light so subduing. He was what man should be to woman ever—gentle, and yet a guide" (361–62). "What man should be to woman ever": in a short space of time, Sybil travels a long way—from faith in the people and in herself to faith in the aristocracy and reliance on Egremont, from putatively having the power to guide his aspirations and govern his ambitions to being subdued by him and finding, that, although he did not at first appear in that light, in fact, he is "gentle, and yet a guide."

"Such shameless hussies as our Harriet."—*Sybil*

There is a final group of women in *Sybil* who are also involved in politics—the factory girls, Caroline, Julia, and Harriet. Although they are very minor characters—the working class is primarily represented by their male counterparts, Devilsdust and Dandy Mick—these women join in discussions of the issues of the day by voicing their enthusiasm for the Charter and the Ten Hours Bill. As the battle drags on, Mick declares: "The gals is the only thing what has any spirit left. Julia told me just now she would go to the cannon's mouth for the Five Points any summer day" (424). Interestingly, these three girls remain the most politically involved and unsubdued of all the women in *Sybil*. In many ways their lives are the Victorian nightmare of female rebellion. They have all the forbidden fruits: money, sexual freedom, fancy dress. They desert their families and set up housekeeping on their own so that they can spend their money on themselves and live free of parental supervision. They leave the moral supervision of Trafford's mill for factories that do not impose such regulations on their employees: "'At the Trafford's,' said Caroline, 'the greatest fun we ever had was a singing class'" (130). They dress "gaily" with "their hair scrupulously arranged," wearing "coral neck-laces and earrings of gold" (121). They pal around together and keep company with men when and where they please. When Dandy Mick invites them to the pub, the Temple of the Muses, Caroline replies, "Oh! I love the Temple! 'Tis so genteel! I was speaking of it to Harriet last night; she never was there. I proposed to go with her but two girls alone,—you understand me. One does not like to be seen in these places, as if one kept no company" (122–23).

Yet the novel does not demonize these women. Boisterous and happy-go-lucky, they are teenage girls out for a good time. Harriet Warner is singled out for the harshest treatment because she has deserted her needy family. But, even so, there are hints that that desertion is not so much monstrous as merely human. Her mother whines, attacking her as a "shameless hussy" and telling her younger daughters, "You are good girls; you will never be like that infamous Harriet. When you earn wages you will give them to your poor mother and baby, won't you?" (156). But her unemployed father, perhaps with a touch of envy, is more sympathetic as he explains, "She has long murmured at her hard lot; working like a slave and not for herself. And she has gone, as they all go, to keep house for herself" (149–50).

Near the end of the novel, long after Lady Marney and Sybil have been silenced, the factory girls still declare their political convictions with enthusiasm. Caroline announces: "I will never marry any man who is not for the Five Points." This provokes the final and most open debate in the novel about women's right to political involvement. The Widow Carey, who runs a food stall and represents a more traditional way of thinking, complains, "I don't like these politics, . . . they bayn't in a manner business for our sex." But the factory girls articulately defend their position, even claiming equality with men. Julia asks: "Ayn't we as much concerned in the cause of good government as the men? And don't we understand as much about it?" Caroline and Harriet join in, comparing their positions with those of the queen and the aristocratic ladies: "'It's fine news for a summer day,' said Caroline, 'to say we can't understand politics with a Queen on the throne,'" and Harriet asks, "[W]hy are we not to interfere with politics as much as the swell ladies in London?" But old Widow Carey gives as good as she gets. About the queen, she says practically, "She has got her ministers to tell her what to do" (451). When Julia celebrates women's political knowledge as the "march of mind," Widow Carey responds, "[W]hat's the use of all that? What we want is, good wages and plenty to do; and as for the rest, I don't grudge the Queen her throne, nor the noblemen and gentlemen their good things. Live and let live say I." When Harriet, skilled in political rhetoric, accuses her of being "a regular oligarch," she misunderstands the nature of the insult and responds: "And perhaps I might call you something if I chose, Miss Harriet; I've heard things said before this, that I should blush to say, and blush to hear too" (452). The innuendo of sexual impropriety concludes the debate, apparently silencing the insurgents. The "experienced" factory girl is always vulnerable to such attacks.

This discussion momentarily abandons the heady abstraction of Sybil as ideal "Woman" and returns the novel to the specifically classed political women. The factory girls' practical commitment to the Ten Hours Bill and the Charter's Five Points, Lady Marney's skill at reading the political tea leaves and canvassing, the queen's resistance to Peel during the Bedchamber Plot—all stand in contrast to Sybil's spiritual and moral symbolism and her eyes suffused with tears in response to the speeches of her father and Egremont. What I want to emphasize, in conclusion, is the revelation in this novel of two very different political roles that women could perform in Victorian England. On the one hand is Sybil, the ideal Woman who transcends class and cannot understand petty politics or sully herself by descending to them. The male politicians who invoke this transclass ideal compete for the moral high ground, even while they use it to secure their own power. On the other hand are women as classed subjects—who are flawed and make mistakes and yet have specific political goals and achievements. The conclusion of *Sybil* might suggest that the first woman has entirely conquered: Sybil herself disappears into marriage with Egremont and the ethereal atmosphere of aristocratic life. Even the junketing factory girls, Julia and Caroline, dwindle into marriage with the newly minted capitalists Dandy Mick and Devilsdust. All the loose ends seem neatly tied up.

But, interestingly, Disraeli leaves one recalcitrant factory girl to represent a different viewpoint. The holdout is Harriet, that shameless hussy, who had deserted her family, set up on her own, and about whose character the Widow Carey had heard things said that made her blush. The narrator reports, "As for Harriet, she is not yet married. Though pretty and clever, she is selfish and a screw. She has saved a good deal and has a considerable sum in the Savings' Bank, but like many heiresses she cannot bring her mind to share her money with another" (496). Harriet is called an heiress, although she earned her money through her own hard work, and she is accused of selfishly refusing to "share" it in marriage, although before the passage of the Married Women's Property Act in 1882 her money would belong to her husband. This curious image of the wealthy factory girl stands in contrast to the true heiress Sybil whose newly restored lands and unimpeachable aristocratic lineage now belong to her husband Egremont. As Lady St. Julians and Lady Bardolf discuss the beautiful Sybil, now Lady Marney, they gossip about "*his* immense fortune" (emphasis mine): "Mr. Ormsby, and there is no better judge of another's man's income, says there are not three peers in the kingdom who have so much a year clear" (493). Self-interested and resistant to domesticity, the shameless factory worker Harriet is the concluding sign that just manages to hint at the need for women to connect with specific class and gender experiences in order to represent their own interests, rather than those of men.

Chapter 4

Hidden Connections/Missing Links

Luddism and Feminism in *Shirley*

"Mad Methodist Magazines."—*Shirley*

THERE COMES a startling moment in *Shirley* when the shy gentlewoman Caroline Helstone theorizes about the possible political connection between her position and that of the working class: "Old maids, like the houseless and unemployed poor, should not ask for a place and an occupation in the world: the demand disturbs the happy and rich."[1] This passage is made even more surprising because it comes just after Caroline and Shirley Keeldar have witnessed a Luddite attack on Robert Moore's mill, an attack during which Robert, whom Caroline loves, is wounded and in which several Luddites are killed. The class violence that has occurred, even directed against the man she loves, does not deter Caroline from making the connection: she recognizes her affinities with the violent male Luddites who have just attacked the mill. Yet, while Caroline thinks this, there is no suggestion as to how she can make the connection work. It remains problematically theoretical, one of those possibilities or prophecies that hangs over *Shirley* but never seems to come to fruition.

Caroline's thoughts are the one place in the industrial novels where a character explicitly parallels the position of women with that of the working class. The context of her contemplations is telling, providing the reader with some clues as to how she comes to make this crucial connection.

After the attack, Caroline spends days alone, with nothing but her sewing to occupy her, pondering its significance and searching for images of visionary possibility that might shed light on the positions of those, like the Luddites and herself, who seem excluded from a place in the world. During this period of contemplation, she turns over the strange books left to her by her Aunt Mary, among them "some mad Methodist Magazines, full of miracles and apparitions, of preternatural warnings, ominous dreams, and frenzied fanaticism; the equally mad Letters of Mrs. Elizabeth Rowe from the Dead to the Living" (376). Both of these are religious texts filled with visionary prophecies. The fact that the narrator specifically labels them "mad" is also significant. As Barbara Taylor points out in *Eve and the New Jerusalem,* only those religious movements that seemed "mad" to the nineteenth century—and have been dismissed as irrational and apolitical by a number of commentators since—could communicate a vision of a world that provided equality for everyone, for working-class, as well as upper-class, women, as well as men.[2] Finally, Caroline turns to the Bible, looking for feminist models and cites Solomon's "virtuous woman" in Proverbs, whom she describes as a manager and agriculturalist (378). This moment in *Shirley* brings together a complex set of references: housework, a woman's criticism of her society, Luddite violence, visionary "mad Methodist Magazines," and rereadings of the Bible are put into relation with one another. It is true that *Shirley* never fully develops these connections, but their presence is more significant and their proximity more explosive than has previously been recognized.

This is the crux of my examination of *Shirley*. What happens to this theoretical connection between Luddism and feminism? How can it be made more than theoretical? Brontë's narrative recognizes a hidden convergence in the histories of women and the working class, but, while at times they run along parallel lines, at other times they seem to be in conflict. One element of the historical connection is that the two groups exist in an ironic relationship to industrial capitalism. That is, both women and workers found their feudal, idyllic, patriarchal ties destroyed by it, and yet this displacement, in part, produced the births of feminism and working-class radicalism. But *Shirley* also recognizes that these intertwined births do not produce a simple kind of "progress" or a conventionally coherent history.

No novel on industrialism is more fascinating or more frustrating than *Shirley*.[3] It covers an extraordinary range of topics: wild-eyed Luddites, determined Captains of Industry, arrogant clergyman, warring female servants, unhappy middle-class women, independent heiresses, and romantic tutors elbow each other on its pages. It is a novel of startling juxtapositions as well as revealing weaknesses. In the first category is the provocative proximities it suggests between Luddism and feminism. Caroline and Shirley follow the Luddites and hear their attack on the mill. Although their class affiliations place them in opposition to Luddite politics, each rebels against the restrictions on women's lives, and each expresses that rebellion within the context of Luddite violence as well as in a millenarian religious rhetoric that has both working-class and feminist implications. A second important theme that brings together both class and gender inequities is the novel's emphasis on housework.[4] *Shirley* opens and concludes with the words of housekeepers. Female servants aggressively voice their opinions, and Caroline and even Shirley are identified with servants. There are also moments, however, where the connections between working-class Luddism and middle-class feminism turn negative. Both share a central weakness: while claiming to serve the interests of working-class women, ultimately each movement fails to address their position and needs. Luddism was the first of many nineteenth-century working-class movements not only to be male-dominated but also to direct its strikes against women's factory work. And although Caroline and Shirley share the problematic position of women with their servants, they still retain their class privileges.

In the center of *Shirley* is a gap, for Robert Moore's mill is operated by mill girls who are never represented and are mentioned only twice in passing. When his sister, Hortense, complains about their servant, Sarah, Robert offers her the choice "of an attendant among all the girls in his mill; only he feared they would scarcely suit her, as they were most of them, he was informed, completely ignorant of household work; and pert and self-willed as Sarah was, she was perhaps no worse than the majority of the women of her class" (112). Sometime later, Robert fantasizes that Caroline is one of his mill girls: "But a week ago, I was standing at the top of one of my long rooms, girls were working at the other end, and amongst half a dozen of them, moving to and fro, I seemed to see a figure resembling yours" (257). In these two mentions, mill girls seem to merge, on the one hand, with domestic servants, and, on the other hand, with the middle-class Caroline. Such displacements and elisions are a part of what haunts this novel which is full of visions that are described but never enacted and rebellions that are heard but never seen. At the center of its story lies a mill that the reader never enters, operated by mill girls that the reader never meets. In place of the mill girls are domestic workers. In place of the mill are such landscapes as Fieldhead Hollow and Nunnely Common where, years ago, Robin Hood and "fairishes" (fairies) roamed. Now Caroline, Shirley, and Robert wander there, reenvisioning Eve as a Titan Mother and discussing the visions of the mad assassin, Michael Hartley.

Shirley builds to two pivotal moments—the Luddite attack on the mill and Caroline's unorthodox challenge to her society. After these moments, the novel seems to retreat: the Luddite Rebellion disintegrates, Caroline becomes ill and then recovers enough to marry Moore, and, most significantly, the connection between women and the working class is never given concrete form. Even so, its residue imbues the novel with repressed possibility and a suggestion of utopian promise. It is present most clearly in the opening and concluding chapters which foreground working-class women and history; in the voices of female servants throughout the novel; and, connecting Caroline's "mad Methodist Magazines" with Luddism, in the mystical visions of Shirley Keeldar and the mad radical and attempted assassin, Michael Hartley. It is this explosion and its residue that makes *Shirley* an important social-problem novel, tantalizing in its insights and frustrating in its truncating of them. This chapter addresses the question of why *Shirley* can make these connections but cannot fully develop them.

> "N.B. All the Males in the Trade may sign but no Women."
> —Framework knitters' petition, 1812

Shirley recognizes the contingency of histories; no one strand can be separated out: women's history is contingent on men's, and vice versa, middle-class history is contingent on working-class history. This points directly to the novel's startlingly deep and broad sense of history—the Napoleonic Wars, the actions of industrialists, the Luddites, and the lives of women are presented in the novel as well as the implication that the histories of industrialism, women, and workers are intertwined and ongoing. Terry Eagleton argues that "Chartism is the unspoken subject of *Shirley*,"[5] showing that Brontë in some sense anticipated E. P. Thompson's thesis in *The Making of the English Working Class* that Luddism was the starting point of a new kind of working-class radicalism. To read Luddism and feminism together in *Shirley* is to read the account of a fractured but potentially explosive connection. As Thompson puts it, "[W]e must see the years 1811–13 as a watershed, whose streams run in one direction back to Tudor times, in another forward to the factory legislation of the next hundred years. The Luddites were some of the last Guildsmen, and at the same time some of the first to launch the agitations which lead on to the 10 Hour Movement. In both directions lay an alternative political economy and morality to that of *laissez faire*."[6] As with industrialism and working-class radicalism, the connection between the Napoleonic period and the 1840s is also important for women. In *Eve and the New Jerusalem,* Barbara Taylor points to the significance of the earlier period for examples of radical feminism while the 1840s saw a resurgence of feminist activity, stimulated by women's exclusion from the 1840 International Anti-Slavery Convention in London and Chartism's decision to call for male suffrage, instead of universal suffrage.

A central reason for the critical disenchantment with the novel's version of this history, however, is that it does not celebrate working-class radicalism.[7] There is a desire in critics, and I admit I have shared it, to rewrite the conclusion of *Shirley* and develop the connections it makes in a more positive direction. Yet in *Shirley* class issues are continually disrupted by gender, while, conversely, gender issues are disrupted by class in increasingly complex ways. One of the elements that makes Thompson's *Making of the English Working Class* so satisfying is, as Anna Clark puts it, his portrayal of working-class radicals as "rational heroes who forged a working-class consciousness"; but, Clark continues, "to make his point he neglected the connections between family and political life."[8] In *The First Industrial Woman* Deborah Valenze concludes that working-class women "dislodge the 'whig history' of industrialization—an unbroken narrative of progress—from its dictatorial role."[9] A "whig history" of Luddism and feminism would insist upon connecting women and workers by producing a history of mutually supportive progress for them. The history that *Shirley* frustrates us with produces "progress" only for the industrialists. The histories of women and workers, on the other hand, are fractured and fragmented, sometimes seeming regressive, at cross-purposes with one another, rather than progressive. But the reasons behind this are more complicated and more revealing than have previously been realized. They cannot be blamed exclusively on Charlotte Brontë's Tory pessimism.

Such issues are also related to criticism of the novel's form.[10] As

Catherine Belsey argues in *Critical Practice,* classic realism is "a privileged, historic narration which is the source of coherence of the story as a whole."[11] Much of the response to *Shirley* is based on the fact that it deliberately defies such "coherence."[12] The lack of coherence in *Shirley,* its refusal to "plot" history, is based on several reasons. Susan Zlotnick defines *Shirley* as "a woman's history of England," and, while Zlotnick's approach suggests that women's history is inevitably disruptive to official histories, it itself is also disrupted by class.[13] In *Reading the Romantic Heroine,* Leslie Rabine argues that *Shirley* is about the relationship between "a submerged feminine historicity and an official masculine historicity."[14] But historically privileged coherence is even further undone by Brontë's breaking apart of male history with her Luddite setting, with her introduction, in other words, of a submerged masculine historicity. In fact, Asa Briggs points out that "the 12,000 troops employed against the Luddites greatly excelled in size the army which Wellington took into the Peninsula in 1808."[15] Yet, despite that statistic, until E. P. Thompson recuperated Luddism as the starting point for working-class political consciousness, it had disappeared from official histories, leaving barely a trace. Thus *Shirley*'s relationship to "masculine historicity" is doubly complicated as well.

As feminist historians have established, to fully understand Luddism as the making of the English working class, one must also recover the importance of women as political actors and take account of the role of gender in defining a male-dominated working-class movement that would often exclude women from its unions and, by the 1840s, from its demand for the vote. Thus, the Luddite Rebellion reveals the complex gender politics of working-class radicalism. On the one hand, Luddism undoubtedly drew on a broad base of support from working-class women, especially those who were attached to the families of male artisans. In fact, Luddite violence grew out of a tradition of food riots that was associated particularly with women participants. As a remnant of that tradition, women appear as symbols within the movement, with men dressed in women's clothes calling themselves Lady Ludd and General Ludd's wives. On the other hand, specific gender tensions do appear. The organization and nocturnal strikes of Luddism appear to have excluded women from direct participation. As Malcolm I. Thomis and Jennifer Grimmett argue in *Women in Protest, 1800–1850,* women "doubtless contributed a lot to the community backing and protection that the Luddites received, but their role was probably described accurately by Frank Peel in his imaginative account, written in 1880, in which the wives waited anxiously at home for the return of their husbands from their dangerous and illegal nocturnal missions."[16] Another significant factor to take into account is that Luddism was directed against the work of mill girls, who were supplanting male weavers as workers, and it drew upon the energies of radical Jacobins and artisans who were part of a male working-class culture that included significant strains of misogyny.[17] Thus, although many working-class women supported Luddism, it was also a movement in which they were not directly represented and that tended to subordinate their political voices and independent economic interests. For example, in 1812 framework knitters circulated a petition to Parliament which collected 10,000 signatures. The petition concluded with the note, "All the Males in the Trade may sign but no Women."[18]

The male-dominated structure of working-class politics is reflected in the presentation in *Shirley* of five working-class men who represent different political viewpoints: Moses Barraclough, Noah o' Tims, and Michael Hartley represent Luddism; Joe Scott represents those men who identify with the masters; and William Farren represents Brontë's idea of a good working man, dissatisfied with the masters but unwilling to join in direct rebellion. Critics such as Terry Eagleton and Igor Webb have effectively critiqued Brontë's middle-class bias, especially revealed in the negative representation of Barraclough, the hypocritical Luddite leader, and the humble Farren, who, according to Webb, uses language a working-class man never would.[19] This is a place where class and gender issues undercut one another. Brontë's negative treatment of Barraclough, for example, has a feminist aspect to it, but her unbalanced treatment of him relative to the male leadership of the upper classes emphasizes the way in which class muddies her vision here. Problems arise, on one level, because dominant, patriarchal culture recognizes political movements only when they reproduce its male, middle-class identity politics. *Shirley* demonstrates how middle-class men, such as Robert Moore and the Reverend Matthew Helstone, construct their identities as powerful by using "the great men of history" as models. Moore and Helstone argue over who is the greater man, Napoleon or Wellington, and they use a further historical reference, each arguing that his favorite is like Moses. The reference to Moses is evocative because, although he is seen by these men as the ideal leader, his meaning for women might be different. As a student at Constantine Heger's school in the 1840s, Brontë was required to write a series of *devoirs* on "great men." Like Shirley, who adapts the writing assignments her tutor Louis gives her to her own purposes, Brontë approached the assignments from her own perspective. Two of them, entitled "The Death of Napoleon" and "The Death of Moses," indicate the limitations of the model even by their titles. The essays do reproduce expected praise for the great and powerful (male) individual, but they also make explicit that this is a historical world that did not "count the women and children."[20]

The significantly named Moses Barraclough similarly attempts to model himself on a hero when he comes to see Moore at the head of a working-class deputation. He compares his role in relation to his class to that of Moses: "I'm a very feeling man, and when I see my brethren oppressed like my great namesake of old, I stand up for 'em" (155). What Brontë is recognizing here is that Luddism and working-class movements in the nineteenth century tended to construct themselves on a male identity. Male working-class movements achieved success in so far as they reproduced the patriarchal family relations of the middle class. Pressured to reproduce an identity politics that divides them against themselves and from each other, women and workers remain subordinated to the larger patriarchal order. On the other hand, *Shirley* clearly cannot credit individual leadership or heroism in the working class, as it can with the upper classes. Even though Brontë criticizes men like Moore, she also praises him at some points, showing that Brontë was still attached to traditional ideals of heroism, seeing them very much within a class-biased framework.

But the presentation of working-class issues is more complex than this, first, because the voices and the work of working-class women are also presented, and, second, because Luddism in the novel is most effective when it discards the model of individual male heroism and becomes communal and visionary. Luddism is powerful when it is unseen but felt and heard, as demonstrated in Michael Hartley's visions and in the attack on the mill. If Brontë does not present an effective, honest working-class leader, she does show respect for the invisible force of Luddism which strikes at night. In fact, here she locates a primary source of Luddite success and a significant way in which it undercut the expectations of its opponents. The organized attacks of the Luddites were so effective that the authorities were convinced that there must be some upper-class man directing it. But, as the name Luddism indicates, that was not the case. General or King Ludd, the reputed leader of the movement, did not exist, although letters signed by him were delivered as warnings to mill owners. Many men took on the role of General Ludd and organized raids in their communities.[21] It is the hidden work of working-class women and the invisible power of Luddism that *Shirley* is most in tune with.

> "She doesn't keep a servant, but does the work of the house herself, as her mother did afore her."—*Shirley*

Shirley's opening and concluding chapters foreground its competing yet complementary histories in interesting ways. These chapters provide a frame for the histories of Caroline and Shirley which the central sections of the novel develop, a frame that emphasizes certain subtly recurring themes in the novel and that highlights some unexpected and overlooked intersections between these two middle-class women and working-class women and men. The opening chapter's satire on the curates and the Victorian critics' negative response to it have distracted readers from its other aspects, particularly its significant descriptions of two symbolic working-class characters—the landlady, Mrs. Gale, and "the Antinomian weaver," Michael Hartley (48).

After the narrator describes the curates' habit of dining at one another's lodgings, she cites their landladies' sentiments about this practice: "'[I]t is just for nought else but to give folk trouble.'" Thus, the first words quoted in the novel are the words of working women, as the last words of the novel will be. Then the reader is introduced to Mrs. Gale, who is the present recipient of the clerical invasion: "Mrs. Gale waits on them, but a spark of the hot kitchen fire is in her eye." The terms on which she lets her lodging include "the privilege of inviting a friend to a meal occasionally," but the curates have abused those terms, frequently coming to stay all day and spend the night and expecting to be fed breakfast, tea, and dinner. To add insult to injury, "they treat her with less than civility, just because she doesn't keep a servant, but does the work of the house herself, as her mother did afore her" (41). In *Charlotte Bronte and Defensive Conduct: The Author and the Body at Risk,* Janet Gezari focuses on the symbolic importance of food in this opening scene of a novel that deals with hungry, unemployed workers. The first words heard from the curates are Mr. Malone's "More bread!" (41), followed by the command, "Cut it, woman" (42). The narrator comments, "and the 'woman' cut it accordingly. Had she followed her inclinations, she would have cut the parson also; her Yorkshire soul revolted absolutely from his manner of command" (42). Gezari points out that "in Mrs. Gale, gender, class, and regional motives coincide, and her conflict with the curate reveals the deep relation between oppressive social distinctions and physical violence."[22] The curates also represent the wider culture's disdainful attitude toward the female domestic worker, an attitude so thoroughgoing that her existence is frequently overlooked altogether.[23] If factory and mining women's work was hidden because it threatened Victorian gender ideology, ironically, female servants are invisible because they are seen as a natural extension of it.

Shirley begins with the violent though repressed anger of this female domestic worker, and, as Bruce Robbins points out in *The Servant's Hand: English Fiction from Below,* the novel's final words are also those of a working-class woman, this time the narrator's housekeeper. Robbins's thesis is that such servants' voices can hold elements that are repressed in the novel proper; they can be utopian, suggesting "how much the action has left unresolved"; they can be dangerous, even containing, as he puts it, "a subterranean Luddism."[24] The disruptive significance of this framing of *Shirley* by working women's voices has been underread, as has the pervasive presence of their voices within the novel. In every household in *Shirley,* the personality, and frequently the voices, of the female domestic worker, whether housekeeper or servant, are presented. Their presence and voices do not merely provide a chorus for the main action; often their comments directly affect it.

Brontë has been accused of oddly ignoring work in this novel about industry,[25] but, again emphasizing the decentering focus of her view of history, she points repeatedly to the work most ignored in traditional histories: housework. Susan Zlotnick notes that "she focuses on the contribution of the working woman rather than the working man."[26] Not only is housework quintessential women's work, but it is also work which traditional capitalist and Marxist economics do not recognize as producing value. And female servants were often considered pariahs by their own class, so, despite the fact that the vast majority of women workers during the Victorian period worked as servants—in fact, servants formed the largest single occupational group—they were invisible to working-class political movements. Stereotypical women's work was assumed to produce the stereotypical woman worker, passive, apolitical, unable to be organized. But the "spark of the hot kitchen fire" in Mrs. Gale's eye (41) and her inclination to "cut" Mr. Malone with the breadknife (42) is repeated in the rebellious attitudes and actions of the female servants in other households, suggesting that the woman worker is not as apolitical or as passive as generally believed.

More than most Victorian novels, *Shirley* is saturated with references to servants. The viewpoint of Mrs. Gale on the curates is not an isolated instance. From Fanny and Eliza who are shown assisting Caroline Helstone at the parsonage, to Sarah who battles against the French influence of Hortense Moore at Hollow's Cottage, from Deb and Mrs. Horsfall at Hiram Yorke's Briarmains, to Mrs. Gill, the housekeeper who at first cheats and then supports Shirley at Fieldhead, every household is described from the servants' viewpoint with details that point to the kind of lives they lead. When unannounced guests descend on the Helstone parsonage for tea, the cook, Eliza, complains to Caroline, "What a lot on 'em! And I put off the baking to-day because I thought there would be bread plenty to fit while morning: we shall never have enow . . . I wish these fine folk would stay at home till they're asked: and I want to finish trimming my hat" (135). At Hollow's Mill, Sarah acts as the voice of Yorkshire, asserting itself against Hortense's foreign housekeeping: "The usual affray took place about the dinner, which meal, when Sarah at last brought it into the room, she almost flung upon the table, with a look that expressed quite plainly: 'I never dished such stuff i' my life afore; it's not fit for dogs'"(105). Like Hortense Moore, Mrs. Yorke keeps a "hot kitchen" (113). She is described as the kind of woman who, "while rendering miserable the drudging life of a simple maid-servant, would nurse like a heroine an hospital full of plague patients" (523). As in the cases of Mrs. Gale and Sarah, such treatment provokes rebellion. When Robert Moore is recovering from his wound at Briarmains, Mrs. Yorke forbids the housemaids his room and joins forces with Hortense to keep Moore to themselves (524). The servants communicate their dislike of this interference: "The servants were in the kitchen, breakfasting solemnly with closed doors; [Mrs. Yorke] and Miss Moore were airing themselves on the lawn, and discussing the closed doors aforesaid" (534). The oak-paneled parlor at Shirley's Fieldhead is described as beautiful from the perspective of an aesthete but "execrable" to the maids who have to keep it clean (208). Individualized and opinionated, these working-class voices make housework visible.

Not only is housework made visible here, but there is also a constant sense of chafing about the housework that is performed, whether it is Mrs.

Gale cutting bread, Sarah cooking a ragout, or Caroline sewing. *Shirley* fails to complain about the heavier weight with which housework falls on working-class women, but it does underline its importance to considerations of sexual equality and also points to failings in those political movements that ignore its significance. When working-class men marched to protest unemployment, they sometimes carried washing tubs or other household items to demonstrate their belief that the natural order of things was being reversed by industrialism: women had jobs outside their homes, and men were in danger of being reduced to performing housework. Only the most radical socialist movements, such as Owenism, attempted to address the problem of housework, and even there, they did not argue that it should be shared by men and women but only that it should be done collectively either by women or children, so that its burden could be spread out.[27] The burden of the double shift, in fact, is probably quite sufficient in itself to explain why many working-class women did not participate more fully in political movements and why they acquiesced to the ideal of the male breadwinner.

Shirley also connects female servants with other significant feminist issues. They are the chroniclers of the history of women. For example, they are the repository of the dark secrets of the Helstone family. This oral history shows up as "gossip," but it contains revelations of the most important aspects of Caroline's life. Her uncle never speaks to her about his wife or her father and mother. However, servants pass on the hints of domestic neglect, abuse, and violence that an official historian like Helstone refuses to address. Female servants, for example, uncover and pass on the history of Mary Cave, considered by feminist critics to be a central symbol of the novel's feminism,[28] and discuss how the indifference of Mr. Helstone contributed to her death: Helstone's "dry-eyed and somber mourning scandalized an old housekeeper, and likewise a female attendant, who had waited upon Mrs. Helstone in her sickness; and who, perhaps, had had opportunities of learning more of the deceased lady's nature, of her capacity for feeling and loving, than her husband knew" (82). It is through servants that Caroline remembers the abuse that she suffered at the hands of her father: "Rumours had reached her ear of what that father's character was; old servants had dropped hints: she knew, too, that he was not a good man, and that he was never kind to her. She recollected—a dark recollection it was—some weeks that she had spent with him in a great town somewhere, when she had had no maid to dress her or take care of her. . . .

She knew she had fallen ill in this place, and that one night when she was very sick, he had come raving into the room, and said he would kill her, for she was a burden to him" (126). It is through a servant that Caroline receives her only glimpse of the mother who deserted her: "[A]n old servant, who had lived with Mrs. James Helstone for a short time after her marriage, whenever she referred to her former mistress, spoke with chilling reserve: sometimes she called her 'queer,' sometimes she said she did not understand her" (201). Finally, the servant Fanny suggests to Caroline that she visit the old maids, Miss Ainsley and Miss Mann, again making a female servant the conduit for feminist insights into the hidden lives of women (191).[29] In fact, it might be argued, that without these servants there would be no history of women available in *Shirley.*

Female servants, therefore, are one place where aspects of a class critique and aspects of feminism meet in the novel. Service can be seen as a "bridging" occupation, bringing working- and middle-class women together. So far I have tried to stress, as Bruce Robbins does, the utopian and disruptive potential in such voices. But there are, of course, limitations to this claim, especially in terms of class, which must also be kept in mind. And, although *Shirley* to its last words retains an emphasis on the utopian possibility in working-class women's voices, a significant missing link is its lack of full address to class differences between women. In *Nobody's Angels,* Elizabeth Langland argues against Robbins's position, making the point that middle-class women managed their servants as a workforce in a way that paralleled their husbands' management of working-class men and, thus, they functioned to consolidate middle-class power.[30] Certainly, *Shirley* reveals, as well as critiques, the continuing surveillance of servants by their middle-class mistresses. Through Hortense and Mrs. Yorke, the usual catalog of complaints against female servants is unfolded. When they get together, the two of them "possessed an exhaustless mutual theme of conversation in the corrupt propensities of servants. Their views of this class were similar: they watched them with the same suspicion, and judged them with the same severity" (524). Their clothes—Hortense views Sarah as "an insolent coquette in a flounced gown, and absolutely without cap!" (112)—their independence, and their sweethearts are constant topics. It is not only these middle-class women who are engaged in disciplining this workforce. Caroline reports how Matthew Helstone cooled off their servant Fanny's sweetheart by giving him a shower under the pump (259–60). The emphasis on clothes, insolence, and lovers aligns servants with mill girls whose reputations for independence, love of finery, and freedom with men were often repeated accusations. This connection is made explicit in Robert Moore's comment, comparing his servant Sarah with his mill girls: "[P]ert and self-willed as Sarah was, she was perhaps no worse than the majority of the women of her class" (112).

Shirley and Caroline, by contrast, have a more complicated relationship with servants. The idea of service as a "bridging" occupation comes to the foreground here, pointing to both the strengths and weaknesses of such a concept. Shirley and Caroline are presented as combining forces with their servants, and, demonstrating how much they share with them, their lovers each momentarily picture them as working-class women. Shirley has a serious "servant problem" because her housekeeper Mrs. Gill cheats her. Examining her household account book, she comes across charges for numerous "unaccountable" items, "pounds of candles," huge amounts of "bleaching powder," and exorbitant "butchers' bills" (266–67). Yet the usually commanding Shirley does not respond in the manner of a Hortense Moore and Mrs. Yorke, or even rise to the mild remonstrance of a Caroline Helstone. Mysteriously, by this very lack of household management skill, Shirley manages to bring Mrs. Gill around. Close to the novel's conclusion, when Shirley confesses to Louis Moore that she fears she will die after being bitten by a rabid dog, she tells him, "If female help is needed, call in my housekeeper, Mrs. Gill: let her lay me out, if I die. She is attached to me. She wronged me again and again, and again and again I forgave her. She now loves me, and would not defraud me of a pin: confidence has made her honest; forbearance has made her kindhearted. At this day, I can trust both her integrity, her courage, and her affection" (480). Shirley conquering Mrs. Gill through kindness is perhaps merely a gentler, more subtle form of managing the working class, but she also flies in the face of common wisdom about how to deal with such a situation and she feels so close to Mrs. Gill that she chooses her, along with Louis whom she loves, to deal with her illness. This way of presenting the relationship between mistress and housekeeper tries to stress the cross-class bond rather than class-power relations.

But class privileges, of course, remain very significant, and they come to the foreground particularly in relation to middle-class love and marriage. Curiously and disturbingly, at one point Louis Moore fantasizes about Shirley serving him in a series of working-class roles. He pictures himself as a king and Shirley as his housemaid, then himself as a gentleman and Shirley as the servant who waits on him, and, finally, himself as a comfortable wayfarer and Shirley as the humble peasant woman who gives him a drink of water. Obviously, this daydream represents Louis's desire to establish power over Shirley and to reverse their social and economic positions—a dream, by the way, that the novel fulfills when he marries Shirley and, thereby, becomes the owner of her property and the magistrate of the parish. But, revealingly, the fantasy which strips Shirley of the accoutrements of class also removes Louis's desire to possess her: "I should like her. I should wish to stay an hour: I should linger to talk with that rustic. I should not feel as I now do: I should find in her nothing divine; but whenever I met the young peasant, it would be with pleasure—whenever I left her, it would be with regret" (488). Thus, while Shirley describes herself as joining forces with Mrs. Gill and vice versa, there still exists a noticeable, unaddressed imbalance: Mrs. Gill serves her while, when Shirley is pictured as a server, she loses both economic and sexual power.

Similar patterns emerge in the relationship between Caroline Helstone and servants, although, dependent on the charity of her uncle, she remains much more closely identified with them, psychologically and factually. Servants share her family history with her, and she shares their work with them. Preparing for visitors at the Parsonage, Caroline holds a "privy council" with Fanny and Eliza (135). In preparation for the school feast, the three of them "were busy the whole morning arranging the Rectory-parlours in first-rate company order, and setting out a collation of cooling refreshments—wine, fruit, cakes—on the dining-room sideboard" (291). At Hollow's Cottage, Hortense supervises and complains about Caroline, just as she does Sarah: "The morning passed as usual. Mademoiselle, ever breathlessly busy, spent it in bustling from kitchen to parlour—now scolding Sarah, now looking over Caroline's exercise or hearing her repetition-lesson. . . . She thought incessant reprimand, severe or slight, quite necessary to the maintenance of her authority; and if no possible error was to be found in the lesson, it was the pupil's carriage, or air, or dress, or mien, which required correction" (105). Sarah at Hollow's Cottage and Fanny at the Parsonage sympathize with Caroline, seeming to identify with her. Sarah sees Caroline under the rule of Hortense, too: "How low you seem, Miss! But it's all because your cousin keeps you so close to work. It's a shame!" (108). When Caroline sinks into a depression over Robert's withdrawal from her, Fanny recognizes something is wrong—"Fanny, as she passed in and out of the room occasionally, intent on housemaid errands, perceived her young mistress sat very still"—and suggests, "read, or do something to amuse you . . . you are quite too still—you should visit more" (191). Oddly, there seems to be almost a role reversal here, as if the middle-class Caroline envied the life of her servants. They have the occupations, community, and freedom from the burdens of genteel ladyhood that Caroline lacks.

Thus, the novel does not escape the problem of making working-class women work for it both literally and figuratively. So, after Robert's rejection, Caroline turns her anger inward, telling herself that this is what she deserves for her unmaidenly fault of falling in love with him before he asked her to. But, in the middle of explaining why "a model-heroine" must suffer in silence, the narrator quotes a ballad where the "deeply-feeling, strongly-resentful peasant-girl," Puir Mary Lee, is free to express the anger that Caroline represses: Mary Lee hates the yellow-bellied newt, "the hairy adder," and the milk on the toad's back but, most of all, she hates the man who betrayed her, Robin-a-Ree (129). Neither Caroline nor Shirley will exact revenge for Robert's betrayals, but he will be shot by the Luddite Michael Hartley and pummeled to within an inch of his life by the large working-class nurse Mrs. Horsfall. In *Shirley*, working-class women support middle-class women and voice the anger and sometimes enact the rebellion that middle-class women repress, but the reverse is not nearly as apparent. Both class and gender conflicts clearly demand more radical solutions beyond the friendly cross-class contacts established between Caroline, Shirley, and their servants. In fact, in order to address them, the world needs to be reenvisioned. Just as Caroline turns to "mad Methodist Magazines" looking for answers, so the novel also includes the complementary visions of the Luddite Michael Hartley and the feminist Shirley Keeldar.

"There is a wild interest in his ravings."—*Shirley*

"Mad Methodist magazines" prefigure Caroline Helstone's connection of women and the working class. The association of madness with Methodism may lead a reader to dismiss its significance; however, other elements underline its importance. Several critics have described "the Methodist matrix" of the Brontës' works, a matrix that includes their father, a Church-Methodist; their mother; their Aunt Elizabeth Branwell, who served as their housekeeper and read "mad Methodist magazines";

and Tabitha Ackroyd, their servant for thirty years who was "a class leader at the Wesleyan Chapel, and not only remembered when fairies inhabited the area" but also remembered the "very words" of a famous Wesleyan preacher. In his study of the importance of Methodism for the Brontës, Valentine Cunningham argues that it provided them with "a rhetoric of passion . . . by appropriating the rhetoric of Methodism's love of God, exploiting the language of Divine love for earthly love."[31] Barbara Taylor's *Eve and the New Jerusalem* both expands and complicates Methodism's significance, bringing into play not only personal relations but also the politics of class and gender. In her reading, its visionary language could be about earthly love *and* a new social order that provides equality for all classes, about sexual desire *and* sexual equality: "For the majority of early Socialists, the language of prophecy and apocalypse expressed not a literal faith in millenarian change but an intensity of aspiration for which there was simply no secular vocabulary available—an imaginative straining towards future freedom which found voice in the only language of social optimism possessed by most men and women." One overhears such language in *Shirley,* for example, in the hymns sung in the working-class Briarchapel:

Oh! who can explain
This struggle for life,
This travail and pain,
This trembling and strife?
Plague, earthquake, and famine,
And tumult and war,
The wonderful coming
Of Jesus declare! (163)

This hymn is followed by shouts of "'I've found liberty!' 'Doad o' Bill's has fun' liberty!'" (163–64), and the chapel-goers respond:

What a mercy is this!
What a heaven of bliss!
How unspeakably happy am I!
Gather'd into the fold,
With thy people enroll'd,
With thy people to live and to die! (164)

Taylor argues that, although it is possible to read such language as simply otherworldly and apocalyptic, an interpreter must understand "the significance of *linguistic traditions* within changing ideological contexts": "Words, like ideas, are historical phenomena," and part of the strength of nineteenth-century working-class radicalism came from its ability to "appropriate [religious] language and turn it to new psychological and political purposes." Thus *Shirley's* Wesleyan hymns comment on earthly life as well as the afterlife, so that "famine,/And tumult and war" refer to the French Revolution, the Napoleonic Wars, and the Luddite Rebellion; "I've found liberty!" and "With thy people enroll'd" to democratic political aspirations and working-class solidarity. Taylor points out, "It is important to recall that even the most uncompromising anti-Christians in the movement frequently adopted this mode of speech, not as a way of disguising their anti-theological views but as a way of communicating their own commitment to the construction of a new heaven on earth."[32]

Taylor's thesis is important for understanding not only Wesleyan hymns but also the language of the novel's two declared visionaries, Michael Hartley and Shirley Keeldar. Michael Hartley is the most overlooked character in *Shirley,* and, in many ways, it is easy to understand why.[33] The narrator dismissively describes him as an Antinomian, a radical Jacobin, a Leveler, an alcoholic, and a madman. Yet he is also discussed in the opening and closing chapters of the novel, quoted as a visionary, and it is he who wounds Robert Moore. It takes a careful examination of the scenes in which he is mentioned to realize that this shadowy yet provocative figure never actually appears in the novel. His words are quoted by other people, but the reader hears his voice directly only once, just before he shoots Moore. I would like to interpret the unseen Michael Hartley in two ways: first, as the ultimate representative of the novel's Luddites, who are invisible in their attack on the mill although their yell is described; and, second, as a figure of mad rebellion who has an even wider resonance. If *Jane Eyre* has its madwoman in the attic who emerges at night to light fires and attack the upper-class husband who imprisons her, so *Shirley* has its madman who similarly revenges Moore's treatment of workers and women. Perhaps *Shirley's* mad avenger has to be even more fully repressed from the text than *Jane Eyre*'s because of the dangerous connections he makes so apparent. For, although he is like Bertha Mason Rochester in being associated with alcoholism, madness, and violence, he is unlike her in that he is a working-class man, a political revolutionary, and a religious visionary.

Michael Hartley is first discussed in chapter 1 when the Reverend Mr. Helstone comes to Mrs. Gale's to recruit the curates to defend the mill from a possible Luddite attack. The curate Mr. Sweeting agrees that Moore is in danger and that he should "take warning," specifically because of what he has heard about Michael Hartley: "Mr. Hall [another Anglican clergyman] thinks Mike has no personal hatred of Moore; Mike says he even likes to talk to him, and run after him, but he has a *hankering* that Moore should be made an example of" (48). Thus, Hartley becomes the voice of Luddism; he predicts who will be singled out for attack. Helstone underlines this when he describes Hartley, albeit jokingly, as a visionary and prophet: "He is a very Ezekiel or Daniel for visions" (49). Helstone then offers a lengthy description of one of Hartley's visionary prophecies:

> Mike is out of work, like many others, unfortunately; Mr. Grame, Sir Philip Nunnely's steward, gave him a job about the priory: according to his account, Mike was busy hedging rather late in the afternoon, but before dark, when he heard what he thought was a band at a distance, bugles, fifes, and the sound of a trumpet; it came from the forest, and he wondered that there should be music there. He looked up: all amongst the trees he saw moving objects, red, like poppies, or white, like May-blossom; the wood was full of them; they poured out and filled the park. He then perceived they were soldiers—thousands and tens of thousands; but they made no more noise than a swarm of midges on a summer evening. . . . Mike followed them; they seemed passing Fieldhead, when a column of smoke, such as might be vomited by a park of artillery, spread noiseless over the fields, the road, the common, and rolled, he said, blue and dim to his very feet. . . . Mike, like a wise Daniel as he is, not only rehearsed the vision, but gave the interpretation thereof: it signifies, he intimated, bloodshed and civil conflict. (49–50)

Hartley's prophecy is both generally and specifically fulfilled by the events in *Shirley*—in the Luddite Rebellion and in the attack on Hollow's mill. His vision is also placed in an interesting context. He has been unemployed—a specific reference to the cause of Luddite Rebellion. But now he is working out in nature in the Nunnely priory. The mention of Nunnely priory associates Hartley's visions with both nature and religion. His words are reported through three Anglican clergymen, Mr. Sweeting, Mr. Hall, and Mr. Helstone, indicating their status as a kind of competing doctrine. Finally, there are also mythic associations with the place of Hartley's vision. Nunnwood, where he first hears and then sees the soldiers, is "the sole remnant of antique British forest" in the region. Caroline describes it as "like an encampment of forest sons of Anak" and confirms Shirley's thought that it was "one of Robin Hood's haunts" where "there are mementos of him still existing" (220). Robin Hood, who lived outside the law and attacked the rich to give to the poor, is an ancestor of General or King Ludd, the mythical leader who revenges the working class on its exploiters in 1812.[34] All these connections give Hartley's words a power and a resonance that cannot easily be dismissed as the pointless ramblings of an alcoholic madman.

Hartley's visions are discussed a second time in a scene that repeats many of these themes and connections. One night Caroline watches from a distance while Shirley and Robert walk together, deep in discussion. Caroline believes that the two are falling in love, and throughout the scene Robert's betrayal of both women is hinted at. Their discussion, however, is about business, specifically the rumor that the Luddites will attack Robert's mill. Once again Hartley becomes the specific symbol of Luddite thinking. He is introduced into the discussion when Robert tells Shirley that he likes to roam about the Hollow on moonlit nights. Shirley responds by introducing an image that will recur at the novel's conclusion, one that significantly derives from a female servant: "When I was a very little girl, Mr. Moore, my nurse used to tell me tales of fairies being seen in that Hollow. That was before my father built the mill, when it was a perfectly solitary ravine: you will be falling under enchantment. . . . But there are worse things than fairies to be guarded against. . . . For instance, how would you like to meet Michael Hartley, that mad Calvinist and Jacobin weaver?" Robert confesses that he has already met him and talked with him about politics and religion. Michael again makes a prophecy that later events, in part, fulfill: "God's vengeance, he said, was preparing for me, and affirmed that in a vision of the night he had beheld the manner and the instrument of my doom." Robert's response to this conversation is a strange one, revealing his Romantic-hero side rather than his industrial-capitalist one. He says, "A strange little incident it was: I liked it." His assessment of Hartley's character is also revealing: "There is a wild interest in his ravings. The man would be half a poet, if he were not wholly a maniac; and perhaps a prophet, if he were not a profligate" (242).

All these aspects of Hartley's character come together in his one dramatic actual appearance—or almost appearance—in *Shirley.* Just before he shoots Robert Moore, his hat is glimpsed just above a hedge, and his voice is heard, offering biblical justification for his act. He declaims, "When the wicked perisheth, there is shouting. As the whirlwind passeth, so is the wicked no more (with a deeper growl); terrors take hold of him as waters; hell is naked before him. He shall die without knowledge" (506). Like Caroline and Shirley, Hartley turns to the Bible for inspiration, and, also like them, he changes and reinterprets it. Although it seems to flow as one quotation, his brief declaration is actually a compilation of five different passages drawn from Proverbs and Job. The context of each passage deals with warnings to the rich and powerful of the dangers of their position and with promises that God will defend the poor against their oppressors. Drawing inspiration from the Bible for his prophecies and actions, Hartley revenges the Luddites and also, unwittingly, Caroline and Shirley.

It is the half of Hartley that would be a poet and a prophet that links him to a character who seems far removed: Shirley Keeldar. For Shirley is also a visionary who experiences trances: when the inspiration comes, "she reaches a station scarcely lower than that whence angels looked down on the dreamer of Beth-el, and her eye seeks, and her soul possesses, the vision of life as she wishes it." She, too, would be a poet, if she were not "an indolent, a reckless, an ignorant being" who has too little of "the organ of Acquisitiveness" to write her visions down (374). Like Hartley's, Shirley's visions appropriate religious imagery for other ends, but, whereas Hartley's visions are Luddite in their politics, Shirley's are feminist. To read their feminism, however, it is necessary to recover the ideological context of their historical moment: the language of Shirley's visions has much in common with that of a number of radical working-class movements and sects dating from the last part of the eighteenth century through the 1830s—a language that revealed the working class's desire for a transformed society but was even more necessary in order to imagine a transformation of gender and sexual relations. Thus, as Sally Greene argues in "Apocalypse When? *Shirley's* Vision and the Politics of Reading," Shirley's visions fit into a tradition of utopian feminism. Drawing on Barbara Taylor's discussion of the connection between "religious enthusiasm and sexual heterodoxy," Greene demonstrates the parallels between Shirley's visions and the millenarian religious rhetoric of such radical sects as Southcottianism, Saint Simonianism, and Owenism.[35] For example, just prior to as well as during the Luddite era, Joanna Southcott, significantly a former domestic servant, founded a new religion, announcing herself as "the new Saviour" and the "Bride of Christ." Abandoning Methodism, in 1802 she published an apocalyptic tract, and between that time and her death in 1814, attracted 100,000 followers in London in addition to numerous devotees in the Northern industrial districts. Most of her converts were female, many of them single working women. Southcott's poems are "full of the imagery (mostly biblical) of brides, bridesmaids, bridegrooms, marriages, wedding feasts, wedding guests."[36] Similar images are central to Shirley's visions.

The reader is given two examples of Shirley's visions, the first just before the Luddite attack on the mill, the second near the end of the novel. Shirley shares the first vision with Caroline as they linger outside the church during a service: "The first woman was heaven-born: vast was the heart whence gushed the well-spring of the blood of nations; and grand the undegenerate head where rested the consort-crown of creation." When Caroline says they should go into church for the service, Shirley refuses, claiming, "I will stay out here with my mother Eve, in these days called Nature. I love her—undying, mighty being! Heaven may have faded from her brow when she fell in paradise; but all that is glorious on earth shines there still." Shirley's vision is actually a re-vision of the Judeo-Christian Eve as the first Mother, a "woman-Titan" who remains powerful and "glorious," even after the Fall (315–16). Among the most radical working-class movements, feminist reinterpretations of the Bible, especially of Genesis, were very popular. Taylor explains, "At stake in the myth of the Fall was not merely female culpability for the exile from Paradise but the issue of Eve's innate inferiority to Adam."[37] Thus, Shirley's attack on Milton—whose portrayal of Eve, as Sandra Gilbert and Susan Gubar demonstrate, emphasizes both her secondary status and her responsibility for the Fall[38]—prepares the way for her claim: "So kneeling, face to face she speaks with God. That Eve is Jehovah's daughter, as Adam was his son" (316). The traditional view of Eve, represented by Milton, associates women with evil, with "Satan, and Sin his daughter, and Death their horrible offspring" (314–15). Shirley's Eve is the source of salvation and life: after "millenniums" of bondage and conflict, she could still bring forth a Savior; Shirley identifies her with Nature (315). Shirley's imagery has notable parallels with the language of James Smith, who professed both Owenism and Southcottianism and wrote an editorial for the Owenite newspaper, *The Crisis,* which proclaimed: "This is the marriage of nature. *She* is the only priest, or rather, priestess. Hitherto the world has been ruled by priests; let a priestess be substituted in their stead. Hitherto God has been worshipped as a man; let us now worship the female God; the goddess Nature—the bride—the Lamb's wife."[39]

Shirley's first re-vision of Genesis imagines Eve as first woman, mother, and Nature. Her second vision also critiques Genesis and draws upon utopian feminist imagery. Called "La Premiere Femme Savante" or "The First Blue-Stocking," this re-vision is an old *devoir* that Shirley wrote in French under the tutelage of Louis Moore. It begins with a quotation from Genesis—"that the sons of God saw the daughters of men that they were fair; and they took them wives of all which they chose" (455)—and tells the story of Eva, a lost orphaned child, who searches for purpose in life and finds it in a "glorious Bridegroom" who tells her he is "a Son of God" (459). Like the language of Southcott and Smith, this vision is saturated with images of nature, brides, and marriages. It also shares features with a related radical movement, Saint Simonianism. Founded in the late eighteenth century by the French aristocrat, Claude-Henri de Saint Simon, the Saint Simonians brought a heady mix of socialism and eroticism to England in the 1830s. In 1833, lecturing on the rights of women in premises lent to them by Robert Owen, they attracted attacks from the conservative press which worried that their ideas would appeal to "the weaker sex, upon whom they hope to make a fatal impression, as the serpent succeeded with Eve." In the Saint Simonian cosmology, Nature is structured around sexual difference: Man represents ideas, genius, and power while Woman represents emotion and nature. As Barbara Taylor reports, in 1833 "the sect's leader, 'Pere' Enfantin, announced that he had received a message from God informing him that the establishment of the *systeme sociale* would be inaugurated by the advent of a woman saviour, *La Femme Libre, La Mere,* with whom he would spiritually unite, thereby creating a divine androgyne, the new messiah."[40] This rhetoric has parallels in the courtship described in "La Premiere Femme Savante" where Eva, a child of Nature, marries a son of God who calls himself Genius.

The parallels between Shirley's visions and the radical feminism of Southcottianism and Saint Simonianism are very important; however I want to stress the significance of their proximity to a specifically *working-class* radicalism. Shirley's second vision is less powerful than her first: the heroine is named Eva, not Eve; she is a daughter of Nature, not a mother of men. While the first Eve, although fallen, is all that is beautiful in the world and, after eons of struggle, is still capable of bringing forth a savior, the secondary Eva marries her superior, the son of God, who brings her only battle and death. Eve can still be worshipped in Nature; Eva dies in the arms of Genius, who then "bore her triumphant into his own home—Heaven; restored her, redeemed to Jehovah—her Maker; and at last, before Angel and Archangel, crowned her with the crown of Immortality" (460). The less radical emphasis of this vision reflects the regressive movements of the conclusion of *Shirley.* It is even a literal regression since Shirley wrote it years earlier when she was a schoolgirl.

The contrast between the two visions, the difference between Eve and Eva, points out the stimulus given to Shirley's utopianism by her proximity to Luddism. The second vision is enclosed, shut off, from working-class radicalism: it was written in the schoolroom for her tutor, Louis Moore, who declares: "I approve nothing Utopian" (464). By contrast, the timing and the context of Shirley's first vision of the woman-Titan put her in relation to the working class: it occurs the day of the Luddite attack on Robert's mill; and, demonstrating that the connection is not fortuitous, immediately after Shirley discusses her image of the first Mother with Caroline, they are roused by sights and sounds reminiscent of Michael Hartley's vision: "They listened, and heard the tramp of horses: they looked, and saw a glitter through the trees: they caught through the foliage glimpses of martial scarlet; helm shone, plume waved. Silent and orderly, six soldiers rode softly by." Shirley comments, "Did I not say we should see unusual things erelong?" (317). The appearance of the soldiers is, in turn, followed by a discussion of religion and politics with, first, William Farren and, then, Joe Scott, two working-class men who represent two different relations to feminism. Farren finds Shirley and Caroline enjoyable to talk to and exchanges ideas with them on both topics. Joe Scott openly scorns women's ability to discuss either politics or religion. He quotes

Paul's first Epistle to Timothy to them: "'Let the woman learn in silence, with all subjection. I suffer not a woman to teach, nor to usurp authority over the man; but to be in silence. For Adam was first formed, then Eve'" (322). With that as authority, he summarizes that "women is to take their husbands' opinion, both in politics and religion; it's wholesomest for them" (323).

Thus the visions of Luddism and feminism have been brought close together in *Shirley*, but they never coalesce. Michael Hartley's dreams of battle say nothing about sexual equality, although he unconsciously punishes Robert Moore for his abuses of women. Joe Scott, aligned with his master in more ways than one, represents members of the male working class who will take a conservative stand on gender equality. The argument he has with Shirley and Caroline is a forerunner of the stands working-class politicians would take against "bourgeois feminism." He also provides a grim but revealing glimpse of the working-class women who submitted to such male dominance: His wife does not presume to argue religion and politics with him because she "is a hard-working, plain woman: time and trouble has ta'en all the conceit out of her; but that is not the case with you, young Misses" (323–24). Reading the Luddite movement from the perspective of the late 1840s, Brontë stressed those aspects of it that led to the male dominance of working-class radicalism.

But, if working-class movements are fragmented by gender, Shirley's feminism is fragmented by class. Her visions take place in a pre-class world, and they never make the connection between women and the working class that Caroline, whose life is so much more intertwined with working-class women, does. Perhaps that is one reason that Caroline complains that Shirley's description of the first mother is "very vague and visionary!" (316). More tellingly, Shirley's critique of Milton's misogynistic portrait of Eve uses working-class women as a negative sign. Shirley says that Milton did not see the first woman: "It was his cook that he saw; or it was Mrs. Gill, as I have seen her, making custards, in the heat of summer, in the cool dairy, with rose-trees and nasturtiums about the latticed window, preparing a cold collation for the rectors" (315). The double-edged sword that feminism can become is seen here clearly. For in this image Shirley makes a radical feminist point: that women are not ordained by God to do housework and to serve men. Unhappily, as she does so, she also distances herself from the vast majority of women, the working-class women who keep house for the upper classes and for working-class men. Shirley assumes too easily that the cook and Mrs. Gill are as Milton or she have seen them, submissively serving. The "spark of the hot kitchen fire" in Mrs. Gale's eye has been ignored (41). In the midst of Shirley's utopian feminism, the viewpoint of working-class women has been erased.

> "And that was the last fairish that ever was seen on this country side (though they've been heard within these forty years)."—*Shirley*

The conclusion of *Shirley* has provoked as many different critical interpretations as the novel as a whole. In fact, the conclusion poses in miniature the interpretive problems that hover over the entire novel. Many critics have agreed, however, on finding the conclusion unsatisfying, a kind of retreat on Brontë's part from the crucial questions she has raised.[41] Indeed, on several levels, the parallels between women and workers that fueled the novel seem to end here. Caroline marries Robert, thus abandoning the position of old maid that had led her to compare her life with that of the unemployed workers. Shirley marries the anti-utopian Louis. Michael Hartley dies of delirium tremens a year after his assassination attempt on Moore fails (589). The repeal of the Orders in Council reverses the industrial downturn and makes it possible for the mills to employ more workers, suggesting the end of the Luddite Rebellion. It is even possible to read this conclusion, as Terry Eagleton does, as a celebration of these developments.[42] Bells ring out in Yorkshire to announce the repeal of the Orders in Council almost at the same moment that Robert proposes to Caroline; then, festive bells "clash out" again, this time all over England, to announce a victory by Wellington in Spain, and this coincides with a general celebration of the two marriages. The area that was the ground of the Luddite assault is now the place of merriment: "This night is Briarfield to be illuminated. On this day the Fieldhead tenantry dine together; the Hollow's mill work-people will be assembled for a like festal purpose; the schools have a grand treat" (598). The conflicts of the novel seem to end on a grand note of harmony, a coming together of the national history of England and the regional history of Yorkshire, of the public and the private, of the middle class and the working class. The economy is booming; the optimism and progress so loved by readers of historical fiction are the order of the day. The narrator comments that "the good time seemed come. These prospects might be delusive, but they were brilliant—to some they were even true" (591).

As these comments illustrate, despite so much, apparently, to celebrate, the tone of the final chapter is oddly unsettling. The narrator undercuts the apparent harmony and mocks the reader's desire for a simple, happy ending. At points, the chapter reads like a send-up of conventional novelistic conclusions, but there are deeper reasons for its unsettling effect. Like the novel as a whole, the last chapter is framed by Brontë's sense of history—which means that there are no comforting victories or heroes here or any simple sense of historical coherence. One of its most important framing features is its title, "The Winding-Up," replacing the more conventional "Conclusion" or "Wind-Up." "The Winding-Up" is on some level a mockery of official history and official plotting. Winding-up can suggest action as well as resolution, and, further, it is a textile image, referring to the winding-up of thread before it is put on a knitting machine. Significantly, winding was a female occupation in the factory, and, because the winding room was relatively quiet, the women who worked there were able to talk and tended to develop a special sense of community. It has been pointed out that women winders were disproportionately represented as active suffragists at the end of the nineteenth century.[43] The sense of historical tension, of a winding-up to some kind of action, also appears in the narrator's comments. The narrator describes this historical moment in a way that suggests more turbulence to come: "The nineteenth century wantons in its giant adolescence: the Titan-boy uproots mountains in his game, and hurls rocks in his wild sport" (590). The bells ring out for Wellington's victory at the battle of Salamanca, not Waterloo, suggesting that jubilation is premature, leaving us with a sense of historical incompletion. In fact, the reader in 1849 and later knows that this is not the end, that the Napoleonic Wars still have several years of bloodshed to struggle through, that industrialism's impact on the landscape and class relations is in its infancy, that this is just the first stage of working-class radicalism, that the position of women will become increasingly problematic. Like a top that has been wound up, this is a moment of stillness, but just a pause, before the forces that have been constricted are let loose again, and the top begins to whirl. So the issues raised by Luddism and feminism have not been resolved but only contained within patriarchal culture to begin new and other submerged historical movements.

Like the novel's opening, the conclusion also emphasizes two emblematic voices in addition to the narrator's. The first is that of the industrialist, Robert Moore. Never averse to mixing business with pleasure, Moore's proposal to Caroline is immediately followed by a lengthy description of his plans. He begins by telling Caroline that he has learned "the downright folly of being selfish" and that "the houseless, the starving, the unemployed, shall come to Hollow's mill from far and near; and Joe Scott shall give them work, and Louis Moore, Esq., shall let them a tenement." Mixed in with these plans for paternal benevolence, however, are others. Robert will "double the value" of the property by rooting up the copse to build a larger mill and "will get an act for enclosing Nunnely Common" (597–98). These places, associated with Robin Hood, fairies, Shirley's Eve, and Michael Hartley's visions, will be destroyed in order to make room for the industrialist's "day-dreams" (598). Despite Robert's claim that Caroline's influence will soften him—"I know the being I seek to entwine with my own will bring me a solace—a charity—a purity—to which, of myself, I am a stranger" (595)—he brushes aside her rather feeble protests: "Horrible! You will change our blue hill-country air into the Stilbro' smoke atmosphere." Even her offered kiss is "taken unfair advantage of, to the extortion of about a hundred kisses" (598). The powerful mercenary imagery that flows through Robert's words, whether of courtship or of business, gives clear indication as to which side of his newly married self will dominate.

Although he dominates Caroline, however, Robert does not have the last word. In the novel's final paragraph, the narrator confirms the fact that at least the negative portions of the industrialist's "day-dreams" came to pass: "I suppose Robert Moore's prophecies were, partially, at least, fulfilled. The other day I passed up the Hollow, which tradition says was once green, and lone, and wild; and there I saw the manufacturer's day-dreams embodied in substantial stone and brick and ashes—the cinder-black highway, the cottages, and the cottage-gardens; there I saw a mighty mill, and a chimney, ambitious as the tower of Babel." By indicating the connections between past and present that had begun the novel, the narrator underscores the temporary nature of the industrialist's dominance. She looks both backward and forward in time—backward to before industrialism when "tradition says the Hollow was green, and lone, and wild" and forward to the new mill "ambitious as the tower of Babel"—and perhaps just as doomed to failure (599).

Then, opening history again to the voices that official histories suppress, the narrator makes a dialogic movement, telling us she is speaking to her housekeeper and then quoting her housekeeper, who further quotes her mother. The novel had begun with a gathering of curates around a supper table and the jaundiced reactions of the landlady, Mrs. Gale, who is waiting on them and despised by them, as she says, "because she doesn't keep a servant, but does the work of the house herself, as her mother did afore her" (41). Here, again, is the voice of women's work and of working-class women, the voice most muted by history, but emphasized by Brontë's narrative frame. The final exchange in the novel between the narrator and her housekeeper emphasizes, not male achievements, but the memories of women's lives. The housekeeper recalls the founding of the new mill—"the two Mr. Moores made a great stir about it"—but what is important to her is the memory of Caroline and Shirley. They become, in fact, mythologized: "[T]here is no such ladies now-a-days." Then the housekeeper repeats the narrator's historical shifts by reaching even farther back in time, remembering, "My mother coming running in just at the edge of dark, almost fleyed out of her wits, saying, she had seen a fairish (fairy) in Fieldhead Hollow; and that was the last fairish that ever was seen on this country side (though they've been heard within these forty years)" (599).

A last vision, passed from woman to woman, keeps alive another tradition, one that may not be embodied in the "substantial stone and brick and ashes" of society but that still maintains a submerged importance (599). As an ending, too, of a novel that deals with the Luddite Rebellion, whose name derives from General or King Ludd, that mythical Robin Hood-like defender of the working class, the housekeeper calls up associations with other traditions that imagine ideals outside of a culture's dominant myths—like Michael Hartley's visions and Shirley's mysticism and that of working-class millenarianism. Thus, the narrator returns to the connection between woman and woman, between women and the working class, indicating that its apparition has not been permanently laid to rest but will continue to haunt official histories. *Shirley* disrupts those official histories with other voices—domestic servants, Luddite prophets, and feminist visionaries. In these ways it underlines the importance of the most marginalized and hidden elements in Victorian society. But *Shirley* also points to, and partially reenacts, ongoing failures in working-class movements and in feminism to connect class and gender issues, especially in their treatment of working-class women. Caroline Helstone's ambitious desire to understand the relationship between women's and the working class's positions does not come to fruition, as the industrialist's does. Still, within the pages of *Shirley,* one can actually hear some of the "fairishes" who have disappeared from history's countryside and, therefore, can examine the beginnings of the slow, difficult process of mapping the problematic, still unresolved connections between women's history and working-class history.

PART THREE

Class Relations

Chapter 5

Domesticating Violence
Hard Times for Working-Class Women

It has become quite a truism that our women are like dogs, the more you beat them the more they love you.

—"Wife-Torture in England," Frances Power Cobbe, 1878

AFTER THE turbulent debates of the 1840s, working-class women largely disappear from public discourse in the 1850s. The emerging consensus among upper- and middle-class spectators and the male-dominated union movement was that working-class women should be returned to the domestic sphere. The newly domesticated image of working-class women was not without its price, however. Such enforced domesticity was haunted by the specter of domestic violence. In fact, one of the ongoing markers in representations of working-class life in the second half of the nineteenth century is violence between men and women: the violence that was previously represented in the public sphere is removed to the working-class home. Dickens's *Hard Times* (1854) presents this dynamic in its subtle images of working-class domestic violence. Coketown's factory discipline does not provoke political violence or union strikes; instead, violence haunts the Jupe and Blackpool households, suggesting that domestic violence provides society with a safety valve for working-class protest. Dickens's indirect portrayal of domestic violence is followed by increasingly blunt fictions that eventually suggest such violence is an inevitable feature of working-class life. Frances Hodgson Burnett's *That Lass O' Lowries* (1877) provides one of the few nineteenth-century representations of a heroine who works in an industrial setting. Joan Lowrie, a pit-brow lass who picks coal on the surface of the mines, is gifted with courage and beauty and seems at times to shatter both class and gender barriers. But this novel directly tells the story that *Hard Times* only hints at: Joan's coalminer father beats her regularly, and Joan's bruises appear right at the juncture of class and gender distinctions. In the 1880s and 1890s, the Darwinian slum worlds of George Gissing and Rudyard Kipling envision working-class life as a jungle where the strong prey upon the weak. In these worlds women evolve into naturally violent creatures, who compete with each other for men, and sometimes into monsters who are deadlier than the male. Such is the case with the overpowering Clementina Peckover who wreaks havoc in Gissing's novel, *The Nether World* (1889). A sadist who tortures the weak to amuse herself, Clem is the novel's most dangerous creature and is finally put on trial for attempting to murder her own mother. In Kipling's 1892 short story about life and death in London's East End, "The Record of Badalia Herodsfoot," women fight among themselves but always lose out when they go up against their men. Here, in fact, the flip side of Clem Peckover's sadist appears; Badalia, an intelligent and resourceful working-class woman, masochistically wants the husband who beats and finally murders her. Now removed from the context of working-class protest, these later fictions demonstrate the ways in which imagined class and gender differences can be made to reinforce one another and how they combine to naturalize both poverty and violence.

> If [a working-class man] discovered his wife with a paramour, or found that by her drunkenness she had caused the death of a child, would he appeal to the laws—would he in the former case sue for damages in Doctors' Commons, or petition Parliament for a divorce? No. He would give his wife a sound thrashing, and all the world would think it a very natural act, considering his condition and circumstances.
>
> Editorial, *Times* September 10, 1850

In the 1840s working-class unions and middle-class politicians found common ground in the idea that working-class women should be returned to the domestic sphere where they could perform their destined function. By the 1850s this consensus had begun to take effect in a general decline in working-class women's quality of life—fewer opportunities for outside employment resulting in greater dependency on men, worsening diet and health, and a corresponding psychological deterioration. By the 1850s their jobs were less secure, and they had largely disappeared from the public sphere, even as objects of debate—except, that is, in their domestic role. Middle-class rhetoric, which working-class leaders often adopted, positioned the newly domesticated working-class woman as the savior of her class. Through her softening influence, she was to create a happy home for husband and children. Through careful household management, she was supposed to stretch the portion of her husband's meager paycheck that was turned over to her to provide adequate meals, clothing, fuel, and medicines for her family. Significantly, too, for the middle classes, such happy, well-run working-class homes were meant to keep men from two threats to public peace—drink and politics.

The cost to working-class women is revealed in their declining quality of life after 1850 and in cases of domestic violence. Critics have long associated the treatment of Stephen Blackpool's marriage in *Hard Times* with the contemporary debate over the reform of the divorce laws.[1] In 1854, Parliament debated the Matrimonial Causes Act, which was finally passed in 1857 and which made divorce less expensive and easier to attain. For men, grounds for divorce included the wife's adultery or desertion; for women, adultery needed to be aggravated by desertion or physical cruelty. But in 1853, another piece of matrimonial reform legislation was passed, the Prevention and Punishment of Aggravated Assaults on Women Acts. These acts gave police magistrates the summary power to punish wifebeaters by giving them a maximum sentence of up to six months' imprisonment with hard labor; in 1868, the acts were amended to extend the maximum penalty to one year. Although historians debate whether incidents of domestic violence declined in the second half of the nineteenth century, they agree that historically wifebeating was tolerated and that, as Nancy Tomes puts it, "the working-class community recognized violence or threats of violence as legitimate means of maintaining the husband's superiority in the family." As the breadwinner, the husband "expected his wife to run errands for him, prepare his food, and keep the house." Failure to perform these tasks could provoke the husband's abuse. For example, Tomes cites a case of a man who sent his wife to pick up his boots which were being mended; the boots were not ready and, when the wife returned without them, he beat her.[2]

Abuse was most likely to occur when the husband's authority was challenged or in cases where the husband was unemployed. Money was a major battleground. The household budget was the wife's province. When the husband received his pay packet, he kept money for himself and turned the rest over to her. After that, he typically took little interest in the running of the household. In fact, working-class men and women often lived in separate worlds and on separate budgets—one for the husband, the other for the wife and children. Conflicts could occur when the husband did not provide enough money to support the household or when he considered that his wife had mishandled household money. Wives operated in a hidden world where they struggled to make ends meet by eating less nutritional food than their husbands, by pawning clothes and household furnishings, and by working to earn additional money at home.[3]

The responses of the working-class community and nineteenth-century law to domestic violence make clear its ambiguous tolerance by both. Neighbors controlled the level of domestic violence through surveillance. Normally, they would interfere only if there was danger of murder. Otherwise, the "[f]emale neighbours took the responsibility for tending the wife's injuries and putting her to bed after a beating." Middle-class responses to working-class domestic violence tended to draw upon two stereotypes—on the one hand, the working-class woman as an overpowering virago who deserved whatever abuse she received and, on the other, the working-class man as a drunken brute who lived outside the state of civilization. Edward Cox's 1877 handbook on sentencing guidelines, *Principles for Punishment,* provides an example of the first stereotype: "In the vast majority of these cases the suffering angel of the sensation 'leader' is found to be rather an angel of the fallen class, who has made her husband's home an earthly hell, who spends his earnings in drink, pawns his furniture, starves his children, provides for him no meals, lashes him with her tongue when sober and her fists when drunk, and if he tries to restrain her fits of passion, resists with a fierceness and a strength for which he is no match." The magistrate Thomas Holmes provides an example of the second attitude: "How their wives suffer! . . . Is there any misery equal to theirs, any slavery to compare with theirs? If so, I have never heard of it. I have seen thousands of them, and their existence is our shame and degradation."[4] Such bifurcated images of working-class women as either viragos or passive victims typically serve to naturalize working-class violence.

Other middle-class observers offer more nuanced analyses of the problem. Frances Power Cobbe's 1878 essay, "Wife-Torture in England," provides an insightful critique of the economic, political, and social circumstances resulting in domestic violence. Written twenty-five years after the passage of the Punishment and Prevention of Assaults on Women Acts and just prior to the passage of an updated Matrimonial Causes Act, Cobbe's essay argues that the present laws are ineffective at both punishment and prevention and urges passage of more stringent ones, particularly ones that guarantee women protection from abusive husbands. A prominent suffragist, Cobbe points to the inferior status of women before the law and as wives, mothers, and citizens as the key feature that prevents any effective address to the problem.

The first of Cobbe's tactics is to shock her audience into an awareness of the serious nature of domestic violence. She suggests that it is no accident that "Punch and Judy" shows are England's most popular form of street entertainment: social attitudes treat "wife-beating" with a humorous tolerance. To counteract those attitudes, Cobbe provides several pages of crime reports, delineating "wife-torture" and murder. Instead of a jolly battle of the sexes, here women are kicked with hob-nailed boots, lit on fire with paraffin lamps, strangled, thrown down fourteen flights of stairs, struck with pokers, have bulldogs set on them, have vitriol thrown in their faces, and are hacked to pieces with hatchets. This grim litany illustrates her point that "the familiar term 'wife-beating' conveys about as remote a notion of the extremity of the cruelty indicated as when candid and ingenuous vivisectors talk of 'scratching a newt's tail' when they refer to burning alive, or dissecting out the nerves of living dogs, or torturing ninety cats in one series of experiments."[5]

At the center of Cobbe's presentation is the direct connection she draws between domestic violence and class. In fact, she claims that domestic violence is almost exclusively a working-class problem, stating that while upper- and middle-class Englishmen are world-renown for their courteous treatment of women, working-class men treat their wives like chattel. Cobbe further connects domestic violence to class issues by claiming that it is especially endemic to industrial cities such as Liverpool, places that she nicknames "the kicking districts." Cobbe comments, "Wife-beating exists in the upper and middle classes rather more, I fear, than is generally recognized; but it rarely extends to anything beyond an occasional blow or two of a not dangerous kind. . . . The dangerous wife-beater belongs almost exclusively to the artisan and labouring classes."[6]

As explanations for this difference, Cobbe lists such factors as the close quarters in which workers live, the high incidence of heavy drinking and prostitution, and the general assumption that middle- and upper-class men are more sensitive to public censure while working-class men are free to give way to their most brutal urges.

Some of Cobbe's most interesting comments critique Victorian representations of working-class women, suggesting the ways in which they contribute to attitudes toward domestic violence. Stereotypical views of working-class wives positioned them as either masochists, who clung whimpering to the men who beat them, or as viragoes, who gave at least as good as they got. Cobbe replaces these stereotypes with complex human faces and motives. She dismisses the view of "[a] specially experienced gentleman" from Liverpool who claims that "[t]he women of Lancashire are *awfully fond* of bad husbands. It has become quite a truism that our women are like dogs, the more you beat them the more they love you." Cobbe argues that this is the coward's way out of the problem, simply "a welcome excuse for the 'policy of non-intervention.'" She repeatedly points out that women cannot be expected to place complaints against their husbands unless the law protects them from retribution. Her views on the frequent assumption that working-class women deserve or provoke attack, including murder, are even more strongly asserted. She goes so far as to defend "that universally condemned creature, the drunken wife" by asking how many of them "have been *driven* to intemperance by sheer misery"?[7]

Finally, Cobbe argues that the popular belief that "nagging" justified abuse and even murder was the most destructive. Her most telling point is that accusations of "nagging" usually arise out of conflicts over money: sometimes a husband has spent money on drink or other women and his wife asks him for money for herself and their children; at other times, the wife herself is the breadwinner, and the husband becomes enraged when she refuses to give the money that she has earned to him. In fact, Cobbe argues that the women who are most likely to be attacked and murdered are those who are the sole support of their families. The new law that Cobbe advocates would protect these women in particular: "A Bill should, I think, be passed, affording these poor women, by means easily within their reach, the same redress which women of the richer classes obtain through the Divorce Court. They should be enabled to obtain from the Court which sentences their husbands a Protection Order, which should in their case have the same validity as a judicial separation. In addition to this, the Custody of the Children should be given to the wife."[8] Cobbe's analysis was persuasive enough to affect Parliament; the recommendations about protection orders and the custody of children became part of the Matrimonial Causes Act of 1878 largely through her efforts. Her comments also present an interesting template against which to measure fictions about domestic violence. Like her, they present such violence as widespread among the working classes. Unlike her, however, they do not contain a progressive feminist analysis of the women's position. Yet, although their images of viragoes and victims often draw on the stereotypes Cobbe attacks, the fictions also place those images in a broader context, demonstrating how they develop and the social purposes that they serve.

> "Father, father! Pray don't hurt the creature who is so fond of you!"—*Hard Times*

In a climactic moment in *Hard Times,* the circus girl, Sissy Jupe, shares a glimpse of lower-class family life with the middle-class Louisa Gradgrind. Despite the fact that her father has deserted her, Sissy remains loyal to him, believing that he left her for her own good and will return for her. Taken into the Gradgrind household as an educational experiment *cum* female companion, Sissy is expressly forbidden by Mr. Gradgrind to talk about her previous life as the daughter of a circus clown. In a chapter entitled "Sissy's Progress," however, Sissy and Louisa hold a confidential conversation that moves from Sissy's troubles at school to the secrets of lower-class family bonds. As Louisa tries to help her with her lessons, Sissy confesses her miserable failure at the M'Choakumchilds' school. But, although Sissy seems incapable of learning the lessons of political economy and statistics that Louisa knows by heart, she has more crucial things to teach Louisa about love and pain.[9]

Their violation of Mr. Gradgrind's taboo begins with a discussion of education that is usually read within the context of the novel's attack on utilitarianism but also has implications for the education of girls and women. The educated Louisa already recognizes that she "might not be the better for [her schooling]" (96). In the previous chapter, she had confessed her sense of her own deficiencies, and how she has been miseducated, to her brother, Tom, saying that "as I get older, and nearer growing up, I often sit wondering here, and think how unfortunate it is for me that I can't reconcile you to home better than I am able to do. I don't know what other girls know. I can't play to you, or sing to you. I can't talk to you so as to lighten your mind, for I never see any amusing sights or read any amusing books that it would be a pleasure or a relief to you to talk about, when you are tired" (91). Sissy's behavior in the Gradgrind home has shown Louisa that Sissy's "education" in the school of hard knocks has prepared her for the Victorian woman's ideal role in the novel, a kind of companion/nurse: "You are more useful to my mother, and more pleasant with her than I can ever be. . . . You are pleasanter to yourself, than *I* am to *my* self" (96). Louisa, then, presses Sissy to enter "on forbidden ground" by asking her about her father, assuring her, "No one hears us; and if any one did, I am sure no harm could be found in such an innocent question." As the secrecy and intensity of the scene mount, Louisa asks questions "with a strong, wild, wandering interest peculiar to her; an interest gone astray like a banished creature, and hiding in solitary places." She asks, first and foremost, about love: "Did her father love [her mother]?" And, though her mother died when she was born, Sissy responds on faith, "O yes! As dearly as he loves me" (98). Sissy defends her father's abandonment of her, claiming that "[n]obody understands him as I do; nobody knows him as I do" (98). Then, she describes life with father.

What Sissy has to reveal does not, at first, seem to warrant the prohibitions and secrecy with which it is surrounded. She makes the "terrible communication" that her mother was a dancer and "whisper[s] the awful word" that her father was a clown (98–99). But, as Sissy describes her life with her father, darker secrets do appear, surrounding his growing failure at his job and Sissy's struggle to comfort him—physically, with the nine oils that she buys to soothe his bruises; mentally, with the stories she tells to distract him from his pain; and, most of all, emotionally, with the love and trust that she maintains in him even in the face of violence and abandonment. The bottle of nine oils is all she has to remember him by, and she always keeps it in expectation of his return. This image of a girl nursing the physical and psychic bruises of a man on his return from work is the first level of what the novel communicates about the role of the woman in the working-class home.

The second level unveils a more disturbing secret. Sissy's description of her emotional bond to her father reaches its climax when she describes the only time he lost his temper: "He was angry only one night, and that was not to me, but Merrylegs," his performing dog. Senor Jupe returns home after a performance that has brought his frustration to the boiling point: "Everything of father's had gone wrong that night, and he hadn't pleased the public at all." When he enters the room, he orders Merrylegs to perform a trick, but the dog only "looked at father, and didn't do it at once" (99). Merrylegs's hesitation to obey Senor Jupe crystallizes his anger: "He cried out that the very dog knew he was failing, and had no compassion on him. Then he beat the dog, and I was frightened, and said, 'Father, father! Pray don't hurt the creature who is so fond of you! O Heaven forgive you, father, stop!' And he stopped, and the dog was bloody, and father lay down crying on the floor with the dog in his arms, and the dog licked his face" (99–100).[10]

This dramatic scene of family attachment in the face of male job failure and consequent loss of authority, culminating in a beating, contains the tabooed secret that Sissy shares with Louisa about women's ultimate role in *Hard Times*. It is also one of the few glimpses that *Hard Times* offers of life inside a lower-class family. Significantly, the other working-class home the novel dramatizes, Stephen Blackpool's, is also threatened by violence. What is even more telling about Sissy's revelations is the way that she and the performing dog, Merrylegs, accept the violence. Many critics agree that Sissy Jupe is the real reformer in *Hard Times,* although they may debate her effectiveness as a persuasive character.[11] She, along with Rachael, Stephen Blackpool's loyal and virtuous beloved, are the novel's angels in the house. By giving this role to two lower-class women, Dickens reverses the more typical class relations between women.[12] Here lower-class women instruct the middle class in the duties of womanhood and household management. But the nature of the lessons Sissy has to offer—all-suffering devotion in the face of domestic violence and desertion—open a window on the domestic role of working-class women and its political and economic functions that has disturbing implications.

> "Is it possible, I wonder, that there was any analogy between the case of the Coketown population and the case of the little Gradgrinds?"—*Hard Times*

The issue of domestic violence not only shadows Sissy Jupe's relationship with her father and Stephen Blackpool's marriage, but it also forms a crucial connection between two other problematic aspects of *Hard*

Times—its treatment of class conflict and the family. A distinctive feature of *Hard Times* is that, unlike other industrial novels, it contains no direct representations of class violence—no riots such as punctuate the conclusions of *Sybil*, *Alton Locke*, and *Felix Holt*, or assassinations like that described in *Mary Barton,* or even a rock thrown by an angry striker as in a pivotal scene in *North and South*. There seems, in fact, to be a deliberate suppression of class violence in the novel. Even a strike is apparently too much of a threat to public order to be represented.[13] When the union meets in *Hard Times,* it debates the problem of Stephen Blackpool's refusal to join, not the problem of negotiating with the masters. Their solution is not to attack him physically but to shun him quietly. The story of Rachael's little sister, whose arm is ripped out by a machine, is erased. Now the factory girl is replaced by the lower-class but entirely domestic Sissy. This is not to say, however, that *Hard Times* is not a violent novel. So much active suppression seems to demand some kind of release. *Hard Times* represses active violence, on the one hand, but its language fairly explodes with it, on the other. As David Sonstroem asserts, "In reading *Hard Times* one senses a pervasive violence which the action of the book cannot completely account for." Sonstroem points to the violence of the novel's imagery as one solution to this mystery: the names of characters—the "grind" in Gradgrind, the "bite" in Bitzer, the "choke" in M'Choakumchild; the way that Mr. Gradgrind is described as "a kind of cannon loaded to the muzzle with facts, and prepared to blow [the students at the M'Choakumchilds' school] clean out of the regions of childhood at one discharge" (48) or Mrs. Gradgrind as one "who, whenever she showed a symptom of coming to life, was invariably stunned by some weighty piece of fact tumbling on her" (59).[14]

There is one place, however, where violent metaphor becomes metonymy,[15] and that is in the novel's references to, and, in the case of Senor Jupe's beating of Merrylegs, actual instance of, domestic violence. *Hard Times* displaces the violence that should occur in the economic and political spheres on to the domestic sphere in order to contain and redirect it, because, unlike political violence, which strikes at the power structure, domestic violence seeks out the least powerful for its victims. Dickens's desire to construct the family as a refuge from the world and an escape from economic conflict has been recognized. Yet in tension with that desire is his need to construct the family as a disciplinary agency. In *The Novel and the Police,* D. A. Miller interprets Dickens through the lens of Foucault: "The novels continually imply the family's advantages over other agencies in producing acceptable citizens of the liberal state both in quantitative terms—as its greater economy—and in qualitative ones—as the superiority of the bonds between its members."[16] Gallagher's analysis of the use of the family-society metaphor in *Hard Times* goes right to the heart of the paradox: "Dickens's special use of the family-society metaphor . . . gives family reform priority over social reform and tries to substitute family solidarity for social cohesion." But, she concludes, the book undercuts this central metaphor because it "seems suffused with a fear of making connections in a world where relationships are almost without exception destructive."[17] The tensions that are always present in the Dickensian family become even more acute in the industrialized atmosphere of Coketown because of the competing needs to construct the family both as a haven from that atmosphere and as a source of factory and social discipline.

In another Foucauldian reading of Dickens, "The Fixed Eye and the Rolling Eye: Surveillance and Discipline in *Hard Times,*" Cynthia Northcutt Malone traces the novel's preoccupation with watching that links family, factory, school, and circus. As she also demonstrates, discipline does not preclude punishment. She points to the specific instances of the bruised body of Signor Jupe—"The metaphorical figure that marks his absence, the bottle of nine oils, functions as a visible spectacle of the undisciplined body's fate"—and the broken body of Stephen Blackpool as it is pulled from the Old Hell Shaft.[18] In *Hard Times* Dickens's distaste for factory discipline and Gradgrind's utilitarianism suggests, in fact, a hidden preference for old-fashioned beatings. Therefore, the family is the perfect vehicle for discipline not just because it sublimates violence but also because if the problem becomes acute enough, it becomes the place where physical punishment can take place secretly and where bonds can become bondage.

The displacement of social violence on to the domestic sphere is not direct and not at all simple in its effects, however. Images of domestic violence appear in a complex and unstable series of displacements. The references to it take the reader through a hall of mirrors where Dickens seems to imagine a number of different possible relations between domestic violence and wider political and economic relations. In a sense, the novel demands that the reader peel away the layers of references to uncover what is really happening. Dickens gives domestic violence its full political and psychological dimensions. In the political realm, it becomes a metaphor for industrialization, with England represented as a large abusive family. In the psychological realm, it uncovers three related problems: first, Dickens's insight into the fact that social control will always produce violence as a reaction; second, his belief that the maintenance of social order requires that that violence be absorbed in some way; and, finally, his portrayal of domestic violence as powerfully attractive because it absorbs violence in a way that does not threaten the social order as a whole and because he understands the intense psychological bond it establishes between the victim and the victimizer and sees it as, in some way, a justification of violence. Thus, the political and the psychological realms continually interpenetrate each other and function in mutually supportive ways, and domestic violence is revealed as a guilty secret, a safety valve, and, finally, part of the glue that keeps society together.

> "I read in th' papers every 'Sizes, every Sessions—and you read too—I know it!—with dismay—how th' supposed unpossibility o' ever getting unchained from one another, at any price, on any terms, brings blood upon this land, and brings many common married fok to battle, murder, and sudden death."—*Hard Times*

On the level of the middle-class family the violence is kept metaphoric and psychological. Mr. Gradgrind is compared to a wife killer, but in Gradgrind's case the parallel is invoked only to be denied: "Although Mr. Gradgrind did not take after Blue Beard, his room was quite a blue chamber in its abundance of blue books" (131). Mrs. Gradgrind, Louisa, and Tom suffer in various ways from Mr. Gradgrind's utilitarian emotional repressiveness, but no physical discipline is needed to enforce his system. This is also true of the middle-class Bounderby household—despite the fact that Bounderby himself is harsh and aggressive. Perhaps thankfully, Dickens drops a veil across Bounderby's marriage to Louisa where they seem to exist in separate spheres even when in the same room—he bombastically asserting himself while she coldly withdraws. Harthouse observes that Louisa was "ashamed of her husband's braggart humility—from which she shrunk as if every example of it were a cut or a blow" (161). But there is no hint of Bounderby exerting force on Louisa or asserting his "conjugal rights," again, surprisingly, because he had felt no compunction about forcing himself on her when he was a forty-seven-year-old man and she was a fifteen-year-old girl. At the novel's opening, when Bounderby smooths over their father's anger at finding Louisa and Tom peeping at the circus, he claims a sexual reward: "Well, Louisa, that's worth a kiss, isn't it?" After Bounderby has taken his kiss, Louisa's violent response is inflicted on herself: "He went his way, but she stood on the same spot, rubbing the cheek he had kissed, with her handkerchief, until it was burning red. She was still doing this, five minutes afterwards. 'What are you about, Loo?' her brother sulkily remonstrated. 'You'll rub a hole in your face.' 'You may cut the piece out with your penknife if you like, Tom. I wouldn't cry!'" (64). This pattern of hurting oneself is seen in both Louisa and Tom, almost as if they longed for physical punishment, rather than their father's utilitarian discipline. Louisa repeats it when she returns to the father who hurt her after the failure of her marriage.[19] When she finally confronts her father with the truth, asking him why he had inflicted an education on her that had destroyed her heart, she strikes *herself,* "with both hands upon her bosom" (239).

The worlds of the circus and of Fancy are, apparently, opposed to those of industrialism and utilitarianism, yet stories of familial abuse predominate there as well. At the end of the novel, the circus master, Mr. Sleary, celebrates fecundity when he reveals that, because the circus families have so many children, "'we're thtrong in the Fairy bithnuth and the Nurthery dodge." But the specific performance he recommends is the Babes in the Wood, the story of two orphaned children who are abandoned in the woods to die (297). To comfort her father after his failures, Sissy reads him stories from *The Arabian Nights:* "They kept him, many times, from what did him real harm. And often and often of a night, he used to forget all his troubles in wondering whether the Sultan would let the lady go on with the story or would have her head cut off before it was finished" (99). In *Women and Romance: The Consolations of Gender in the English Novel,* Laurie Langbauer discusses Dickens's fascination with *The Arabian Nights,* interpreting it as a secret attraction to narrative forms in which plot is constantly led astray by a devious woman. In her reading, Dickens's own narratives are also identified with women, and, just as in the case of Scheherazade, the archetypal female storyteller, they are constantly shadowed by the intertwined threats of sex and death. Thus, Sissy's innocent reference to *The Arabian Nights* has a dark underside, suggesting what her storytelling postpones as she plays the roles of both Scheherazade and her mother who died in childbirth. Langbauer also points to Dickens's "need to beat wayward women into line," best represented by his famous, obsessively repeated performance of Sikes's murder of Nancy in *Oliver Twist,* another example of working-class domestic violence.[20] In the case of *Hard Times*, this need appears not only in the treatment of Mrs. Blackpool but also, perhaps even more chillingly, in that of the loyal Merrylegs.

Another layer of violent imagery is provided by Bounderby who organizes a fictional life of "hard knocks" around the image of himself as an impoverished and physically abused child. In reiterated stories he describes himself as deserted by his mother and left to the care of his drunken grandmother. In a way that inverts the psychological reality of abuse, Bounderby brags about the beatings he claims he received. He tells Sissy, "By George! . . . when I was four or five years younger than you, I had worse bruises upon me than ten oils, twenty oils, forty oils, would have rubbed off. I didn't get 'em by posture-making, but by being banged about. There was no rope-dancing for me; I danced on the bare ground and was larruped with the rope" (69). He claims that his grandmother was "a she-wolf" who "didn't give any milk, ma'am; she gave bruises. She was a regular Alderney [small dairy cow] at that" (227). Replacing mother's milk with mother's blows, Bounderby's lies form his justification for treating other people harshly. He took the initiative and ran away from his abusive grandmother, and, then, "instead of one old woman knocking me about and starving me, everybody of all ages knocked me about and starved me. They were right; they had no business to do anything else. I was a nuisance, an incumbrance, and a pest" (60). Bounderby's vision of a society where abuse is the norm provides a tricky overlay for other images of domestic violence, because it both discredits the reality of abuse and disguises its more subtle social and political functions. Bounderby's stories of abuse prove to be just that, complete lies; by describing himself as a victim, he is able to justify victimizing. His stories also suggest that public display of domestic violence automatically calls it into question.

If, for Bounderby, domestic violence provides both a rhetorical release and justification of aggression, however, two other characters—the novel's representative working-class man, Stephen Blackpool, and the novel's representative of the circus's life of Fancy, Sissy Jupe—reveal the secret psychological power of domestic violence and that power's interconnection with the structure of class and gender relations. In Stephen Blackpool

Hard Times comes the closest to a direct displacement of violence from the economic on to the domestic sphere. If Bounderby invents for himself a drunken abusive grandmother, Blackpool actually has a drunken abusive wife. On a structural level, Blackpool's life makes the possible political use of domestic violence the clearest because all his dissatisfactions—any anger that he might feel about his miserably limited life as a factory worker—are directed at his wife. During the course of the novel, he is actively mistreated by Bounderby, the union, and Tom Gradgrind, but he is never tempted to strike back at anyone except his wife. His one active thought, which he expresses to Bounderby when he goes to ask him for advice about getting a divorce, is "how I am to be ridded o' this woman" (111).

In his meeting with Bounderby, Blackpool argues that, because of unjust divorce laws, domestic violence between husband and wife becomes inevitable for the working class. The way he presents his case is revealing, especially because, on every other subject, he is passive and quite inarticulate. Here, however, standing in front of his employer as well as his employers' well-born companion, Mrs. Sparsit, Blackpool is unmuddled and almost lawyerlike in arguing for divorce law reform. First, Blackpool states that the structure of the law and economic circumstances make domestic violence unnecessary for the upper classes: "I ha' read i' th' papers that great fok (fair faw 'em a'! I wishes 'em no hurt!) are not bonded together for better for worse so fast, but that they can be set free fro' *their* misfortnet marriages, an marry ower agen. When they dunnot agree, for that their tempers is ill-sorted, they has rooms o' one kind an another in their houses, above a bit, and they can live asunders. We fok ha' only one room, an we can't." Then, he points to the unfair structure of law as it bears on working-class life, one that denies working-class spouses a divorce but punishes them for domestic violence: "If I do her any hurt, sir, there's a law to punish me?" he asks rhetorically—an interesting question, given popular attitudes (112). Finally, he summarizes his case by generalizing the results of these injustices: "I'm a weaver, I were in a fact'ry when a chilt, but I ha' gotten een to see wi' and eern to year wi'. I read in th' papers every 'Sizes, every Sessions—and you read too—I know it!—with dismay—how th' supposed unpossibility o' ever getting unchained from one another, at any price, on any terms, brings blood upon this land, and brings many common married fok to battle, murder, and sudden death" (112–113). Here Blackpool directly connects his life as a factory worker with widespread domestic violence, and, like Frances Power Cobbe, sees such violence as endemic to working-class life.

The scene also provides the only history the novel offers of Mrs. Blackpool who begins life as a factory girl and ends it as a drunken, repulsive monster. Mrs. Blackpool is the blue book stereotype of the factory girl writ large: undomestic, unattractive, aggressive, loud-mouthed, drunken, sexually uncontrolled. But Richard Fabrizio poses the questions that the novel leaves unasked and unanswered about her:

> How did the woman become "a self-made outcast"? What made her "drunken," "begrimed," "foul"? The marriage took place some eighteen or nineteen years before we meet them. Little is said of her background, but nothing indicates that she was unlike any other working-class girl. Indeed, she worked with and was a friend to Rachael, which shows that at least she kept good company. Before marriage, Blackpool himself admits that as a girl she was quite "pretty" and had "good accounts of herseln." After marriage Mrs. Gradgrind's head began to ache; after marriage, Blackpool's wife drinks. Blackpool professes that he was not "unkind to her." But this is a negative response. When she began to go bad, he says he tried to be "patient" with her.[21]

Actually, Blackpool tells Bounderby, "Gonnows I were not a *unkind husband* to her" (emphasis mine), which, given working-class mores, could suggest that Blackpool was tempted to beat her into submission when she began to go bad. Bounderby apparently thinks Blackpool should have played a stronger hand because, in response to Blackpool's claim that he was "patient wi' her," Bounderby comments to himself, "The more fool you, I think" (110). Like the *Times* editorialist, if Blackpool gave this uncontrolled woman a sound thrashing instead of looking to the law for a solution, Bounderby would find it a very natural, and intelligent, way of handling his difficulties.

The violence and murder that are directly named in this scene with Bounderby, however, are repressed in the later scene when Blackpool is presented with the opportunity to be rid of his wife. His desire to murder can only be deduced indirectly from the long, troubled dream he has while he sleeps in a chair with his wife unconscious on the nearby bed, and the murder that he is tempted to commit is an entirely passive one, a sin of omission rather than commission. Given the very specific shape that Blackpool gave to his anger verbally in his presentation to Bounderby, and his direct naming of blood on the land, and battle, murder, and sudden death, the indirect, muted nature of this scene stands in important contrast. In fact, here the novel seems to play a kind of brinkmanship with domestic violence. Because of Blackpool's despair, the way the novel underlines his entrapment within marriage, and the dehumanized image of his wife, who is repeatedly described as a mere form or shape, his desire to murder her is given every possible justification. But the actual moment of the attempted murder is drained of all violence, almost all volition, on Blackpool's part. In this case, domestic violence provides no release for him; with his usual bad luck, Blackpool has to feel just as guilty as if he had committed murder without accruing any of the possible benefits he might have gained from it. The result is that Blackpool turns the violence back on himself, which helps to explain why from this point on he will function as the consummate victim, used in turn by the union, by Bounderby, by Tom Gradgrind, and finally falling into an abandoned mine shaft. The structure of domestic violence in relation to working-class life as presented here is one that forces one to choose between being victimizer or victim, and, having refused the first role, Blackpool will occupy the feminized position of victim for the remainder of his life.[22]

Significantly, it is angelic Rachael who prevents the death of Blackpool's wife, and she is connected to the ultimate image of domestic violence presented in the novel because of her parallels with Sissy Jupe. Thus, Rachael's role in the novel provides another template of the working-class woman in the working-class home, although the home the reader sees her in is not her own, but Stephen Blackpool's. She, too, is a factory worker, but the reader only sees her doing domestic work for Stephen. Not only that, but Rachael's work combines politics and domesticity in ways that represent the ideological burdens working-class women were made to assume. Her relationship with Stephen and its important political implications are immediately set up in the occasional conversations they hold in the streets before or after work. Although they cannot marry, even these brief meetings have improved Stephen's behavior: "Thou hast been that to me, Rachael, through so many year: thou has done me so much good, and heartened of me in that cheering way, that thy word is a law to me.

Ah lass, and a bright good law! Better than some real ones." Rachael performs the domesticated working-class woman's ultimate role by influencing Stephen to submit to the moral law and to the existing legal system. Stephen's glancing critique of the "real" laws brings her kind rebuke: "'Never fret about them, Stephen,' she answered quickly, and not without an anxious glance at his face. 'Let the laws be.'" Stephen grumbles and resists, "Yes, . . . Let 'em be. Let everything be. Let all sorts alone. 'Tis a muddle, and that's aw." But Rachael completes her work when she touches him: "'Always a muddle?' said Rachael, with another gentle touch upon his arm, as if to recall him out of the thoughtfulness, in which he was biting the long ends of his loose neckerchief as he walked along. The touch had its instantaneous effect. He let them fall, turned a smiling face upon her, and said, as he broke into a good-humoured laugh, 'Ay, Rachael, awlus a muddle. That's where I stick. I come to the muddle many times and agen, and I never get beyond it'" (105). Recalling him from what might be dangerous "thoughtfulness," the touch of Rachael's hand converts Stephen from bitterness and anger to good humor and acceptance. The narrator later describes it as "the touch that could calm the wild waters of his soul, as the uplifted hand of the sublimest love and patience could abate the raging of the sea" (114–15). Like Sissy, Rachael keeps her man from what would do him "real harm," whether it be drink or intoxicating ideas of legal, economic, and political change (99).

Thus, the way that Dickens structures Stephen's life, his real problem seems to be that he cannot always live with Rachael's softening influence: "He thought of the home he might at that moment have been seeking with pleasure and pride; of the different man he might have been that night; of the lightness then in his now heavy-laden breast; of the then restored honour, self-respect, and tranquillity, now all torn to pieces" (118). This is emphasized when, after speaking with Rachael in the street, Stephen enters his home to find his drunken wife there. Her reappearance obliterates Rachael's influence and makes Stephen determined to complain about the law.

After he is rebuffed by Bounderby, Stephen again waits for Rachael after work "because he knew himself to want that softening of his anger which no voice but hers could effect." His home occupied by an evil working-class harridan, Stephen does not return: "He ate and drank, for he was exhausted—but, he little knew or cared what; and he wandered about in the chill rain" and, dangerously, all the while, he is "thinking and thinking, and brooding and brooding" (118). When he returns home, the reader again witnesses the ideal working-class woman in the working-class house. After working all day in the factory, Rachael has gone to Stephen's house, cleaned it, and begun nursing his wife. When Stephen at last enters, hidden hands have performed their work: "Everything was in its place and order as he had always kept it, the little fire was newly trimmed, and the hearth was freshly swept" (120). Most importantly, Rachael hides the existence of Stephen's wife with a curtain and fills the room magically with her own soothing influence: "Quiet and peace were there. Rachael was there" (119). Like a good working-class neighbor, when the landlady came to tell her that Stephen's wife was wounded and bruised, she came to nurse her. She tells Stephen that she will stay until 3 a.m., so that she can clean his wife's wounds again. When Stephen worries that she will miss her night's sleep, Rachael embraces her double shift and puts his welfare and work before hers: "I slept sound last night. I can wake many nights, when I am put to it. 'Tis thou who art in need of rest—so white and tired. Try to sleep in the chair there, while I watch. Thou hadst no sleep last night, I can well believe. Tomorrow's work is far harder for thee than for me" (121).

Rachael's nursing of Stephen's wife has many parallels with Sissy's nursing of her father. Like Senor Jupe, Mrs. Blackpool is wounded and bruised: "The wounds of which she had spoken, seemed to be about the neck of the self-made outcast. She dressed them now, still without showing her. She steeped a piece of linen in a basin, into which she poured some liquid from a bottle, and laid it with a gentle hand upon the sore" (121). In his article on *Hard Times* and the Matrimonial Causes Acts, John D. Baird argues that Mrs. Blackpool's wounds are "the eruptions of syphilis" and that the poisonous medicine that Rachael applies to them is perchloride of mercury which was frequently used to treat it.[23] The signs are, essentially, that Mrs. Blackpool is a prostitute. In connection with that, Nancy Tomes comments that prostitutes were likely to encounter violence from their working-class clients.[24] Rachael describes Mrs. Blackpool as "[w]ounded too, and bruised" (120). It is possible that she has syphilitic sores and has also been beaten. Like Sissy's bottle of nine oils, the bottle of medicine Rachael uses becomes symbolic. Like Sissy, Rachael is there to prevent violence or, if necessary, to absorb it. When she wakes in time to prevent Mrs. Blackpool from drinking the poison, she has to fight her to keep the bottle from her lips: "The creature struggled, struck her, seized her by the hair" (124). At the end of the struggle, Rachael has "the red marks of fingers on her forehead" (125). Thus, Rachael fulfills the ultimate role of the working-class woman: to prevent violence and to do so, if necessary, by taking it on herself.

Rachael and Sissy will come together when Blackpool disappears like Sissy's father; they discover the Old Hell Shaft and organize the rescue of Blackpool's mangled body. But, while working-class men are bruised by their contacts with the world, working-class women are bruised by the violence of home. Finally unable to save their men, they must take the punishment. Sissy's disturbing, ambiguous memory of the beating of Merrylegs best illustrates the secrecy, sexualization, and feminization necessary to the domestic sphere's absorption of violence. It parallels Freud's essay on memories of child abuse, "A Child Is Being Beaten," where he argues that the memory of being beaten by the father is primarily a female fantasy, that in its early phases it takes the shape of fantasizing that another, rival child is being beaten, and finally, that the fantasy is both masturbatory and masochistic.[25] So Sissy and Merrylegs, the dog that he took with him when he abandoned her, are both rivals for the father's affections and interchangeable, as is underlined by her words, "Pray don't hurt the creature who is so fond of you!" And the reaction to the beating suggests sexuality and masochism as the bloody dog licks the face of the crying father.

Not only is this beating scene at the center of Sissy's memories of her father, but Merrylegs, the performing dog, returns in the novel's penultimate chapter to deliver a final message. After the circus people help Tom Gradgrind escape the law, the ringmaster, Mr. Sleary, talks to Mr. Gradgrind about the remarkable instincts of dogs and reveals that he believes Sissy's father is dead because Merrylegs returned to the circus, and, once again, Sissy and the dog are interconnected in their loyalty to her father.[26] In thinking about how the dog stayed with Mr. Jupe until his death and how Sissy still keeps the bottle of nine oils for him, Mr. Sleary philosophizes, "It theemth to prethent two thingth to a perthon, don't it, Thquire? . . . one, that there ith a love in the world, not all Thelf-intereth after all, but thomething very different; t'other, that it hath a way of ith own of calculating or not calculating, whith thomehow or another ith at leatht ath hard to give a name to, ath the wayth of the dogth ith!" (308). Self-interest versus a love like that of a beaten dog: the more you beat them, the more they love you. Dogs are domesticated animals, and these images of the dog and of Sissy's doglike instinctive loyalty suggest the investment that society has in domestic violence as a means of maintaining social order. In its contrasting use of different images of domestic violence, *Hard Times* also indicates that domestic violence performs this function best when it is secret, feminized, and sexualized.

"For women is cruel put upon in Gunnison Street."
— "The Record of Badalia Herodsfoot."

Frances Hodgson Burnett's *That Lass O'Lowries* also has a working-class heroine who is both represented as a savior and compared to a dog. Also, like Sissy Jupe, Joan Lowrie will eventually be taken into a middle-class household. Before that moment, however, she will literally endure the beatings that are just hinted at in *Hard Times* as well as literally place her body between a middle-class man and violent working-class attack. *That Lass O' Lowries* is one example of the increasing bluntness of late-nineteenth-century fictions about working-class domestic violence. Whereas *Hard Times* repressed the violence and also subtly suggested its origins by placing it in the context of industrial protest, later fictions, such as *That Lass O' Lowries* and Gissing's *The Nether World,* display domestic violence openly; but, because working-class protest is downplayed, such violence is seen simply as an habitual element of the environment. In fact, one could argue that one plot that now becomes narratable for working-class women is the plot of domestic violence. With its focus on an admirable working-class heroine, *That Lass 'O Lowries* returns to the question of self-determination that *Helen Fleetwood* and *Mary Barton* had addressed. Joan Lowrie is physically as well as morally strong, and she needs both types of strengths because she exists in a much more openly brutal world. She directly confronts the class and gender conflicts that were more hidden in the earlier novels discussed here, and she will bear the marks of those confrontations literally on her body.

Frances Hodgson Burnett made her name as the American author of such popular children's fictions as *Little Lord Fauntleroy* and *The Secret Garden,* but she was born and raised in Manchester until she was sixteen years old when her family emigrated to the United States. *That Lass O' Lowries,* her first novel, drew upon her background and was one of the most unusual novels of its period. Not since Tonna's *Helen Fleetwood* had a novel focused on a heroine directly involved in industrial labor. And not only does Joan Lowrie work, but she also works in one of the most despised and controversial of women's jobs—as a pit-brow lass. Thus, the novel reverberates with some of the most charged images and questions that had surrounded women's labor in the Victorian period.

Set in the fictional coal town of Riggan, *That Lass O' Lowries* revisits the debates of the 1840s, although in a different register. When the 1842 Mining and Collieries Bill excluded women from underground work, about 4,500 women remained at work sorting coal at the top of the shafts. Controversy surrounding their work—especially focused on the 1,500 Wigan pit girls who worked in trousers—surfaced at regular intervals after the midcentury. In 1863 an article, provocatively entitled "A Real Social Evil," appeared in *Once a Week* accompanied by illustrations of Wigan pit girls dressed in trousers. In 1865 miners presented a petition asking Parliament to exclude women from surface labor at the mines. Again, in 1874 the new *Pictorial World* tried to rouse public controversy with front-page illustrations of pit girls at work. In 1886–87 the matter was finally laid to rest when another attempt to outlaw such labor was made, and public opinion swung decisively in the pit girls' favor.[27] Published in 1877 in the midst of these debates, *That Lass O' Lowries* registers these conflicts by presenting a strong working-class heroine who directly faces both class and gender contradictions.

Like her mother before her, Joan Lowrie has sorted coal at the mouth of the mine since childhood. Powerfully built, covered with coal dust, and dressed in trousers, she is the antithesis of the middle-class Victorian heroine, at first glance a seeming reemergence of the uncivilized working-class woman of earlier industrial literature. Yet, although the women she works among are described as "half-savage," Joan carries herself with a native nobility.[28] Middle-class observers such as the engineer Fergus Derrick and the curate Paul Grace confirm this by pronouncing her "a fine creature," and also a problem: "Here . . . is a creature with the majesty of a Juno—though really nothing but a girl in years—who rules a set of savages by the mere power of a superior will and mind, and yet a woman who works at the mouth of a coal-pit,—who cannot write her own name and who is beaten by her fiend of a father as if she were a dog. Good Heaven! What is she doing here? What does it all mean?" (12). From the beginning, Joan is a living contradiction, a strong, admirable heroine who, at one and the same time, belongs to her environment—she could not exist anywhere else—and yet is seen as divorced from it.

The novel revolves around the question of "what can be done with Joan Lowrie?" How can such a fine creature be left in this environment? Its understandable, although unsatisfactory, conclusion is to make Joan over, to "middle-class" and feminize her, in order to prepare her for marriage to Derrick. Before that happens, however, Joan's life poses some questions about class and gender lines and how permeable or rigid they are. Joan's working-class life is represented as masculine: she dresses like a man, in trousers; like a man, too, she is tall and strong, adept at physical labor; according to the novel, she works at a man's job. Middle-class life is represented as feminine: when Joan first sees Anice Barholm, the rector's daughter, standing in her garden, she immediately recognizes her as a pattern of proper femininity. Tired and dirty after a long day's work, Joan stands behind a hedge and measures the distance between herself and "Anice in her soft white merino dress, with her basket of flowers, with the blue bells at her belt and her half audible song. She struck Joan Lowrie with a sense of beauty and purity. As she watched her she grew discontented—restless—sore at heart. She could not have told why, but she felt a certain anger against herself" (38). As Joan understands, Anice is inside the hedge; she is outside: "theer's th' difference. It a'most looks loike the hedge went aw' around an she'd been born among th' flowers, and theer's no way out for her—no more than there's a way in fur me" (39). Here, too, is a contradiction. Joan envies Anice her soft, feminine beauty and pleasures, yet this paradise is also a trap: the hedge of middle-class femininity that excludes Joan encloses Anice, and, if there is no way in, there is also no way out.

In or out is the structure that the novel finally imposes on Joan, not a destruction of the hedge itself. But its most interesting moments are those that violate that structure. Derrick will fall passionately in love with the coal-covered Joan, not the middle-class feminine ideal, Anice Barholm. Joan has a beauty and a purity that are unique, entirely her own. And Joan's most noble actions involve the kind of physical strength and moral courage that are identified as masculine, although, at the same time, she is never presented as "masculinized" or "unsexed." When the girl Liz returns to Riggan with an illegitimate child, Joan defends her from attack by the community and takes her in with the conscious idea of protecting and supporting her and her little girl. Even more strikingly, she takes on the role of protector for Derrick, guarding him from violent attack, and finally she joins an all-male crew and rescues him from an explosion in the mine.

Joan's violations of class and gender lines do not come without cost, however. The most dramatic, ongoing feature of her life is its association with domestic violence, a violence that appears right at the juncture of class and gender lines, seeming to allow their breach and exact punishment for it at one and the same time. Like Sissy Jupe, Joan lives with her father, but in this novel there is no loyal Merrylegs to receive the father's anger; instead, Joan is presented as the beaten dog. Grace reports, "She has borne, they tell me, such treatment as would have killed most women. She has been beaten, bruised, felled to the earth by this father of hers, who is said to be a perfect fiend in his cups. And yet she holds to her place in their wretched hovel, and makes herself a slave to the fellow with dogged, stubborn determination" (3–4). The first time Derrick talks to her, her father has beaten her and thrown her out of the house at night: as Joan puts it, "I'm turned loike a dog into th' street" (10). But, if the beatings Joan receives mark her as feminine, her consciousness of her position allows her to draw a kind of strength from her endurance. Finally, her "dogged . . . determination" will not subjugate her to her father but, instead, will bring him down.

Another contradictory view of violence is present in the Joan/Derrick relationship. The two have been attracted to one another at a distance; Derrick had marveled at the existence of this fine creature in the midst of the coal mines while Joan had admired Derrick's strength and integrity, although her pride would never let her approach him. Later, Derrick ponders, "She followed her own path as if she were a creature of a different world,—a world so separated from his own that nothing could ever bridge the gulf between them" (130–31). But he is wrong: violence bridges the gulf and allows them to draw close to one another as man and woman, despite the class barriers. When Derrick finds Joan on the street, he examines her bruised face and gently binds up her wound, and in one moment Derrick and Joan come very close to one another, physically and emotionally. A similar scene later in the novel makes the violence at the base of their meeting ground even more explicit. Joan's father has again beaten her, but this time for defending Derrick to him. When Derrick meets her after this, for the first time he declares his feelings for her: "There was that in his manner which moved her as his light touch had done that first night of their meeting, when he had bound up her wounded temple with his handkerchief. It was that her womanhood—her hardly used womanhood, of which she had herself thought with such pathetic scorn—was always before him, and was even a stronger power with him than her marvelous beauty" (132). Joan's bruises represent her womanhood, and Derrick's tender care of them symbolizes his love. In this way, Joan and Derrick reverse the typical gender relations as he nurses her wounds, although, at the same time, her wounds represent her womanhood. This complex role reversal—which allows the transgression of class lines and the violation of gender norms, although always with a price tag of violence—continues throughout their relationship as Joan positions herself as Derrick's defender.

An engineer who works for the mining company, Derrick is presented as a reformer caught between the upper and lower classes. He confronts the owners because they refuse to make needed safety improvements in the mine, and he conflicts with the miners when he demands that they abandon the dangerous habit of using their lanterns to light their pipes underground. This innovation brings him into direct conflict with Joan's father, a man who refuses any control over his actions. When Lowrie refuses to obey the new rule, he and Derrick have a fistfight; when he continues to flout safety regulations, Derrick has him fired. Knowing that her father plans to ambush Derrick in order to exact revenge, Joan begins to shadow Derrick whenever he goes out at night in order to guard him from attack. Thus, much more directly than either Merrylegs or Rachael, Joan takes the working-class violence that is directed at the upper classes on herself. When Derrick catches sight of her following him, she warns him of her father's determination to get revenge at any cost and explains her equal determination to protect him, "If I'm behind thee, theer is na a mon i' Riggan as dare lay hond on thee to my face, if I *am* nowt but a lass" (66). Later, she tells him, "It is na wi' me as it is wi' other women. Yo' munnot judge o' me as yo' judge o' other lasses. What mowtn't be reet fur other lasses to do, is reet enow fur me. It has na been left to me to be lass loike, an' feart, an'—an' modest" (131–32). She makes her intention even more explicit when her father confronts her with her actions. He mocks her for defending a man who is so far above her, who, he says, "as cares no more for yo' than he does for th' dirt at his feet, an' as laughs, ten to one, to know as yo're ready to be picked up or throwed down at his pleasure!" He tells Joan quite clearly that her presence will not thwart his revenge and that, if she persists in getting in the way, he will kill her, too. Joan, however, makes her intentions clear: "'[I]f it's murder yo' mean, theer's yo' an me for it before it's done; an' if theer's deathly blows struck, the first shall fa' on *me*.

Theer!' and she struck herself upon her breast" (129–30). As she promised, when the crucial moment comes, Joan's presence protects Derrick. Her father and some cohorts plan to jump Derrick in the dark, beat him, and burn him with vitriol; but the plan backfires when her father, thinking he has spotted Joan dogging him, is mistaken for Derrick and attacked himself. As he lies dying, he and Joan have a final confrontation as he realizes she has thwarted him. His last words are, "Tha went agen me, did tha? . . . Dom thee!" (160). Joan takes beatings and curses on herself for Derrick's sake.

Joan's final heroic rescue effort takes place when there is an explosion in the mine and Derrick is trapped below. Women, of course, always remain above during such emergencies, waiting. When Joan requests permission to join the rescue team, the coarser men say, "We'n ha' no wenches," while the well-bred Grace tells Joan, "You are a woman. We cannot let you risk your life" (178–79). But Joan insists she can work as well as the men, and the women agree: "She's worth two o' th' best on yo'. Nowt fears her" (178). The men give in when Joan finally tells them that "theer's a mon down theer as I'd gi' my heart's blood to save" (179). Joan's rescue mission is a success, but with Derrick now injured and Joan nursing him, their role reversals are at an end. Danger and violence allowed them to break class and gender barriers. Now class and gender designations return with a vengeance. Joan had once longed for "woman's work" and complained that she was tired of "bein' neyther th' one thing nor th' other" (103). Now, despite the fact that she and Derrick admit they love one another, she asserts the gulf between them is impassable: "Am *I* fit wife fur a gentlemon? Nay, my work's done when the danger's ower" (188). There seems to be no middle ground. Either Joan and Derrick exist in the world of working-class violence or they must retreat behind the hedge of middle-class respectability. Before Derrick recovers completely, Joan abandons Riggan and goes south to stay with Anice Barholm's aunt and learn how to be feminine and middle class. The novel's brief conclusion shows the new Joan standing in a flower garden where Derrick finds her and proposes to her. She is now inside the hedge, dressed in fine new clothes with flowers in her hair; trembling and humble, struggling to learn a new way to speak, she answers Derrick: "Give me th' time to make myself worthy . . . be patient with me until th' day comes when I can come to yo' an' know I need not shame you" (206). The novel thus ends "happily" but at the cost of Joan's character. Having erased her uniqueness and abandoned the violations of gender and class lines that had charged her relationship with Derrick, the novel both saves its pit girl from working-class life and betrays what made her interesting.

Although *Hard Times* and *That Lass O' Lowries* suggest the political uses of domestic violence in managing class and gender relations, the epidemic violence in the late-Victorian slum worlds of George Gissing and Rudyard Kipling seems to produce only the beaters and the beaten. Violence is a given in these environments, where Darwinian competition and the law of natural selection rule, and women adapt themselves to the circumstances either by becoming monsters of cruelty themselves or by masochistically accepting violence as part of the marriage compact. In George Gissing's *The Nether World,* the virtuous fight their environment with lives of miserable self-sacrifice, while the vicious struggle to succeed by trampling on those around them. In one story line, a father abandons his daughter and then returns to her, only to cheat her of her inheritance and destroy her chance of happiness by dividing her from the man she loves. In another, a beautiful, ambitious girl abandons her poor family to pursue the stage; as she is about to have her chance at stardom, a jealous rival throws vitriol in her face. In the midst of these stories of crime and cruelty, Gissing places an overpoweringly vicious woman, transplanting the monstrous working-class female born of Northern industrial conditions to the late Victorian London slums.

In *The Working Classes in Victorian Fiction,* P. J. Keating calls Clementina Peckover "the triumph" of Gissing's novel and argues that "[n]owhere in earlier English fiction had such a portrait of a working-class woman appeared."[29] But, from the viewpoint of the history I am unfolding, she might be considered both the fruition of earlier ideas and the inaugural character in a new age of frankness. In her character, Gissing replays and develops the charges made against factory girls and coalmining women. In 1844 Lord Ashley had warned, "The females not only perform the labour, but occupy the places of men; they are forming various clubs and associations, and gradually acquiring all those privileges which are held to be the proper portion of the male sex. . . . They meet together, to drink, sing, and smoke; they use, it is stated, the lowest, most brutal, and most disgusting language imaginable. . . . Whence is it that this singular and unnatural change is taking place? Because that on women are imposed the duty and burthen of supporting their husbands and families, a perversion as it were of nature, which has the inevitable effect of introducing into families disorder, insubordination, and conflict."[30] In this 1889 novel, Clementina Peckover seems proof that Ashley's predictions have come true: the sign of a broken civilization, she lives like a man and is, therefore, worse than a man—crueler, more malevolent.

First introduced as a strapping sixteen-year-old who works in an artificial flower factory, Clem, as her friends call her, is both masculinized and highly sexualized, just as her predecessors were. Coming, like the mining women, from below, hidden from civilized eyes, Clem is physically overpowering, with large muscular hands and arms that are "as strong as a carter's."[31] Her mother, of whom she is a more developed type, is described as having an arm "like a coal-heaver's" (39). At sixteen Clem is a sexual animal, "coarsely magnificent" (8), with abundant hair and elaborate dress. She is shown to have strong physical appetites for beer and meat, and, presumably, sex. Paying careful attention to her dress and conscious of her charms, she fights, drinks, and curses like a man. In fact, Gissing's most effective innovation is to make clear that Clem's particular brand of sexual attractiveness is based precisely on her "uncivilized," masculine, physical powers and appetites. Clem is "sexed" rather than "unsexed" by her working-class fusion of masculine and feminine.

Although Clem enjoys her male admirers, sex is a secondary passion for her. She takes more pleasure in inflicting pain than in sexuality. Survival in the nether world is not of the fittest but of the cruelest. Gissing has not only transplanted but also updated her character by developing those aspects of the stereotype that are best adapted to life in the post-Darwinian slums. Indeed, Clementina Peckover is the nether world's most malevolent form of life. With her reddish glossy hair and her eyes shining with the red of the fire, she seems the embodiment of "Nature red in tooth and claw," as she puts away a huge meal of beer and sausages while plotting to enjoy herself by tormenting some "defenseless creature" (5). Her first act in the novel is to devise physical and mental torments for its pure heroine, Jane Snowdon; her last is to attempt to poison her own mother for her money. *The Nether World* is ruled by money, power, and cruelty, and Clementina is its most unrelenting force of evil.

The narrator of *The Nether World* is clearly fascinated by Clem, although puzzled about how to explain her origins. He claims, "Civilisation could bring no charge against this young woman; it and she had no common criterion." At points the narrator theorizes that Clem is the natural product of inevitable evolutionary forces: "Who knows but this lust of hers for sanguinary domination was the natural enough issue of the brutalising serfdom of her predecessors in the family line of the Peckovers? A thrall suddenly endowed with authority will assuredly make bitter work for the luckless creature in the next degree of thraldom." (6). Yet at other times the narrator denies that she is a "natural" product and argues, instead, that she is the diseased outgrowth of a poisoned environment. So, despite the evidence that she is a strapping physical specimen, however morally underdeveloped, the narrator claims that "[h]er health was probably less sound than it seemed to be; one would have compared her, not to some piece of exuberant normal vegetation, but rather to a rank, evilly-fostered growth. The putrid soil of that nether world yields other forms besides the obviously blighted and sapless" (8). Here Clem herself is an artificial flower, attractive but poisonous, produced by the diseased environment of the nether world. At still other moments, the narrator suggests that Clem might be some sort of evolutionary throwback—physically magnificent and cruel as an ancient Roman, a savage, or a bloodthirsty red Indian (191–92).

Gissing's reinterpretation of this working-class monster emphasizes that her savagery displays itself not so much in sex, although that is a factor, but in violence. In this novel, Clem is the originator of domestic violence. When Bob Hewett, the man she fancies, courts and marries another girl, Clem attacks her and tears the clothes off her back. When she marries Jane Snowdon's father on the expectation that he will inherit money, he lives "in a sort of fear of the animal" who would not blink at murdering him if it provided her with any advantage (380). Not only is she cruel herself, but she infects others with it as well. When she reunites with Bob, she does so with the purpose of talking him into murdering their spouses. Although unlike her, he shrinks from this ultimate act, he "was infected by the savagery of the woman who had taken possession of him. Her lust of cruelty crept upon him like a disease" (333). After an assignation with Clem, when Bob's poor wife drops and breaks a cup, he releases his fury on her: "With his clenched fist he dealt blow after blow at the half-prostrate woman, speaking no word, but uttering a strange sound, such as might come from some infuriate animal" (334). Clem's schemes backfire when Bob is killed and she herself is arrested for attempted murder, but, though she does not get what she wants for herself, she does succeed in inflicting lifelong injury on everyone she comes in contact with. If the estimation of "the sex" is the measure of a civilization, then Clem is a dire omen of an

England on the brink of disaster. Uncivilized, spreading like a disease, crueler than any man, Clem functions ultimately as a metonym for the darkest depths of a society gone wrong.

Perhaps no story better indicates the view that working-class marriage and domestic violence are inseparable than Rudyard Kipling's "The Record of Badalia Herodsfoot." Kipling continues Gissing's themes of a Darwinian slum world of struggle and violence but shifts the terms on which the battle of the sexes is fought. Unlike Gissing's nether world where predators of both sexes rule, Kipling's divides along the gender lines of natural selection. Men have sex, women have babies; men are sadists, women, masochists—and so the world goes on. Set on Gunnison Street in London's East End, the story is a brief, grim record of working-class women's struggle to live in a world ruled by the law of the jungle. The story begins with the well-known ironic epigraph from Robert Browning's "Pippa Passes": "God's in his heaven/All's right with the world," and its plot of violence, struggle, and murder retains that tone of jolly inevitability.[32] In Gunnison Street men follow "the law of [their] kind" and chose mates "according to the laws of free selection," then leave them for others while the women bear the children and the blows (368). But what can be done? Although the story is aware of the injustice, aid is ineffectual. Bands of well-meaning religious workers, forerunners of the welfare state, try to help the women and children, but they make no appreciable difference. The battered women of Gunnison Street accept their fates and, when given a choice, defend their men rather than themselves. Thus poverty and violence are naturalized through gendered action.

"The Record of Badalia Herodsfoot" presents a slum world in which working-class men are inevitably violent, drunken, and unfaithful and in which working-class women not only endure but finally even embrace that reality. The full acceptance of the way this world works is made all the more striking because Badalia, its working-class heroine, is unusually strong and thoughtful with a kind of instinctive feeling for justice and an inherent integrity. Her story begins when her husband, Tom, leaves her for another woman, "pass[ing] out of Badalia's life, over Badalia's senseless body; for he stifled protest with blows" (357). After his departure, Badalia refuses other suitors and resourcefully sets up a unique business of her own by offering her services to the district charities. The local clergymen give Badalia charge of monies for distribution, using her knowledge of East End slum life to make sure that the money goes where it is needed most. As she explains, "I'm Gunnison Street . . . I know what's what, I do." She knows the way her world works; the men take care of themselves but the women can't, "'specially bein' always confined. 'Ow should they? They wants things if they can get 'em anyways. If not they dies, an' a good job too, for women is cruel put upon in Gunnison Street" (360). Badalia's "record" is the book where she writes down the money she dispenses and how it was spent. Each entry is a working-class woman's life chronicled in Badalia's large, unschooled handwriting:

> —Mrs. Hikkey, very ill brandy 3d. Cab for hospital, she had to go, 1s. . . .
> —Mrs. Vincent. Confid. No linning for baby. Most untidy. In money 2s. 6d. . . .
> —Mrs. Lockhart took a baby to nurse to earn a triffle but mother can't pay husband summons over and over. He won't help. Cash 2s. 2d. (362–63).

Life for Gunnison Street's women is made up of a constant struggle over food, babies, and absent husbands.

Thus, Badalia's life proceeds until Tom reenacts his marital pattern with his new "wife" Jenny. At first things go well, but, when a baby is born, "following the law of his kind, Tom, little interested in the children he helped to produce, sought distraction in drink." And once heavy drinking begins, regular beatings follow, "sometimes across the head, and sometimes across the breast" (368). Like Badalia, Jenny accepts these as a regular part of life, for "the bruises furnished material for discussion on doorsteps among such women as had been treated in like manner by their husbands" (368). Like Badalia, Jenny does not really object until Tom decides to move on to another woman. Then Jenny berates him for the entertainment of the street, complaining, "Oh, women, look you, I've bore 'im one an' there's another on the way, an' 'e'd up an' leave me as I am now—the stinkin' dorg!" When the row attracts a policeman, she demands, "Ain't there no Law for such as 'im? 'E's took all my money, 'e's beat me once, twice an' over." But when the policeman asks, "D'you charge 'im? . . . E'll get a month for it, per'aps," Jenny immediately backs down (371–71). She doesn't want to send him to jail; she wants to keep him. Tom's humiliation before the street leads him to return to Badalia not out of love or desire but out of the certainty that he could "vindicate his authority as a husband" by beating her. He reasons that she doubtless will have taken up with someone else so he will be justified and then, drinking a little more, decides that even if she hasn't done anything wrong "he would smash her for not having gone wrong" (372).

Full of drunken self-righteousness, Tom comes back to Gunnison Street, demanding, "Where's my slut of a wife?" (373). When Badalia welcomes him back and tries to entice him into her bed, Tom responds, "I don't want none o' your kissin's an' slaverin's. I'm sick of 'em" (374). What he does want is to restore his masculine self-esteem by beating her and to get the five pounds that he's learned she received from the clergy: "Give me wot you've got," he demands (375). Badalia, however, while she submissively gives him her own money, will not give him her "trust," the money she has received from the clergy. In fact, one could argue, as Frances Power Cobbe does, that it is Badalia's very resourcefulness and integrity that put her most in danger. She uses her own judgment and stands up for what she believes in, rather than submitting to her husband, and what follows her refusal is as brutal a scene of wife torture as anything reported by Cobbe. The almost humorous style that Kipling employs makes the brutality all the more horrifying. Shrieking: "Give it up, you slut!," Tom punches her in the mouth, then grabs her by the throat, forcing her to her knees, and finally throws her against the bed (376). With Badalia kneeling before him, the narrator explains, "[I]t was impossible for a self-respecting man to refrain from kicking her: so Tom kicked with the deadly intelligence born of whiskey. The head drooped to the floor, and Tom kicked at that till the crisp tingle of hair striking through his nailed boot with the chill of cold water, warned him that it might be as well to desist" (377).

While the narrator describes Tom's drunken savagery in detail, Badalia makes no protest at all. The narrator explains that, if a man other than her husband had attacked her, she would have defended herself like "a wild cat," but she quietly submits to Tom's beating in the hope of winning him back (376). Just as Tom tires of kicking Badalia, her rival Jenny arrives, also wanting to win Tom back and "prepared even to endure an exemplary whacking for her performances in Hennessy's Rents" (377). Joined in their desire for and submission to Tom, Jenny and the dying Badalia silently agree to protect him from a charge of murder: he "must not be taken by the Law" (378). Jenny drags Tom out of the flat and tells him to run. Tom doesn't get off scot-free; he is taken by the law—but for public drunkenness, not wife murder. He is last seen in the story as he falls down in the street and is picked up by a policeman. Watching this, Jenny prays, "Gawd send they don't look at 'is boots!" which are covered with Badalia's blood (379). The clergy attend Badalia's deathbed, and the most worldly among them, the Catholic priest, immediately recognizes that "there's a domesticity about these injuries that shows their origin" (380–81). But with her dying breath, Badalia denies it, "Man from outside. Never seed 'im no more'n Adam," although her bitter knowledge of working-class women's lives leads her to admit "A man come an' 'it me over the 'ead, an' 'e kicked me . . . so it was just the same's if I 'ad 'a' 'ad a 'usband, ain't it?" (382).

According to Badalia's "record," working-class life has ever been thus since the days of Adam, and no amount of legal protection or helpful advice from outside will make a difference. These fictions all underline the connection between working-class life and domestic violence, although each places that violence in a different context. From *Hard Time*'s subtle displacement of violence from the public sphere on to the private to Badalia Herodsfoot's isolated slum world, they demonstrate the powerful social sources of stereotypes about working-class domestic violence. They demonstrate, too, that the narrative of domestic violence can be handled in a variety of ways with regard to the representation of working-class women, producing such contrasts as the monstrous Clementina Peckover, whose violation of gender norms only underscores her diseased nature, and the noble Joan Lowry, where the dirty working girl's heroism can be recognized, although, finally, the novel must wash her clean and reduce her from working-class hero to middle-class heroine. In her analysis of domestic violence, historian Nancy Tomes suggests that in the second half of the nineteenth century, working-class women traded off their political and economic voices in exchange for safety within the home.[33] Thus these fictions also indicate some of the unresolved problems that followed working-class women, even as they obeyed society and retreated into domesticity.

Epilogue

> As it was, I was no more a prostitute than Dickens' Oliver Twist was a thief, if I may draw upon a character of fiction to illustrate what I mean. Yet here I was placed in this category, and indirectly it has affected my whole life.
>
> —Emma Smith, *A Cornish Waif's Story,* 1956

THIS EPILOGUE describes both an ending and a beginning. In examining George Eliot's *Felix Holt, the Radical,* it looks at the last "industrial novel," and it then goes on to discuss some of the autobiographical writings produced by working-class women themselves in the later nineteenth and early twentieth centuries. *Felix Holt* positions itself in relation to the movement toward universal male suffrage, a development that also underlined the reasons that women remained excluded from the vote; and, in a related move, the novel largely erases working-class women and projects many of the traits that had been associated with them on to women as a whole. The contradictory conservative/radical woman who emerges from this mixture, best seen in the character of Mrs. Transome, raises some interesting questions about women and representation in both the literary and political realms. In *The Industrial Reformation of English Fiction,* Catherine Gallagher suggests that English fiction alters dramatically in the 1860s as realists such as Eliot finally reject the connection between literary and political representation that had animated earlier social-problem fiction. Positing a separate realm of "culture," the famous realist texts of the late nineteenth century, she argues, devalue the worlds they describe and transfer that value on to the work of literature itself.[1] Further, I would add, the devaluation of women and their exclusion from the franchise are connected to that particular investment in representations of women found in realist novels in the great tradition. In *Breaking the Chain: Women, Theory, and French Realist Fiction,* Naomi Schor sees the texts of such realists as Balzac and Flaubert as based on the chaining of women.[2] This idea also points to the wider implications of the elimination in *Felix Holt* of disobedient working-class women alongside its creation of the entrapped Mrs. Transome, whose politics are bifurcated between a conservatism that upholds the existing social order and a passionate rebellion against its restrictions on women's lives.

Up until this point in the history I am tracing, while many texts by middle-class authors represent working-class women, working-class women themselves have seemed silent, unable to articulate their own histories. Many of the venues available to them, such as parliamentary reports or union platforms, were heavily male dominated while the structures of their lives—the double shift, their relative lack of education—made writing for publication difficult. Although working-class women did produce some substantial writing in the later part of this time period, it has only recently begun to receive critical attention. My study will conclude by looking at this emerging tradition in the form of working-class women's autobiographical writings, writings which employ some of the images found in Victorian social-problem fiction but appropriate them to different ends.

"A woman ought to be a Tory."—*Felix Holt*

"A woman ought to be a Tory," Harold Transome tells his mother approvingly when she objects to his standing for Parliament as a Radical (194). This comment in George Eliot's *Felix Holt* is just one of the elements that suggests how women's political power had been reconfigured by 1866. In Disraeli's *Sybil,* published twenty-one years earlier, Charles Egremont followed his mother's advice as she arranged his election to Parliament. In *Felix Holt,* Harold Transome summarily dismisses his mother's advice. When he announces his Radicalism, she argues cogently that, having been away for many years, he has lost contact with local conditions, and that, by separating himself from likely allies in the upper class, he is alienating his built-in supporters. But Harold dismisses her viewpoint: "Mother . . . it is natural that you should think this way. Women, very properly, don't change their view, but keep to the notions in which they have been brought up. It doesn't signify what they think—they are not called upon to judge or act. You must really leave me to take my own course in these matters, which properly belong to men" (117). Eventually, events will prove that mother knows best. Harold will lose the election while the candidate who shares the ticket with the Tory Phillip DuBarry wins. Beyond that, Harold brings himself into disrepute because his political agents bribe a group of miners to agitate for him, thus laying the groundwork for the Election Day riot.

Harold's words to his mother, however, represent in miniature a reconfigured relationship among gender, class, and politics in *Felix Holt*. By 1866 political involvement is being redefined as based on gender, more than on class, and Eliot reads that paradigm shift back into the reform movement of 1832. Thus, in *Felix Holt,* men of all classes, whether they have a vote or not, become involved—are expected to be involved—in one way or another with the election. When Rufus Lyon asks Felix Holt, "Then you have a strong interest in the great political movements of these times?" (145–45), Felix responds, "I should think so. I despise every man who has not—or, having it, doesn't try to rouse it in other men" (146). Manhood has become imbricated with the idea of political involvement. Women as a group, however, are excluded.

Although the occasional wife will urge the vote upon her husband as a manly duty, women, by and large, do not even express an interest in the political questions of the day. *Felix Holt* has no argumentative factory girls as in *Sybil* or rebellious servants as in *Shirley.*[3] Harold's response to his mother's questions about his political intentions indicates why. Politics "properly belong to men"; women's "natural" viewpoint is conservative to the point of being unchanging. His words imply that men are inherently politically active and responsible, and women are apolitical and incapable of responsibility. Such a contrast reveals much more than just Harold's healthy sexist egotism. Set back in the days of the First Reform Bill, yet written on the eve of the passage of the Second Reform Bill, *Felix Holt* registers the political moment when the franchise is increasingly being extended to men while the exclusion of women is insisted upon.

In order for gender rather than class to become the dividing line for the franchise, women needed to be constituted as a separate group, divorced from the class distinctions that apply to men. This development can be seen in both the gendered language of the first two reform bills and the representation of women in *Felix Holt.* Before the passage of the 1832 Reform Bill, in principle at least, some women had the right to vote, although that right had fallen into disuse. The old patriarchal rule of aristocracy did allow occasional women to exercise power, however limited in scope, as in the case of Mrs. Transome who runs the Transome estate for years because her husband and eldest son are weak minded and her younger son is abroad. In the 1832 Reform Bill, however, the impact of male Liberalism began to be felt and, while it battled to extend the vote to a new class of men, for the first time in English law the phrase "male person" was used in order to make it clear that the franchise would not extend to women. When the Second Reform Bill was introduced in 1867, John Stuart Mill proposed an amendment to replace the word "man" with "person" and thereby admit women to the vote on the same basis as men. The amendment was defeated, but another amendment which proposed to replace the word "man" with "male" was also defeated. This left open the hope that women would be allowed to vote because Lord Romilly's Act, passed in 1850, mandated that, unless explicitly stated otherwise, the term "man" was generic and included women. But when a Manchester widow voted in a by-election in 1867, the Court of Common Pleas ruled that "every woman is personally incapable" of exercising the vote, arguing that such an application of Lord Romilly's Act was a misinterpretation that might also be used to enfranchise "a dog or a horse."[4] I would argue that this progression from the introduction of "male person" in 1832 to the ruling that women were not to be included in the generic "man" in 1867 is symptomatic of the constitution of women as a separate class in the political realm.

This sequence of events, as well as Eliot's handling of gender and politics in *Felix Holt,* is not an isolated phenomenon but, in fact, grows out of ideas well established in classic political philosophy. In *The Disorder of Women: Democracy, Feminism, and Political Theory,* feminist political philosopher Carol Pateman returns to the seventeenth- and eighteenth-century social contract theorists who laid the philosophical foundations of democracy and dislodges the idea that their use of the word "man" was generic, rather than gendered. She argues that the concept of democracy itself was founded upon a political distinction between the roles of men and women. As she puts it, "In the patriarchal construction of the difference between masculinity and femininity, women lack the capacities necessary for political life. 'The disorder of women' means that they pose a threat to political order and so must be excluded from the public world. Men possess the capacities required for citizenship, in particular they are able to use their reason to sublimate their passions, develop a sense of justice and so uphold the universal, civil law. Women, we learn from the classic texts of contract theory, cannot transcend their bodily natures and sexual passions; women cannot develop such a political morality." To illustrate her point, Pateman analyzes such comments as Rousseau's claim in *Politics and the Arts* that "never has a people perished from an excess of wine; all perish from the disorder of women." Similarly, Hegel states: "Womankind perverts the universal property of the state into a possession and ornament for the family."[5] Such concepts about women's lack of political capacity underlie their exclusion from the franchise in the nineteenth century and, not coincidentally, are central to the questions Eliot raises about women in *Felix Holt* through the characters of Esther Lyon and Mrs. Transome. Finally, too, all these disorderly women who disrupt the civilization established by men have important elements in common with the dangerous working-class women who emerged from parliamentary blue books.

Felix Holt repeats ideas about women's disruption of the political order and also, although to a lesser extent, unsettles them. On the one hand, there is the frequent suggestion that women are disorderly creatures who must be excluded from the political process. On the other hand, as Harold Transome's comment, "A woman ought to be a Tory," suggests, women are also seen as innately conservative, preservers of the traditional social order. The first stereotype is the traditional one that is ingrained in classic political theory. The second stereotype, although it seems to conflict with the first, is, in fact, just the flip side of the coin. It will become even more prevalent as women pursue and then win the vote. Interestingly, in the late nineteenth century, Liberal politicians, in particular, opposed women's suffrage because they assumed that women would vote conservative. For example, in 1874 a Liberal politician gave a speech to the Electoral Reform Conference claiming that

> the tendency of most women is favourable to arbitrary government and clerical supremacy. They seem to be incapable of sympathizing with great causes—they have a strong predilection for personal Institutions. . . . It may take two or three generations to awaken public spirit in the majority of women, and to educate them out of their instinctive submission to whatever is and their dread of ideas,

> which have not the sanction of custom; and in the mean time what is to be our fate? The hands of the clock are to be put back that women may pass through men's accomplished experiences, and we are to be delivered over for a long period of uninterrupted Tory rule![6]

Of course, a claim that all women are Tories excludes the possibility of politically engaged working-class women. Thus in *Felix Holt* one indication of women's transformed relationship to politics is the collapse of class categories where women are concerned. Working-class women almost disappear, having been subsumed under the larger category of disorderly "women"; and all the women in the novel, regardless of circumstance, have much more in common with each other than otherwise. Despite widely disparate temperaments, lower-class Mrs. Holt and upper-class Mrs. Transome lead lives that are strikingly similar. Both women have exercised power, taken on the patriarch's traditional role and run businesses/estates in their sons' absences; and both are summarily removed from power when their sons return home. Finally, both sons view their mothers' work with contempt and dismiss their advice preemptively, confining them to exclusively domestic roles that chafe them. So, if before, working-class women's nondomestic work was considered inappropriate and even dangerous, now this extends to all women.

Along with a general denigration of women working at any task outside of domestic ones, the novel records a shift upwards of other negative traits that had been assigned to lower-class women. That mounting swirl of accusations that had been leveled at the factory girl—vanity, frivolity, misapplied income, inappropriately masculine behavior, sexual license, child neglect, and even murder—now belong to "women" generally and are transferred particularly to the characters of Esther Lyon and Mrs. Transome. Esther has worked as a governess in an upper-class household and now teaches French while living in the frugal household of her adoptive father, the Dissenting minister Mr. Lyon. Esther literally enacts some of the vanities that factory girls were accused of. She spends *all* her income on small luxuries like wax candles (140) and expensive clothing for herself. Her gloves, handkerchiefs, shoes, and hosiery are always of the best kind (158); "her money all went in the gratification of these nice tastes, and she saved nothing from her earnings" (160). She even has a "little gold watch, which had cost her nearly a quarter's earnings" (207–8).

This upward shift of negative traits is especially noteworthy in Mrs.

Transome, whom critics have described as everything from a reactionary feudalist, to a liberated woman, to a saboteur.[7] It is an oddity of *Felix Holt* that its most disruptive, revolutionary character is an aristocratic, Tory woman. Perhaps one reason that she is such a striking and disturbing character is that she represents and combines both traditional and emergent stereotypes about women's political and social effects. Mrs. Transome is the key representative of women's innate conservatism and Toryism. Not only in her political disagreement with her son, but also throughout the novel she is identified with traditional aristocratic rule. She is described as having "that high-born imperious air which would have marked her as an object of hatred and reviling by a revolutionary mob" (104). Yet, contradicting this Toryism, Mrs. Transome also lives a constant, mental rebellion against every fact of her existence as a woman—marriage, the sexual double standard, motherhood, her treatment by men, her aging body. Compared with her rage, the miners who drink at Chubb's are sedate, law-abiding individuals. And Mrs. Transome has not just thought her rebellion; at many points in her life, she has enacted it. She disrupts the social order. She marries a man who is socially, mentally, and physically her inferior, and she runs both him and his estate, thus reversing the "natural hierarchy" where men are superior to and rule women. She carries on an adulterous relationship with a social inferior, Matthew Jermyn, the man who works as her lawyer. Her actions as mother are even more disruptive of the social order. She despises her eldest and legitimate son, the weak-minded, dissolute Durfey, and wishes him dead. Her hatred is so vivid that it almost seems a form of child murder: "Somehow the hated Durfey, the imbecile eldest, who seemed to have become tenacious of a despicable squandering life, would be got rid of" (98). Her disorderly desires and actions as both wife and mother result in the ultimate subversion of the patriarchal order: her illegitimate son, Harold, becomes the owner of the Transome estate, "for she'd got another son, quite of a different cut . . . and she wanted her favourite to be heir" (83). As the past begins to close in on her, she repents her motherhood of him, too. She seems to envy her woman servant, Denner, when she tells her, "You never even had a child" (487), and then she confesses that "if I could choose at this moment, I would choose that Harold should never have been born" (490).

In *Felix Holt* the ghost of the factory girl which had haunted the earlier industrial novels appears to have been laid to rest, replaced by Mrs. Transome's bitter, faded shadow defiantly rebelling against "the nature of woman's lot." Mrs. Transome's rebellion seems to be a merely private one—Esther Lyon sees no future there—and, to traditional thinking, a revolt against nature itself. At fifty-six, with only her past to confront, she is left in the novel with nowhere to go. So *Felix Holt* intertwines the coming enfranchisement of working-class men with the political exclusion of women and the erasure of working-class women with Mrs. Transome's contradictory mixture of Toryism and the seeds of a yet-to-be-named feminist radicalism that would eventually challenge liberal democracies to address the issues of women's work, the sexual double standard, motherhood, and ageism. Demonstrating, again, the uncanny resonance between literature and history, *Felix Holt* also happens to fall at the historical juncture, not just of the Second Reform Bill, but also when the British women's movement is about to begin. Significantly, just as the U.S. women's movement was dynamically interconnected with abolitionism and issues of race, so the British movement was energized by the campaign against the Contagious Diseases Acts, which protested the coercive treatment of disorderly working-class women. With it, new possibilities in the relationship of class and gender begin to emerge.

> A common lot she had, and lived a common life, and remains for me one of the most singular and individual women I have ever known.—Kathleen Woodward, *Jipping Street: Childhood in a London Slum,* 1928

Clearly, a continuing problem in evaluating Victorian social-problem fiction lies in the class position of its writers. They are an exclusively middle-class group, and, although there is a considerable range of opinion and approaches among them, none is identified fully with the working class or with working-class women. It would obviously be useful to examine the words of working-class women themselves in regard to the variety of issues that are raised in relation to them. But the same dynamics that make working-class women hard to represent in these fictions were also at work in the larger culture, silencing them in other venues as well. In parliamentary blue books, working-class women are quoted with some frequency, but the fact that middle-class men asked the questions and interpreted the answers limits the usefulness of that testimony. In the Victorian union movement, too, the leadership was male; the few women who did speak from union platforms frequently followed the party line, calling for women's return to domesticity and supporting the ideal of the male breadwinner. Many historians argue that such positions reflect the actual views of many working-class women, but they also suggest that the women were simply taking the best option open to them, given the available "choices." There were problems with this strategy, however, not the least of which is that it left many women—the unmarried or widowed, for example—entirely out in the cold.

Working-class autobiography is also male dominated. Of the 783 autobiographies listed in *The Autobiography of the Working Class, 1790–1900: An Annotated Critical Bibliography,* only seventy, or less than 10 percent, are by women. Of these, too, most were published in the twentieth century.[8] So, for example, William Dodd's *A Narrative of the Experience and Sufferings of William Dodd, A Factory Cripple Written by Himself,* which describes how he went to work in the mills at age six and details the series of injuries that left him crippled and unemployable, was published in 1841. By contrast, the autobiography, "A Little of My Life," by child worker Lucy Luck did not appear until 1925, three years after her death. The political context of Dodd's narrative indicates both why it was written and how it came to be published in its time period. Placed alongside his letters to Lord Ashley in 1842, Dodd's work was instrumental in the passage of factory legislation limiting the hours of work of children and women.[9] As Regenia Gagnier comments in *Subjectivities: A History of Self-Representation in Britain, 1832–1920,* although physically destroyed by his battle with the machine, Dodd's self-conscious narrative reveals that he does achieve "a political identity."[10]

What political cause of the time, however, could Lucy Luck's autobiography serve? What "political identity" is available to her? Born in 1848, Luck was raised in a workhouse after her alcoholic father deserted her family and was set to work in the silk mills when she was eight years old. Her memories of her early life are primarily of how the workhouse system abused and then abandoned her: the relief officer, Black Garner, would "treat [her] like a dog" if she needed to have her boots mended, and, when the workhouse halted its responsibility for her at age thirteen, she was put to work in a public house. Luck comments that "if they had found me a good place for a start, things might have been better for me." But Luck makes her way by her own determination. Leaving a series of jobs where her employers exploit her, she finally manages to become skilled at straw-plait work. She marries at age nineteen and has seven children, and it is the proud achievement of her life that every one of them turned out well. Although married to a hardworking man, throughout her married life she must continue to work for pay herself, at straw-plaiting when she can get it, and at sewing, cleaning, and laundering when she can't. Luck's life story is one that contradicts the dominant beliefs, exposing the myths of domesticity and the male breadwinner, and underlining the vulnerability of working-class women and the failures of the system to address their needs. It also reveals that Luck's survival and achievements are due, in large measure, to her own hard work, courage, and resourcefulness.[11]

Working-class women autobiographers like Luck have also tended to be overlooked because they are seen as falling between two stools. On the one hand, they are judged as not meeting the aesthetic standards set by the middle class. When Virginia Woolf was asked to provide a preface for *Life as We Have Known It,* an anthology of autobiographical writings by participants in the Women's Cooperative Guild that appeared in 1931, she asserted that the writings failed on aesthetic terms: "It cannot be denied that the chapters here put together do not make a book—that as literature they have many limitations. The writing, a literary critic might say, lacks detachment and imaginative breadth, even as the women themselves lacked variety and play of feature."[12] On the other hand, they are judged as not meeting the political standards set by working-class male writers and as being too interested in private or personal matters. Julia Swindell's *Victorian Writing and Working Women: The Other Side of Silence* struggles with the fact that the writers she examines often define their lives through images out of romance fiction.[13] In *Class Fictions: Shame and Resistance in the British Working-Class Novel, 1890–1945,* Pamela Fox's discussion of twentieth-century fiction by working-class women describes a similar problem and, comparing the women with their male counterparts, she challenges the gendered paradigms that have been applied to the women writers, arguing that "[t]he very act of confrontation involved in being a working-class writer seemingly guarantees its masculinity." Fox also points out that images of working-class life might carry different meanings for men and women; elements that are signs of pride for men are signs of shame for women. For example, for working-class men dirt and stained clothes come to symbolize hard, manly labor, while for working-class women they signify an uncontrolled body, menstruation, and sexual impurity.[14]

Examining the autobiographies of working-class women in the context of nineteenth-century social-problem fiction underlines some different aspects of it, aspects that also undercut the views that working-class women writers are aesthetically naïve or politically uninvolved. Victorian social-problem fiction was rife with certain powerful images of working-class women taken from the larger culture, and, of course, it also helped to form them—the factory girl, the fallen woman, the passive beaten wife, the virago. And autobiographies of working-class women both reveal the impact of such images in numerous, subtle ways and appropriate them for their own purposes. Interestingly, it is not a matter of simply rejecting such images. For one thing, the images themselves do contain truths, however partial, about working-class women's lives; for another, they often become labels that attach themselves to women and take on a life of their own. They shape the lives they touch, sometimes in very powerful ways.

One example of the complex process of struggling with such images is the way working-class women writers deal with the charge that they are fallen women. When such a label is applied to a working-class woman, it can obviously have a major effect on her, and in several autobiographies this emerges as a central theme. The autobiographies of Ellen Johnston, "The Factory Girl" poet, and Emma Smith, the "Cornish waif," reveal the continuing power of the fallen woman stereotype. Published in 1867, Johnston's brief autobiography paints her as a free, Romantic spirit struggling against a repressive society. A large portion of that repression takes the form of attacks on her sexual reputation. After a happy early childhood, Johnston's troubles begin at age eleven when her mother remarries and her stepfather both puts her to work in a factory and begins to abuse her. Johnston never specifies the nature of this abuse, but, since she describes it as "the mystery of my life" and refuses to reveal it to her mother until she is on her deathbed, the implication is that it was sexual in nature. Trying to escape her "tormentor," Johnston runs away from home at regular intervals, spending time wandering the banks of rivers and dreaming of becoming an actress or poet before being dragged back home again. This behavior is judged by her community as sexual misconduct on her part, and this charge shapes much of what happens to her. At first, Johnston is unaware of the "misrepresentations" of her behavior, but, finally, when she becomes aware of it, she pleads her case with the reader and describes the almost impossible position she was placed in: "Dear reader, should your curiosity have been awakened to ask what form fate had then so hardly dealt with the hapless 'Factory Girl,' this is my answer:—I was falsely accused by those who knew me as a fallen woman, while I was as innocent of the charge as the unborn babe. Oh! How hard to be blamed when the heart is spotless and the conscience is clear. For years I submitted to this wrong, resolving to hold my false detractors at defiance."[15]

Johnston quickly summarizes the crucial aftermath of these accusations: the other women in the factory turn against her; her first, "true" love abandons her; and, when she accepts another man as "my friend and protector," he too deserts her, leaving her pregnant. In this frank account of her complicated sexual history, Johnston would seem to have moved from being falsely accused to actually becoming a fallen woman, but she rejects that label, describing her joy at being pregnant—"what the world falsely calls a woman's shame"—and her delight at the birth of her daughter. Johnston goes on from these inauspicious beginnings both to become the "Factory Girl" poet and to support her daughter, as well as her mother and stepfather, with her earnings as a factory worker. Later in her life she once again faces down attacks on her character. In 1863 she sues a supervisor for dismissing her without cause; and, although she wins her case, she finds herself again "persecuted beyond description—lies of the most vile and disgusting character were told upon me, till even my poor ignorant deluded sister sex went so far as to assault me on the streets, spit in my face, and even several times dragged the skirts from my dress."[16] Enthusiastically embracing her title as "the Factory Girl" poet as well as openly countering the charges of sexual misbehavior, Johnston's brief history suggests how the sexual reputation of working-class women was used to control their behavior and police any sort of irregularity. Whether abused at home or suing a supervisor, Johnston stood up for her rights and was punished for it by attacks on her character.

Emma Smith's *A Cornish Waif's Story* (1956) offers a similar but darker history of a childhood shaped and haunted by forces the writer cannot understand. The illegitimate daughter of a former pit-brow lass, Emma Smith (a pseudonym; born 1894) must deal not only with her society's construction of her as a prostitute but also with the personal tragedy of her family's abandonment of her. Smith's mother places her and her younger brother in a workhouse, and, later, when her mother marries, her new husband agrees to take only the boy. So her mother abandons her a second time, giving her to Mr. Pratt, a hurdy-gurdy man who wants a child to perform with him. For the next few years Smith alternates between living in Mr. and Mrs. Pratt's filthy flat and traveling the road with Pratt who sexually abuses her.

Throughout her childhood, Smith's life is shadowed by mysterious words and hints of sexual misbehavior whose threat she perceives but whose actual import her childish mind does not comprehend. As a very small child, she remembers hearing the word "bastard" applied to herself and understanding its negativity but not its real meaning. The first time she is able to leave Pratt, her mother puts her in a Salvation Army home where she lives happily for a few months until she is suddenly ejected for having "done something very naughty." As an adult, she has frequently wondered what "crime" she had committed that led the Salvation Army to reject her too. She claims that only in the process of writing this memoir has a suspicion of the truth occurred to her, that perhaps she had sung an obscene song that Pratt had taught her: "I, as I have said, sang them because everybody else sang them, but did not have the faintest idea of what they meant. Now—I wonder—could I possibly have sung this song to the other children? It is sadly possible. If I *did,* then no wonder I was turned away. And yet—and yet—I was, after all, only nine, and they might have known I didn't understand what I was doing."[17]

Ironically, it is only when she is finally and officially categorized as a prostitute that her society, in an effort to reform her, offers her any protection. Running away from Pratt at the age of twelve, she is handed over to the police, who place her in a convent-penitentiary. Here the nuns express shock that so young a girl has been "on the streets" and also expressly forbid her to discuss her previous life. Smith comes to love the convent with its order, peace, and cleanliness; eventually, the nuns train her to be a laundress. But she is forced to purchase safety at the price of self-knowledge. It takes years before she realizes that she has been classified as a prostitute. As an adult, Smith is very conscious of the fictional nature of the charge—"As it was, I was no more a prostitute than Dickens' Oliver Twist was a thief, if I may draw upon a character of fiction to illustrate what I mean. Yet here I was placed in this category, and indirectly it has affected my whole life." But the silence with which the convent surrounds the issue leaves her no way of coming to terms with it herself, although, when she leaves its walls, she wears the clothing of a girl from the "Home," so that other people continually think that they know her history. Even worse, the rule of silence causes her to fear describing the "sordid memories" of her life with Pratt even in the confessional, so that she "was burdened the whole time now with an awful sense of guilt which made me feel older than my years." Although at age sixteen she finally "confesses" her early life to her priest and eventually leaves the convent and marries, *A Cornish Waif's Story* continues to be haunted by her early abuse and abandonment, revealing the enormous psychological price a working-class woman paid when sexual abuse was defined as sexual corruption and when she herself was forbidden to speak about her own history.[18]

Other working-class women autobiographers have less traumatic histories to share and, in fact, can describe different measures of success and triumph. Three women who began their working lives as girls in factories or workshops—the suffragist Annie Kenney; the "Felt Hat Worker" Mrs. Scott, whose autobiographical sketch appears in *Life as We Have Known It;* and the London dressmaker Kathleen Woodward—reveal some parallel themes. Each, especially in comparison to Johnston and Smith, is blessed with a secure home life. Each spends some time defining herself in relation to the communities of girls and women that she works with. Each describes the importance of books and self-education in her life. And, finally, each discovers a sense of herself and the significance of her voice in relation to the union and suffrage movements.

Annie Kenney is by far the best known of these autobiographers, achieving success during her own lifetime as the best-known working-class suffragist to work in association with Emmeline and Christabel Pankhurst. The greater part of her *Memories of a Militant* (1924) details her association with them, but its first section reveals how much she has in common with other working-class women. Born in 1879 into a large, happy family, Kenney lives by the motto that "[j]oyous laughter is one of the best antidotes against the serious disease of depression." A self-described "happy-go-lucky-devil-may-care-come-and-go person," her buoyant personality is apparent in every line of her autobiography. Going to work at age ten as a half-timer in a mill, full-time at age thirteen, Kenney registers the shock of factory discipline and particularly her hatred of her harsh female supervisor, whom the other girls truthfully warn her is "a tartar." But the vast majority of her memories of factory life focus on the escapades she shares with the other girls—the escapist romances in the weekly girl's paper that they went shares on, the turns they took being "ringleaders" in harmless mischief making, such as skating on a forbidden pond or coaxing the coal carter into letting them ride his horse. Kenney retains her sense of childlike playfulness well into her teenaged years, admitting that she played with her doll even at age fourteen.[19]

As she matures, however, Kenney becomes more "serious," spurred on by her religious upbringing and her family's extensive reading (the latter of which has parallels in many working-class autobiographies) and includes such writers as Herbert Spencer, Charles Darwin, John Ruskin, Walt Whitman, William Morris, and Voltaire. With the dawning of political consciousness, Kenney launches into a career, first as a union organizer, and, then, after meeting Christabel Pankhurst, as a suffragist speaker. Her factory overseer predicts: "You ought to make a fortune with that tongue of yours!" and events soon prove him right as Kenney becomes a trailblazer, elected the first female representative in her trade union, which had 96,000 female members. Kenney leaves factory work behind her when she is taken up by the Pankhursts, but she reports that when she spoke at suffrage rallies she "had to start by telling them I was a factory-girl and a Trade Unionist."[20] Like Johnston, Kenney is able to find a niche for herself where being a factory girl is a boon rather than a liability.

Although she does not achieve Kenney's prominence, Mrs. Scott's brief autobiography sketches a similar trajectory. Much more serious, even as a child, than Kenney, she recalls her reading from an early age, and her father taking her to lectures on William Morris, Charles Bradlaugh, and Annie Besant. Beginning work at age twelve sewing men's hats, Scott describes the long hours—beginning at 6:20 A.M. and lasting sometimes until 8 or 9 P.M., if she had to finish work at home—and the hard labor, including the stress on the wrists of having to push needles through felt or leather and the difficulties of getting a hat brim sewn on just right or having to rip it out if it was a quarter of an inch off. But she also recalls the beauty of some of the workrooms—one, in particular, "six stories up, with big windows and a splendid view of the hills"—and the camaraderie of the workers. In one workshop, she says, many of the girls were prostitutes or "fast," but at age fourteen she did not understand this, and she used to listen to their stories of good times and even write their love letters for them. In later workshops, Scott fondly recalls the "full dress debates" they would hold around the worktables: "[S]omeone would call 'Parliament is now sitting,'" and the women would argue point after point with all political positions well represented—Radicals, Socialists, "good old Tories" who loved Queen Victoria and "thanked God they had all married Conservatives," and Irish Catholic girls who quoted their priests saying that all married women who did not have children would go to hell. Later, when Scott becomes active in the Felt Hatter's Trade Union, her supervisor tries to fire her, and she reports that all the women, even those most against the union, refused to go back to work until she was rehired: "I always feel proud of the way they all stood by me." Scott's firm political commitments—first to labor, then to women's rights—obviously guide her choices. Still later, she recalls the abuse she took when she ran for and was elected the first woman delegate to the Cooperative Wholesale Society. Like Kenney, Scott's political activity takes her out of the workroom, and, like her too, it gives shape to her adult life which she describes as a partnership with her husband pursuing their shared political goals.[21]

The last work I will discuss is Kathleen Woodward's *Jipping Street: Childhood in a London Slum* (1928). *Jipping Street* is a fictionalized autobiography and, perhaps for that reason, seems to combine the darker images found in Ellen Johnston and Emma Smith with the path to self-discovery found in Kenney and Scott. *Jipping Street* also most fully represents a pattern of appropriating cultural images. In fact, Woodward's "autobiography" often seems less her own story than the stories of the women around her. In general outline, the lives of these women would seem to represent a whole range of conventional images of working-class women: the beaten wife; the noble all-sacrificing mother; the romantic escapist; the unchaste factory girl; the uneducated, inarticulate older worker. But in Woodward's hands, each image first appears in outline, only to be later exploded. Woodward's own history, as revealed here, is her quest to understand the lives of working-class women and to understand herself. It is also the story of her ambivalence, for she is at once one of these women—they are a part of her—and yet she longs to separate herself from them.

The first lines of *Jipping Street* encapsulate its narrator's double strategy of appropriation and individuation. She opens by describing, not herself, but her mother, and her mother is one of "the masses": "The circumstances of my mother's life in no manner differed from the circumstances of the lives of those inarticulate people without number who compose the 'lower' classes."[22] Yet the narrator immediately inflects this image of her mother with individuality and complex emotion, giving us a different, personal perspective: "A common lot she had, and lived a common life, and remains for me one of the most singular and individual women I have ever known" (2). She goes on to draw the familiar outlines of her grandmother's and mother's lives—her grandmother married to a man who mistreats her for years before drowning himself in the Thames; her mother married to his gentle, sickly opposite and struggling to support him and their children. The two women who emerge from her portraits are neither pathetic victims nor battling viragoes, but they have a kind of steely self-possession and determination that she both admires and fears. Her mother recalls with satisfaction the time she split her father's back open with an ax during one of his rampages. When he commits suicide, her grandmother refuses to go down to identify his body but does keep one memento, which she passes on to her mother: his framed death certificate is one of the few pictures adorning the walls of Woodward's childhood home (3).

The narrator's mother seems to embody a life of total self-sacrifice for her family. One of the narrator's most enduring childhood memories is helping her do the laundry she took in to support them: her mother's face "pinkish purple" with steam; hands, crinkled and bleached with soda water; and "standing, standing, standing" with her "bad leg" propped up on a box, wishing she had "six pairs of feet" (12). But, although her mother is tender and gentle with her sickly father, that sacrificial love does not extend to her six children. In fact, the narrator says: "She had no love to give us and, thank God, she never pretended what she did not feel" (21). Nonetheless, she is the towering presence in the narrator's life, and she knows she remains inextricably tied to her through a complex mixture of love, pain, fear, and admiration. As she explains the paradox, "I lived close to my mother, held fast by strong ties which existed without love or affection; indissolubly I was bound . . . I humbly acknowledge all my debt to her, although I can never know really its nature or dimension" (20).

The narrator's closest childhood friend, an older woman named Jessica Mourn, is another victim of domestic violence. Again, the outline of Jessica's life story reads like a series of clichés: Jessica's mother, who was never "churched" herself, determines her daughter's life will be different. She raises her on a diet of romances and, before she dies, sees her properly married to Mr. Mourn, a man who, Jessica says, saw her as "only a punchball" (45). Sweet, shy, and loving, Jessica seems one of those working-class women born to be a doormat. Another acquaintance describes Jessica's large brown eyes as reminding her of the eyes of a dog she had once seen run over in Jipping Street (30).

But, again, the narrator finds something else in Jessica, whose sufferings have never embittered her but only made her more sensitive and generous to the sufferings of others. Whenever there is trouble in Jipping Street, Jessica is sent for. She attends many deathbeds, offering simple comfort and saying the Lord's Prayer, the only prayer she knows, because "[a]ll I ses is, it won't do no 'arm and it might do some good" (132–33). The narrator's own love of Jessica is obviously based on that emotional generosity, finding in Jessica some of the tenderness that her mother's strength and toughness cannot supply. Jessica also represents a religious hopefulness that is comforting as well and, when the narrator tries to imagine God, she thinks "he must be like Jessica, who would not hurt the meanest creature and found forgiveness and understanding for everyone" (129–30).

The narrator begins her official working life at age twelve as an errand girl in a sweatshop that manufactures men's collars. This "new slavery" requires her to rise at 6 A.M. and walk into the "city" to begin work by 8. There she uncovers the machinery; serves lunch, dinner, and tea to the women workers; cleans up after closing time at 7:30 P.M.; and walks home dead tired. The only ray that briefly lightens this new work life is a nineteen-year-old named Lil Reeds, who transforms yet another image inherited from the Victorian past, the promiscuous factory girl. For, while, as everyone predicts, she comes to a "bad end" and dies giving birth to an illegitimate child, in the narrator's eyes, Lil, whose dancing feet barely seem to touch the pavement, is the very spirit of life and happiness. Whether walking with her to work or helping her fend off her numerous beaux, the narrator shares Lil's pleasures and basks in her "irresistible sunshine" and her "gift of unending laughter" (75–76). The narrator's mother had given her a cheap pair of ill-fitting hockey boots for her long walk, but Lil buys her a pair of patent leather high-button boots that fill her with "pride and pleasure" (81). While her subterfuges sometimes seem as fragile as soap bubbles even to her younger companion, Lil still takes a shabby world and makes it bright, just as she would, "as if by magic," transform her pale face by licking the red cover of a penny dictionary and rubbing the color on her lips and cheeks (76). Against the dark background of factory and slum life—her father a wizened, evil-faced old printer, her mother a drunk whom the narrator sees only once lying at the foot of some steps with her head cut open—Lil's "preternatural brightness" and "quenchless spirit" stand out all the more poignantly (75), although, perhaps for that very reason, they burn out so quickly.

After Lil's death, the narrator's restlessness and ambition emerge more fully as she struggles to find a life for herself. She lies about her age so that she can get a better-paying, full-time factory job and moves away from home into a room of her own, which she keeps clean and uncluttered. She begins, as she puts it, to take her place, "a woman among women" (101). But these advances only intensify her inner conflict because the lives of working-class women, as she sees them, are grim and oppressive, and, while she is both suffocated by them and enraged at the injustice they reveal, she cannot find a way out, although she searches: she attends suffrage lectures and union meetings, and she reads everything she can find, whenever she can—Edward Gibbon, John Ruskin, Ralph Waldo Emerson, a list familiar from other working-class writers—once even driving a needle through her finger while reading a book that is propped up against her machine (137).

The narrator's appropriation of Victorian images works as a writing strategy, but it is not a living strategy, and this leaves her in a difficult position. As she comes to define her own consciousness, she both identifies with the women she describes and longs to transform their lives; she feels herself bound to them yet comes to fear their lives are untransformable. Her questions and desires lead her to join the union and suffrage movements, but, in contrast to Kenney and Scott, those movements provide no upward trajectory for her either personally or politically. In her mind, both are fatally separated from the very women she hopes most to help. Her union meetings are dominated by a man named Jaspar, who is given to passionate, windy attacks on the rich. But the aspect of his personality that the narrator finds most instructive is his treatment of the woman who accompanies him: with a face deformed by some childhood accident, she sits listening to him with silent adoration while he ignores her. When the narrator brings the most sympathetic of the middle-class suffrage leaders to meet her friend Jessica Mourn, the two women stare at each other with uneasy incomprehension. While she firmly believes in the goals of each movement and continues to work for them, struggling, for example, to unionize her tired, indifferent coworkers, her confidence in their success is undercut. Thus, class and gender conflicts seem still prevalent in the union and suffrage movements, leading the narrator to conclude that both may ultimately fail to help her reach her goals.

Woodward's fictional autobiography ends without ending. She concludes,

> Within me, ever more clear and insistent, is the urge that knows no rest; but whither, to what end?
>
> I must talk with some one. Mother would only laugh: "Life kicks you downstairs and then it kicks you upstairs." But I know that there is more. I cannot shape this knowledge even to myself; but in my books, in beautiful words, there is something strangely like my dreams; they smile on me, beckon to me.
>
> I must go on, following without seeing where they lead. (149–50)

These words suggest that she will leave Jipping Street and childhood behind but do not describe where she will go or what her adulthood will be like. She states that she is now separate from the women she has written about—Lil and Jessica are dead, she must leave her mother behind—but does not say who she will be connected with in the future. In fact, the very process of writing itself separates Woodward from these women. A part of the "inarticulate" masses, her mother is illiterate and can only write her name, just as the woman with the deformed face listens adoringly to Jaspar but never speaks herself. According to *Jipping Street,* these "inarticulate" women would be able to reveal the truth, if they could speak; but the very process of "articulating" that Woodward is engaged in seems, on some level, to corrupt and discredit the result. Her mother, Jessica, Lil, the woman with the deformed face, cannot follow where she wants to go. But, if Woodward's autobiography does not point forward to what she will become, it does point forward to later working-class writings, to other books and dreams. Her descriptions of the lives of working-class women with their strategies of appropriation and deconstruction resonate with works such as Pat Barker's *Union Street* and *Blow Your House Down,* while her personal struggle over identification with, and separation from, her class also troubles writers such as Alan Sillitoe. Thus, in the working-class writings of Woodward, Johnston,

Kenney, Scott, and Smith, the lives that had been "hidden" begin to be revealed in different ways, beginning a new series of developments.

> [I]n my books, in beautiful words, there is something strangely like my dreams.—Kathleen Woodward, *Jipping Street: Childhood in a London Slum*

The history of representations that I have traced here is a long and complicated one, starting with the uproar over working-class women provoked by the 1842 Mining and Collieries Report and ending with the emergence of working-class women as writers themselves. Throughout this period of intense historical change, there are continual fluctuations and developments in the relationships of class and gender that particularly affect the ways in which working-class women are represented and the means by which they can represent themselves. On an important level, representations of working-class women reveal both the power and the instability of class and gender ideologies. For middle-class men—and to a significant, although lesser, degree, working-class men and middle-class women—class and gender ideologies can seem to fuse and to buttress one another and can thus appear quite stable; however, representations of working-class women are almost always contradictory, their very incoherence a sign of the cultural conflicts they at once hide and reveal. So, no matter how marginalized, the women at the bottom—the hidden hands who perform both the housework that domestic ideology requires and the factory work that industrial capitalism employs—appear, and they become, not victims, but revelations of what cannot be said, of what, perhaps, cannot even be imagined, offering glimpses of the labor and the lives upon which both systems depend.

One of Victorian social-problem fiction's fascinations is its drive to be all-inclusive, to describe its world in its entirety. While it protects this world from revolutionary violence and often supports its class and domestic ideologies, it also reveals the operations of these ideologies and pushes them to, and sometimes beyond, their limits, with its broad vision. Although working-class women are on the margins of this world in terms of power, they are a necessary, even central, part of its ideological and material functioning. From this complex of forces, individual Victorian writers uncover and draw out what I think are a remarkable group of images.

From Elizabeth Gaskell's Bessie Higgins in *North and South,* whose lived conflict with domestic ideology is matched only by the anger and desperation of her apocalyptic religious visions, to Charlotte Elizabeth Tonna's Helen Fleetwood, whose uncanny descriptions of workplace harassment still resonate 160 years later, even from the margins, factory girls can articulate conflicts and offer challenges that undercut their culture's certainties. Disraeli's *Sybil,* with its saintly heroine and politically committed factory girls, and Brontë's *Shirley*, with its Luddite and feminist visionaries and hot-tempered servants, demonstrate in different ways how crucially class and gender are related in political struggles and political movements and how necessary it is that such traditionally silenced groups as working-class women be heard. These earlier Victorian works contain a breadth and a fluidity that retain the power to surprise with their imagined meetings and conjunctions, where middle-class women befriend factory girls, aristocrats fall in love with overseers' daughters, and mill owners and clergymen debate with Luddite weavers. In *Hard Times* and *Felix Holt,* one finds a hardening of the boundaries of class and gender, as domestic ideology takes its toll on women as a whole, but especially on working-class women. In fact, the connections that the earlier works had drawn upon between representations of working-class women and the broad political and economic issues of the Victorian period begin to be severed here, although Dickens and Eliot subtly gesture to such issues through their critiques of unionism and the reform movement. Yet here, too, these fictions' indirect recognition of the violence and entrapment inherent in domestic ideology—the beating of Merrylegs, Mrs. Holt's powerful image of amputated hands—exposes both its political and social purposes and their costs and limitations, while the ultimate price of working-class women's increasing symbolic isolation is found in the violent slums of Gissing and Kipling.

My concluding discussion of working-class women autobiographers is tentative: much more needs to be investigated here that lies beyond the scope of my study. But, certainly, the autobiographies of such writers as Johnston, Smith, and Woodward reveal the ongoing social and psychological power of some of the representations of working-class women—fallen factory girls, beaten wives—that took root in the Victorian period. At the same time, they comment, sometimes tragically, on the sheer inadequacy of those images to represent the complex lives of these women. New ideas also begin to emerge—factory girls like Johnston and Scott who find different degrees of pleasure and reward in their work, the importance of labor and feminist politics and self-education, the exploding of female domesticity as either an attainable or attractive goal. But it is not quite so simple as finding a "truth" here that was missing in Victorian social-problem fictions. Twentieth-century working-class writings will go on to transform and expand the possibilities of representation for working-class women, but, as Kathleen Woodward's *Jipping Street* makes clear, books and dreams exist as well as mothers and factories, and the changing dynamics between them continue to give shape to human lives and the ways in which we can imagine them.

Notes

Introduction

1. Raymond Williams introduced the term "industrial novel" to define a special category of Victorian social-problem fiction in *Culture and Society, 1780–1950* (New York: Harper & Row, 1958). Catherine Gallagher's *The Industrial Reformation of English Fiction: Social Discourse and Narrative Form, 1832–1867* (University of Chicago Press, 1985) underlines the importance of the industrial novel for an understanding of Victorian fiction at large. Also see Louis Cazamian's *The Social Novel in England, 1830–1850*, trans. Martin Fido (Boston: Routledge & Kegan Paul, 1973); Arnold Kettle's "The Early Victorian Social-Problem Novel," in vol. 6 of *The Pelican Guide to English Literature*, ed. Boris Ford (Baltimore: Penguin, 1958), 169–87; Kathleen Tillotson's *Novels of the Eighteen-Forties* (New York: Oxford University Press, 1961); Ivan Melada's *The Captain of Industry in English Fiction, 1821–1871* (Albuquerque: University of New Mexico Press, 1970); Ruth Bernard Yeazell's "Why Political Novels Have Heroines: *Sybil, Mary Barton,* and *Felix Holt,*" *Novel* 18 (winter 1985): 126–44; and Sheila M. Smith's *The Other Nation: The Poor in English Novels of the 1840s and 1850s* (Oxford: Clarendon Press, 1980).

A number of critics have approached the social-problem novel from a feminist perspective. Joseph Kestner's *Protest and Reform: The British Social Narrative by Women, 1827–1867* (Madison: University of Wisconsin Press, 1985) provides an excellent survey of major and minor works. Rosemarie Bodenheimer's *The Politics of Story in Victorian Social Fiction* (Ithaca, N.Y.: Cornell University Press, 1988) contains persuasive interpretations of the roles of middle-class heroines such as Shirley Keeldar in *Shirley,* Louisa Gradgrind in *Hard Times,* Margaret Hale in Elizabeth Gaskell's *North and South,* and Esther Lyon in *Felix Holt.* Constance D. Harsh's *Subversive Heroines: Feminist Resolutions of Social Crisis in the Condition-of-England Novel* (Ann Arbor: University of Michigan Press, 1994) tries to argue that such heroines as Disraeli's Sybil and Sissy Jupe in *Hard Times* exert significant influence, interpretations that I will argue against. Harsh points to certain empowering aspects in domestic ideology, but she overlooks its limitations, especially with regard to working-class women.

Critics tend to ignore the specifics of working-class women's experiences when examining social-problem literature. For example, Patricia Ingham's *The Language of Gender and Class: Transformation in the Victorian Novel* (London: Routledge, 1996) claims several times that working-class women are rendered entirely invisible or silent (23, 54, 90, 136). See, however, Susan Zlotnick's *Women, Writing, and the Industrial*

Revolution (Baltimore: Johns Hopkins University Press, 1998) for discussions of the representation of the factory girl (15–17, 40–42, 124–25). Wanda Fraiken Neff's *Victorian Working Women: An Historical and Literary Study of Women in British Industries and Professions, 1832–1850* (New York: Columbia University Press, 1929) is the only other book-length study to address the representation of the factory girl as well as other working women in a variety of fields. She points out that it was the Victorians who discovered that the working woman was both "an object of pity" and "a problem" (11). She also notes the discrepancy between the prominence of the female factory worker in parliamentary blue books and her relative absence in novels and speculates that the reasons for this contrast are that "Parliament attended so steadily to the factory question between 1832 and 1850 that novelists burning with a zeal for reform left her to powers stronger than theirs" and that the factory girl—being unattractive, dirty, and hard-laboring—"lacked all the qualifications for the ideal Victorian heroine" (85–86).

2. Kestner, in *Protest and Reform* (175–77), describes several minor works that deal with women factory workers, such as Paul Pimlico's *The Factory Girl,* published in 1849.

3. See Gallagher, *Industrial Reformation of English Fiction,* 128–30; and Harsh, *Subversive Heroines,* chap. 2.

4. See Cora Kaplan's "Pandora's Box: Subjectivity, Class, and Sexuality in Socialist Feminist Criticism," in *Sea Changes: Essays on Culture and Feminism* (London: Verso Press, 1986), 147–76, and "'Like a Housemaid's Fancies': The Representation of Working-Class Women in Nineteenth-Century Writing," in *Grafts: Feminist Cultural Criticism,* ed. Susan Sheridan (London: Verso Press, 1988), 55–75, for discussions of monstrous presentations of working-class women in the works of women writers.

5. Kaplan, "'Like a Housemaid's Fancies,'" 61.

6. Sonya O. Rose, *Limited Livelihoods: Gender and Class in Nineteenth-Century England* (Berkeley: University of California Press, 1992), 184. Feminist historians emphasize the central role that women played as factory workers during the eighteenth and nineteenth centuries. Ivy Pinchbeck's *Women Workers and the Industrial Revolution, 1750–1850* (London: Virago, 1981) documents women's work in the textile industries, coalmining, the metal trades, and millinery. As Deborah Valenze argues in *The First Industrial Woman* (New York: Oxford University Press, 1995), women as a source of cheap labor were crucial to industrialization: "The rise of the merchant capitalist was inevitably gained at the expense of the woman at the bottom. She was not destined to be the hero of the classic story of the industrial revolution, but she clearly made it possible" (75). Also see Anna Clark's *The Struggle for the Breeches: Gender and The Making of the British Working Class* (Berkeley: University of California Press, 1995); Marianna Valverde's "'Giving the Female a Domestic Turn': The Social, Legal, and Moral Regulation of Women's Work in British Cotton Mills, 1820–1850," *Journal of Social History* 21, no. 4 (1988): 619–34; and Wally Seccombe's "Patriarchy Stabilized: The Construction of the Male Breadwinner Wage Norm in Nineteenth-Century Britain," *Social History* 11 (January 1986): 53–76.

7. H. I. Dutton, and J. E. King, *"Ten Per Cent and No Surrender": The Preston Strike, 1853–1854* (New York: Cambridge University Press, 1981), 94.

8. See Anita Levy, *Other Women: The Writing of Class, Race, and Gender, 1832–1898* (Princeton: Princeton University Press, 1991), 32–43.

9. See Lynda Nead, *Myths of Sexuality: Representations of Women in Victorian Britain* (Oxford: Basil Blackwell, 1988); and Elsie B. Michie, *Outside the Pale: Cultural Exclusion, Gender Difference, and the Victorian Woman Writer* (Ithaca, N.Y.: Cornell University Press, 1993), 113–41, for discussions of the disruptive yet controlled effects of representations of prostitution.

10. See, for example, Williams, *Culture and Society,* 104–5.

11. Benjamin Disraeli, *Sybil, or The Two Nations* (Harmondsworth: Penguin, 1980), 213–14; further citations will appear in the text.

12. Elizabeth Langland, *Nobody's Angels: Middle-Class Women and Domestic Ideology in Victorian Culture* (Ithaca, N.Y.: Cornell University Press, 1995), 4.

13. Pierre Macherey, *A Theory of Literary Production,* trans. Geoffrey Wall (London: Routledge, 1978), 79, 94. Catherine Barnes Stevenson's "'What Must Not Be Said': *North and South* and the Problem of Women's Work," *Victorian Literature and Culture* 19 (1991): 67–84, also draws on Macherey in order to critique Gaskell's erasure of women's work in factories. Stevenson emphasizes the contradictions that this involves Gaskell in since she herself is writing for money. She comments, "*North and South* seems to have appeared at the historical moment of the triumph of domestic ideology. Its author's struggle with that ideology determines the text's silence about women's non-domestic labor, whether as mill workers or as writers" (69).

14. A. J. Greimas and François Rastier, "The Interaction of Semiotic Constraints," *Yale French Studies* 41 (1968): 86–105.

15. Fredric Jameson, *The Political Unconscious: Narrative as a Socially Symbolic Act* (Ithaca, N.Y.: Cornell University Press, 1981), 48.

16. Joan Wallach Scott, *Gender and the Politics of History* (New York: Columbia University Press, 1988), 27.

17. Rose, *Limited Livelihoods,* 127.

18. Scott, *Gender and the Politics of History,* 65.

19. Quoted in Angela V. John, "Colliery Legislation and Its Consequences: 1842 and the Women Miners of Lancashire," *Bulletin of the John Rylands University Library of Manchester* 61 (autumn 1978): 78.

20. Valenze characterizes the factory reform movement as bringing "many different interests, including working men, into dialogue over the proper extent of the factory's power over working-class life. Through public discussions about female and child labor in the factories, philanthropists, parliamentary commissioners, and factory operatives thus applied a standard of domesticity to working-class women. In effect, working-class women were harried home by a multitude of voices" (*First Industrial Woman,* 100).

21. In "Women, Class, and Sexual Difference," *History Workshop Journal* 17 (spring 1984), Sally Alexander argues that "the 1830s and 1840s saw the confirmation of men as responsible political subjects while women were largely condemned to public silence" (145). Similarly, in "'A Thousand Times I'd Be a Factory Girl': Dialect, Domesticity, and Working-Class Women's Poetry in Victorian Britain," *Victorian Studies*

35 (autumn 1991), Susan Zlotnick describes the dialect tradition as "consistently den[ying] working women their class identity by refusing to recognize them as laborers" and comments that the "working-class voice" was "a distinctly male one" (8). Scott notes: "Class, after all, was offered as a universal category even though it depended on a masculine construction. As a result, it was almost inevitable that men represented the working class. Women then had two possible representations. They were either a specific example of the general experience of class and then it was unnecessary to single them out for separate treatment; for they were assumed to be included in any discussion of the working class as a whole. Or, women were a troubling exception, asserting particular needs and interests detrimental to class politics" (*Gender and the Politics of History,* 64). P. J. Keating's *The Working Classes in Victorian Fiction* (New York: Barnes & Noble, 1971) reflects the habit of casting men as the sole representatives of the working class. For example, he outlines six types of working-class characters, all implicitly or explicitly males, such as the respectable skilled artisan, the intellectual working man, and the criminal who mistreats or murders his wife or child (26–28).

22. Dorothy Thompson, "Women and Nineteenth-Century Radical Politics: A Lost Dimension," in *The Rights and Wrongs of Women,* ed. Juliet Mitchell and Ann Oakley (Harmondsworth: Penguin, 1976), 115.

23. For example, in Stockport in 1841, 55 percent of factory weavers were women, in 1851 women made up 60 percent, and in 1861 women made up 65 percent (Dutton and King, "*Ten Percent and No Surrender,*" 14).

24. Barbara Taylor, *Eve and the New Jerusalem: Socialism and Feminism in the Nineteenth Century* (London: Virago Press, 1983), xvi.

25. Mary Poovey, *Uneven Developments: The Ideological Work of Gender in Mid-Victorian England* (Chicago: University of Chicago Press, 1988), 200.

Chapter 1

1. See Angela V. John, *By the Sweat of Their Brow: Women Workers at Victorian Coal Mines* (London: Croom Helm, 1980).

2. Celina Fox, "The Development of Social Reportage in English Periodical Illustration during the 1840s and Early 1850s," *Past and Present* 74, no. 74 (1977): 97.

3. *Hansard,* Series 3, House of Commons, "First Report of the Commissioners on the Mines," *Sessions: 3 February–12 August 1842,* 15 May 1842, vol. 16 [381]: 181.

4. *Hansard,* Series 3, House of Commons, "First Report of the Commissioners on the Mines," *Session: 3 February–12 August 1842,* 15 May 1842, vol. 17 [382]: 75.

5. "Murder of the Working Classes," *Bell's Penny Sunday Chronicle,* 15 May 1842.

6. *Illustrated London News,* 20 May 1842.

7. *Northern Star,* 23 Oct. 1842.

8. *Edinburgh Review,* 25 June 1842, 154.

9. Ashley, quoted in John, *By the Sweat of Their Brow,* 49.

10. "Lines on the Lord Ashley's Motion," *Bentley's Miscellany* 12 (1842): 31–32.

11. John, *By the Sweat of Their Brow,* 52–57; John, "Colliery Legislation," 79–80, 113.

12. Peter Gaskell, *The Manufacturing Population of England: Its Moral, Social, and Physical Conditions, and the Changes Which Have Arisen from the Use of Steam Machinery* (London: Baldwin & Cradock, 1833), 68–69.

13. Cited in Margaret Hewitt, *Wives and Mothers in Victorian Industry* (London: Rockliff, 1958), 49, 50.

14. *Hansard,* Series 3, House of Commons, *Session: 5 February–14 August 1844,* 15 March 1844, vol. 10, cols. 1088, 1099, 1100.

15. Anna Jameson. "Condition of the Women and the Female Children," *Athenaeum,* 18 Mar. 1843, 257–58.

16. Fox, "Development of Social Reportage," 99, 96.

17. Charlotte Elizabeth Tonna, *Helen Fleetwood,* in *The Works of Charlotte Elizabeth,* vol. 2 (New York: M. W. Dodd, 1844), 538, 537; further citations will appear in the text.

18. Elizabeth Gaskell, *Mary Barton* (Harmondsworth: Penguin, 1970), 40; further citations will appear in the text.

19. Amanda Anderson, *Tainted Souls and Painted Faces: The Rhetoric of Fallenness in Victorian Culture* (Ithaca, N.Y.: Cornell University Press, 1993), 116; also see Marianna Valverde, "The Love of Finery: Fashion and the Fallen Woman in Nineteenth-Century Social Discourse," *Victorian Studies* 32 (winter 1989): 169–88.

20. Clark, *Struggle for the Breeches,* 198, 119, 121–23.

21. David Vincent, *Bread, Knowledge, and Freedom: A Study of Nineteenth-Century Working-Class Autobiography* (London: Europa Publications, 1981), 40–44.

22. Charles Kingsley, *Alton Locke, Tailor and Poet: An Autobiography* (reprint, New York: Oxford University Press, 1983), 53; further citations will appear in the text.

23. See, for example, Deirdre David, *Fictions of Resolution in Three Victorian Novels* (New York: Columbia University Press, 1981), 38–39; and Ingham, *Language of Gender and Class,* 60; however, see Stevenson, "'What Must Not Be Said,'" 70–71; Harsh, *Subversive Heroines,* 69–71; and Zlotnick, *Women, Writing, and the Industrial Revolution,* 115–18, for revealing commentaries on Bessy's role.

24. E. P. Thompson, *The Making of the English Working Class* (New York: Vintage Books, 1966), 391.

25. See Taylor's discussion of feminism and millenarianism in *Eve and the New Jerusalem,* 118–82.

26. Elizabeth Gaskell, *North and South* (Harmondsworth: Penguin, 1970), 131; further citations will appear in the text.

27. Based on the words of a male factory worker in the 1833 Factory Report; cited in Valverde, "'Giving the Female a Domestic Turn,'" 626.

28. See Joseph Butwin, "*Hard Times:* The News and the Novel," *Nineteenth-Century Fiction* 32 (September 1977): 166–87.

29. Charles Dickens, *Hard Times* (Harmondsworth: Penguin, 1969), 125; further citations will appear in the text.

30. George Eliot, *Felix Holt, the Radical* (New York: Penguin, 1972), 624; further citations appear in the text.

Chapter 2

1. Deborah Epstein Nord, *Walking the Victorian Streets: Women, Representation, and the City* (Ithaca, N.Y.: Cornell University Press, 1995), 117.

2. In *City of Dreadful Delight: Narratives of Sexual Danger in Late-Victorian London* (Chicago: University of Chicago Press, 1992), Judith R. Walkowitz describes the "new social actors" who began to share space with the male flaneur in late-nineteenth-century London: "protesting workers and 'gents' of marginal class position, female philanthropists and 'platform women,' Salvation Army lasses and match girls, as well as glamourized 'girls in business'" (18). The new social mix brought tensions to the surface. For example, Walkowitz writes, "In the West End, the presence of perambulating prostitutes, window-shopping ladies, 'girls in business,' and idle male civil servants in one public area provoked territorial tensions and hostile social acts on the part of men toward women. As a consequence, the West End and the City were notorious areas for street harassment of women" (50). Some women, she reports, "devised personal maps and proscribed zones to organize their walks around the West End," very like Sybil Gerard does in Disraeli's *Sybil.* Discussions of how middle-class women should deal with "male pests" included this advice from *The Girl's Own Paper:* "[A]void strolls where you are annoyed, and always look straight before you, or on the opposite side when passing any man. Never look at them when near enough to be stared at in any impertinent and abrasive way" (51).

3. Nord, *Walking the Victorian Streets,* 3, n.8.

4. Catharine A. MacKinnon, *Sexual Harassment of Working Women: A Case of Sex Discrimination* (New Haven: Yale University Press, 1979), 27, xi, 10–12.

5. Clara Collett, "Women's Work," in *Life and Labour of the People of London,* ed. Charles Booth (New York: AMS Press, 1970), 315–16.

6. Charlotte Elizabeth Tonna, *The Wrongs of Women* (New York: J. S. Taylor & Co., 1843), 79, 83.

7. Cited in Frank Mort, *Dangerous Sexualities: Medico-Moral Politics in England Since 1830,* 2d ed. (London: Routledge & Kegan Paul, 1987), 38.

8. Anna Clark, *Women's Silence, Men's Violence: Sexual Assault in England, 1770–1845* (London: Pandora, 1987), 93–94.

9. Jan Lambertz, "Sexual Harassment in the Nineteenth-Century Cotton Industry," *History Workshop* 19 (1985): 33, 33–34.

10. See Hewitt, *Wives and Mothers in Victorian Industry,* on "Cotton-Mill Morality." She describes the slim evidence on which claims of immorality were based and demonstrates that national statistics about illegitimate births do not bear out the claim that factory women were more sexually active outside marriage than other working-class women (51–53).

11. For example, *The Spectator* refers to "the wholesale prostitution in the mines alleged in the Report of the Children's Employment Commission" and focuses its own report on "gross immorality and indecency," not on wages or working conditions (14 May 1842, vol. 15, 462).

12. Anderson, *Tainted Souls and Painted Faces,* 1–12.

13. In another example from the 1833 Factory Report, James McNish, a leader of the Scottish spinners' union, testified that "it consists with his knowledge that there are at present several girls, who were formerly piecers in his apartment [i.e., department], who are now prostitutes in Glasgow." He also refers to an attempted rape of a ten-year-old mill girl in this context. His considered opinion was "it is the tendency of bringing so many young women together in such an establishment as this [a spinning mill] to render them vicious and dissolute" (Cited in Valverde, "'Giving the Female a Domestic Turn,'" 629).

14. See Anna Clark's analysis in "The Politics of Seduction in English Popular Culture, 1748–1848," in *The Progress of Romance: The Politics of Popular Fiction*, ed. Jean Radford (London: Routledge & Kegan Paul, 1986), 47, 48–70.

15. Mort sketches the biographies of such parliamentary commissioners as Jelinger Symons, James Kay, and Edwin Chadwick, arguing that their professional lives were rigidly divided from the feminized private sphere and that their misogynistic attitudes inevitably found their way into their reports. If they found little common ground with their middle-class wives, they had even less in common with working-class women, who became exotic "others." Mort comments, "In the male-defined culture of these blue-book reports there was space for officials to indulge, sotte voce, their own sexual fantasies" (*Dangerous Sexualities*, 40–41, 38).

16. Deborah Kaplan argues that Tonna's "frank depictions" of working-class women in the workplace "are virtually unique in British industrial novels." In addition to her concrete concerns there, Tonna is alive to the contradictions of domestic ideology. Kaplan comments that her novels expose the "myth of the fall of working women out of the supposedly natural state of female domesticity and into industrial capitalism." See her article, "The Woman Worker in Charlotte Elizabeth Tonna's Fiction," *Mosaic* (spring 1985): 60, 52.

17. MacKinnon argues: "Woman's consciousness erupts through fissures in the socially knowable" (*Sexual Harassment of Working Women*, xii). Perhaps it is for that reason that Tonna is able to describe workplace harassment with the degree of specificity she does. For there are few writers on industrial issues more fissured than Tonna is: as Gallagher has demonstrated, Tonna's novel is split between an intense Evangelicalism that insists on individual free will and an equally intense hatred of an all-powerful factory system (*Industrial Reformation of English Fiction*, 41–44). In *The Reader's Repentance: Women Preachers, Women Writers, and Nineteenth-Century Social Discourse* (Chicago: University of Chicago Press, 1992), Christine L. Krueger argues that Tonna constructs herself as a female prophetic writer in the midst of a heavily patriarchal Evangelical tradition (125–56). In a culminating paradox, while Tonna can be read as conservative, even reactionary, in *The Spirit of Reform: British Literature and Politics, 1832–1867* (Cambridge: Harvard University Press, 1977), Patrick Brantlinger points out that her criticism of the factory system has a great deal in common with that of the most revolutionary factory critics (57).

18. Gallagher, *Industrial Reformation of English Fiction*, 46; Zlotnick, *Women, Writing, and the Industrial Revolution*, 151.

In her discussion, Gallagher praises *Helen Fleetwood* as "the most important work of industrial fiction to emerge from . . . reforming Evangelicalism" (41), but she focuses on Richard Green, who, she argues, "represents the free will actively combating evil in the world." She claims that "he is the character who makes *Helen Fleetwood* a novel" (47). By contrast, I argue that Helen's experience is, indeed, central, while Richard is a bystander, who represents the remnant of an honest but ineffectual paternalism. Richard hopes to marry Helen, but, kept on by his local squire, makes enough money only to support himself. It is Helen's factory wages that help to support, not only herself, but also the Widow Green and her three other grandchildren. Even when Richard visits the factory town M. and discovers that Helen is dying of the work, he cannot rescue her. The best solution he can offer is to help to get her a job in another factory. See, however, Harsh's *Subversive Heroines* for an interpretation of Helen as a powerful Christian martyr (88–91).

19. See Barbara Leah Harman, *The Feminine Political Novel in Victorian England* (Charlottesville: University Press of Virginia, 1998), for a discussion of female publicity and sexual taint in *North and South.* She concludes that the novel "confirms what critics of female emancipation tended to fear—that access to public life means access to potentially dangerous kinds of sexual intimacy for women—and it does so while affirming, and hence finally legitimizing, both female public action and female sexuality" (75). Harman places her interpretation of *North and South* within the context of William Blackstone's definition of married women as existing under the law of coverture and its implications for women in general. She argues, for example, that parliamentary debate over the Married Women's Property Bill in 1868 implied that granting women property rights would enable them to be sexually immoral. Another example Harman offers is the argument that women should not be trained to enter the professions because they would be working in close quarters with men (2–8). The examples Harman chooses of property and careers emphasize a middle-class framework, but there are obviously parallel issues for working-class women.

20. Gallagher categorizes the dog Harold as "both a fellow aristocrat and a kind of portable cloister" (*Industrial Reformation of English Fiction,* 214).

21. See Taylor's *Eve and the New Jerusalem* for a discussion of the property and sexual relations hoped for in the *New Moral World* (19–56), as well as her analysis of why working-class women often distrusted radical attempts to replace marriage with communal relations and ideals of free love, 205–16.

22. Walkowitz, *City of Dreadful Delight,* 81.

23. Yeazell, "Why Political Novels Have Heroines," 127. For Gaskell's treatment of a similar problem in *North and South,* see Harman's argument that women must brave sexual taint in order to act in the public sphere, as well as Bodenheimer's commentary: "Margaret's most significant experience is to become a human agent in her own right—a process that means living with the doubleness of her actions, like the men who act and decide in the public sphere. Gaskell's revision of the myth of the rescuing heroine lies precisely in that refusal to keep her 'pure' and separate from the activities generally associated with the male, the public, and the system" (*Politics of Story in Victorian Social Fiction,* 67).

24. Gaskell again addresses this problem for working-class women in *Ruth,* where, as Michie comments, she "refuses the split between purity and impurity" (*Outside the Pale,* 106).

25. Gallagher, *Industrial Reformation of English Fiction,* 67–87. See also Michael Wheeler, "Two Tales of Manchester Life," *Gaskell Society Journal* 3 (1989): 6–28, which compares *Mary Barton*'s use of the factory girl plot with Elizabeth Stone's *William Langshawe, the Cotton Lord.*

26. In "Private Grief and Public Acts in *Mary Barton,*" *Dickens Studies Annual* 9 (1981), Rosemarie Bodenheimer suggests that *Mary Barton*'s plot is a "muffling of the connection between industrial and sexual exploitation. Harry Carson is a seducer but Mary is not his employee, and he has no direct economic hold over her. He remains a threat only so long as Mary is willing to entertain the idea of a class romance. . . . And, because the stories of sexual harassment and economic exploitation are split between Harry Carson and his father, on the one hand, John and Jem on the other, we are not required by the novel's structure to put them back together into a systematic analysis of industrial oppression" (207–08).

Nord agrees that Mary's experience has "little or nothing to do with [her] work" (*Walking the Victorian Streets,* 151).

27. In fact, Elsie Michie comments that Gaskell's novels "strongly influenced Josephine Butler" and suggests that their influence contributed to her leadership of the campaign against the Contagious Diseases Acts (*Outside the Pale,* 134).

28. Josephine Butler, *An Autobiographical Memoir* (London: J. W. Arrowsmith, 1909), 107–8.

Chapter 3

1. My interpretation underlines aspects of the novel that suggest that it could, in a number of respects, be classified as one of Harman's *Feminine Political Novels.*

Biographers have long been fascinated by Disraeli's relationships with women—from his sister, Sarah, to his many aristocratic confidantes, and from the "perfect wife" to whom *Sybil* is dedicated to Queen Victoria. As early as the passage of the Second Reform Bill, Disraeli was in favor of women's suffrage—in theory, at least. In *Disraeli* (New York: St. Martin's Press, 1967), Robert Blake comments, with a touch of irony directed at the political acumen of both Disraeli and women: "Indeed, few people would have gained more than he by votes for women. But he did not regard the proposal as practical politics" (473). Critics of *Sybil,* however, have tended to downplay the role of women, focusing, instead, on the Two Nations controversy and the novel's depiction of aristocratic and working-class life. Yeazell and Harsh focus on the character of Sybil herself, although interpreting her in contrasting ways. My approach is closest to Yeazell's, who argues that the character of Sybil "has a central place in the novel's design" ("Why Political Novels Have Heroines," 128). She sees Sybil's function as an escape from politics, however, rather than an inextricable part of it. Harsh interprets Sybil as a strictly positive example of womanly influence who is effective both as a guide for Egremont and, within the confines of fiction, as a reformer of society. In "*Sybil,* or the Two Monarchs," *Studies in Philology* 95 (winter 1998): 97–119, Jennifer Sampson discusses the parallels between Sybil and Queen Victoria. See Zlotnick for a brief, negative assessment of all women's political roles in *Sybil* (*Women, Writing, and the Industrial Revolution,* 20–22).

2. Blake, *Disraeli,* 217.

3. Nina Auerbach comments that the concept of the Two Nations might be applied to men and women as well as to rich and poor. See her "Dickens and Dombey: A Daughter After All," *Dickens Studies Annual* 5 (1976): 95

4. Gallagher sees politics as ultimately "unrepresentable" in *Sybil.* She argues that Disraeli's pervasive irony toward politicians, the aristocracy, and the working class finally undermines his own fiction, leaving him no ground from which to create true politics (*Industrial Reformation of English Fiction,* 211).

5. Benjamin Disraeli, *Novels and Tales,* ed. Philip Guedalla, vol. 1 (New York: Knopf, 1927), xv.

6. See the Editorial Collective of *Questions féministes,* "Variations on Common Themes," in *New French Feminisms: An Anthology,* ed. Elaine Marks and Isabelle de Courtivron (New York: Schocken Books, 1981), 222, for a discussion of the political tactic of "kicking women upstairs."

7. Anthony Trollope, *The Prime Minister* (Oxford: Oxford University Press, 1983).

8. Adrienne Munich, *Queen Victoria's Secrets* (New York: Columbia University Press, 1996), 4. Munich also argues that "Victoria's presence on the throne highlighted controversies, debates, concerns, and anxieties about differences between men and women" (7).

9. The idea of politics as a spectator sport, with women favored courtside, is recurrent in Disraeli's own life. When he was first elected prime minister in 1868, his close friend and personal attorney, Sir Philip Rose, reports saying to him: "If only your sister [Sarah] had been alive to witness your triumph what happiness it would have given her," and Disraeli replied: "'Ah, poor Sa! poor Sa! we've lost our audience, we've lost our audience'" (Blake, *Disraeli,* 425).

10. A number of Munich's comments about the symbolic representations of Victoria apply to the character of Sybil as well. Like Victoria, Sybil had a cloistered upbringing (14). Like Victoria, Sybil is a living contradiction—aristocratic yet linked to the common people (3). Munich also discusses the problems that marriage posed to queenly power and suggests that Victoria and Albert's penchant for staging elaborate medieval masked balls symbolically restored male authority because courtly love suggests that "the lady rules by courtesy, but the king forms the apex of the feudal hierarchy, ruling both his lady and his realm" (31). Significantly, courtly love is the ruling motif of Egremont's relationship to Sybil.

11. Thom Braun, *Disraeli the Novelist* (London: George Allen & Unwin, 1981), 108; Yeazell, "Why Political Novels Have Heroines," 128.

12. Gallagher, *Industrial Reformation of English Fiction,* 215; Robert O'Kell, "Two Nations, or One? Disraeli's Allegorical Romance," *Victorian Studies* 30 (winter 1987): 216.

13. John Lucas, "Mrs. Gaskell and Brotherhood," in *Tradition and Tolerance in*

Nineteenth-Century Fiction, ed. David Howard, John Lucas, and John Goode (New York: Barnes & Noble, 1967), 157; Brantlinger, *Spirit of Reform,* 97–104.

14. Gallagher, *Industrial Reformation of English Fiction,* 215; O'Kell, "Two Nations," 216.

15. Gallagher, *Industrial Reformation of English Fiction,* 213.

16. Yeazell also points out that Sybil is "like the ancient prophetesses whom she resembles in name" ("Why Political Novels Have Heroines," 129).

17. See Susan Gubar's "'The Blank Page' and the Issues of Female Creativity," in *Writing and Sexual Difference,* ed. Elizabeth Abel (Chicago: University of Chicago Press, 1982), 73–93, for a full explication of the concept of female virginity and its connection with the image of the blank page.

18. One of the most enjoyable aspects of *Sybil* is that it often includes voices that counter its own apparent agenda—and many of those voices are female. For example, after the beatific entrance of Sybil into the Warner home, Warner's wife remarks: "And is that Gerard's daughter? . . . Only think what it is to gain two pounds a-week, and bring up your daughters in that way—instead of such shameless husseys as our Harriet [one of the factory girls]" (156). In addition to Gerard's salary of two pounds a week, the patronage of the aristocratic Traffords does not hurt, either.

19. Bodenheimer comments, revealingly, that "Stephen Morley makes little sense as a character unless he is understood as a portrait" of such contradictions (*Politics of Story in Victorian Social Fiction,* 183). Also, see Braun for commentary on Disraeli's dismissal of Morley's Owenite politics (*Disraeli the Novelist,* 107). I think my approach deepens these interpretations by explaining why Morley's relationship with Sybil is so central to an evaluation of his politics.

Chapter 4

1. Charlotte Brontë, *Shirley* (Harmondsworth: Penguin, 1974), 377; further citations will appear in the text. The question of what Brontë is doing with the connections she makes between women and the working class in her novels has interested many critics. Interpreting Jane Eyre's statement that "[m]illions are condemned to a stiller doom than mine, and millions are in silent revolt against their lot. Nobody knows how many rebellions besides political rebellions ferment in the masses of life which people earth," Cora Kaplan argues that the passage "does not mark out a moment of conscious reformulation of Brontë's class politics," but, instead, "is a significant moment of incoherence, where the congruence between the subordination of women and the radical view of class oppression becomes, for a few sentences, irresistible" ("Pandora's Box," 173). In *Unbecoming Women: British Women Writers and The Novel of Development* (New York: Columbia University Press, 1993), Susan Fraiman responds to Kaplan with the assertion that "Brontë links Jane's situation as a woman to her plight as a worker for more than a few sentences," an interpretation that *Shirley* also bears out with its more direct connections between women, workers, and rebellion (111). Fraiman's project of stressing the "Chartism" of *Jane Eyre* and pointing out the ways in which it is "inseparable from its feminism" (94) is similar to my own project in reading *Shirley.*

2. Taylor, *Eve and the New Jerusalem,* 159–60.

3. For readings that stress *Shirley*'s failures, see Harsh, *Subversive Heroines,* 115–45; Carol Ohmann, "Charlotte Brontë: The Limits of Her Feminism," *Female Studies* 6 (1972): 152–63; and Donald Stone's *The Romantic Impulse in Victorian Fiction* (Cambridge: Harvard University Press, 1980), 120–26. Readings which positively evaluate *Shirley* on the basis of its feminist power include Helene Moglen, *Charlotte Brontë: The Self Conceived* (New York: Norton, 1976), 152–89; Sandra M. Gilbert and Susan Gubar, *The Madwoman in the Attic: The Woman Writer and the Nineteenth-Century Literary Imagination* (New Haven: Yale University Press, 1979), 372–98; and Janet Gezari, *Charlotte Brontë and Defensive Conduct: The Author and the Body at Risk* (Philadelphia: University of Pennsylvania Press, 1992), 90–124.

4. See Susan Zlotnick, "Luddism, Medievalism and Women's History in *Shirley:* Charlotte Brontë's Revisionist Tactics," *Novel* 24 (spring 1991): 282–95; and Maura Ives, "Housework, Mill Work, Women's Work: The Functions of Cloth in Charlotte Brontë's *Shirley,*" in *Keeping the Victorian House: A Collection of Essays,* ed. Vanessa D. Dickerson (New York: Garland Press, 1995), 259–89.

5. Terry Eagleton, *Myths of Power: A Marxist Study of the Brontës* (New York: Barnes & Noble, 1975), 45.

6. Thompson, *Making of the English Working Class,* 552.

7. See Eagleton, *Myths of Power,* 47–50; and Igor Webb, *From Custom to Capital: The English Novel and the Industrial Revolution* (Ithaca, N.Y.: Cornell University Press, 1981), 132–42.

8. Clark, *Struggle for the Breeches,* 1; also, see Scott on Thompson's *Making of the English Working Class* in *Gender and the Politics of History,* 68–90.

9. Valenze, *First Industrial Woman,* 181.

10. In his influential 1850 review of *Shirley,* George Henry Lewes complained, "The authoress never seems distinctly to have made up her mind as to what she was to do; whether to describe the habits and manners of Yorkshire and its social aspects in the days of King Lud, or to paint a character, or to tell a love story" (unsigned review, cited in *The Brontës: The Critical Heritage,* ed. Miriam Allott [London: Routledge and Kegan Paul, 1974], 165). For later criticism of *Shirley*'s structure and its handling of omniscient narration, see Jacob Korg, "The Problem of Unity in *Shirley,*" *Nineteenth-Century Fiction* 12 (September 1957): 125–36; and Earl A. Knies, *The Art of Charlotte Brontë* (Athens, Ohio: Ohio University Press, 1969), 146–56. For readings that relate the structural problems to *Shirley*'s attempts to link the positions of women and workers, see Marxist-Feminist Literary Collective, "Women's Writing: *Jane Eyre, Shirley, Villette, Aurora Leigh,*" *Ideology and Consciousness* 1 (1978): 35–39; and Bodenheimer, *Politics of Story in Victorian Social Fiction,* 36–53. See, however, Elizabeth Langland's "Dialogue, Discourse, Theft, and Mimicry: Charlotte Brontë Rereads William Makepeace Thackeray" for a defense of Brontë's narrative practice (*Understanding Narrative,* ed. James Phelan and Peter J. Rabinowitz [Columbus: Ohio State University Press, 1994], 246–71).

11. Catherine Belsey, *Critical Practice* (London: Routledge, 1980), 71–72.

12. In *Desire and Domestic Fiction: A Political History of the Novel* (Oxford: Oxford University Press, 1987), Nancy Armstrong classifies *Shirley* as "Charlotte Brontë's most explicitly political novel and one of several less than successful attempts on the part of later novelists to write historical fiction in the tradition of Walter Scott" (213–14). Georg Lukacs's praise of Scott in *The Historical Novel* (reprint, Boston: Beacon Press, 1963) argues that his greatness resides in his ability to represent the contradictions of history yet also to "render visible the generally progressive features of the whole of society, of the whole age" (47): Scott is "a great epic portrayer of the 'age of heroes'" (35), who is able to represent "real, humanly stirring, unproblematic heroism" (50). But, in *Sisters in Time: Imagining Gender in Nineteenth-Century British Fiction* (Oxford: Oxford University Press, 1989), Susan Morgan points out that "Scott was long ago claimed by the men," including Lukacs (56), and she argues that Scott's novels "are historical novels, and history, not as it is lived but as it has been recorded and publicly recalled, has been male. Scott's novels are also about that most masculine of men's activities, armed combat: duels, battles, war" (57). She goes on to argue that women writers, especially the Brontës, "take[s] up and transform[s] Scott's methods and concerns" (57).

13. Zlotnick, "Luddism, Medievalism, and Women's History," 282; also see her *Women, Writing, and the Industrial Revolution,* 88–90.

14. Leslie Rabine, *Reading the Romantic Heroine: Text, History, Ideology* (Ann Arbor: University of Michigan Press, 1986), 112.

15. Asa Briggs, "Private and Social Themes in *Shirley,*" *Brontë Society Transactions* 13, no. 3 (1958): 209.

16. Malcolm I. Thomis and Jennifer Grimmett, *Women in Protest: 1800–1850* (London: Croom Helm, 1982), 49.

17. Clark, *Struggle for the Breeches,* 160.

18. Cited in Thompson, *The Making of the English Working Class,* 537.

19. Eagleton, *Myths of Power,* 49; Webb, *From Custom to Capital,* 135; for a more positive reading, see Bodenheimer, *Politics of Story in Victorian Social Fiction,* 44–45.

20. Cited in Janet L. Larson, "'Who Is Speaking?': *Charlotte Brontë's* Voices of Prophecy," in *Victorian Sages and Cultural Discourse: Renegotiating Gender and Power,* ed. Thais E. Morgan (New Brunswick, N.J.: Rutgers University Press, 1990), 70.

21. See Thompson, *Making of the English Working Class,* 599–601; and Malcolm I. Thomis, *The Luddites: Machine-Breaking in Regency England* (Hamden, Conn.: Archon Books, 1970), 120–21.

22. Janet Gezari, *Charlotte Brontë and Defensive Conduct,* 90.

23. See Leonore Davidoff, "The Separation of Home and Work? Landladies and Lodgers in Nineteenth- and Twentieth-Century England," in *Fit Work for Women,* ed. Sandra Burman (London: Croom Helm, 1979), 64–97.

24. Bruce Robbins, *The Servant's Hand: English Fiction from Below* (Durham: Duke University Press, 1993), 129, 106.

25. Webb, *From Custom to Capital,* 132.

26. Zlotnick, "Luddism, Medievalism, and Women's History," 286.

27. See Taylor, *Eve and the New Jerusalem,* 37–38, 50–52; and Rose, *Limited Livelihoods,* 128.

28. See Gilbert and Gubar, *Madwoman in the Attic,* 376–77; and Gezari, *Charlottë Bronte and Defensive Conduct,* 95–97.

29. See Roslyn Belkin, "Rejects of the Marketplace: Old Maids in Charlotte Brontë's *Shirley,*" *International Journal of Women's Studies* 4, no. 11 (1981): 50–66; Gilbert and Gubar, *Madwoman in the Attic,* 380; and Gezari, *Charlotte Brontë and Defensive Conduct,* 105–6, for discussions of the feminist significance of the old maids.

30. Langland, *Nobody's Angels,* 13–18.

31. Valentine Cunningham, *Everywhere Spoken Against: Dissent in the Victorian Novel* (Oxford: Clarendon Press, 1975), 126, 116, 124–25.

32. Taylor, *Eve and the New Jerusalem,* 159–60.

33. See Eagleton, *Myths of Power,* 45–50, for example.

34. E. P. Thompson cites the following lyric in *Making of the English Working Class:*

Chant no more your old rhymes about bold Robin Hood,
His feats I but little admire.
I will sing the Atchievements [sic] of General Ludd,
Now the Hero of Nottinghamshire. (547)

35. Sally Greene, "Apocalypse When? *Shirley*'s Vision and the Politics of Reading," *Studies in the Novel* 26 (winter 1994): 350–71.

36. Taylor, *Eve and the New Jerusalem,* 162–167, 166.

37. Ibid., 146.

38. Gilbert and Gubar, *Madwoman in the Attic,* 384–86, 394–95; also see Kate Lawson, "Imagining Eve: Charlotte Brontë, Kate Millett, Helene Cixous," *Women's Studies* 24, no. 5 (1995): 411–26.

39. Cited in Taylor, *Eve and the New Jerusalem,* 168.

40. Ibid., 46, 168–70.

41. See, for example, Moglen, *Charlotte Brontë,* 186–89; Rabine, *Reading the Romantic Heroine,* 130–33; and Penny Boumelha, *Charlotte Brontë* (Bloomington: Indiana University Press, 1990), 98–99.

42. Eagleton, *Myths of Power,* 46.

43. Jill Liddington and Jill Norris, *One Hand Tied Behind Us: The Rise of the Women's Suffrage Movement* (London: Virago, 1978), 91–93.

Chapter 5

1. See John D. Baird, "'Divorce and Matrimonial Causes': An Aspect of *Hard Times,*" *Victorian Studies* 20 (summer 1977): 401–12.

2. Nancy Tomes, "A 'Torrent of Abuse': Crimes of Violence between Working-Class Men and Women in London, 1840–1875," *Journal of Social History* 11 (spring 1978): 338, 334, 331.

3. Tomes points out that when husbands and wives fought, neighbors rarely intervened but, if a man was beating a woman not his wife, onlookers would intervene (ibid., 342). Also see A. James Hammerton, "The Targets of 'Rough Music': Re-

spectability and Domestic Violence in Victorian England," *Gender and History* 3 (spring 1991): 23–44; and Ellen Ross, "'Fierce Questions and Taunts': Married Life in Working-Class London, 1870–1914," *Feminist Studies* 8 (fall 1982): 575–602. Hamerton cites an 1850 *Times* editorial that justifies domestic violence while also taking a swipe at working-class men: "If [a working-class man] discovered his wife with a paramour, or found that by her drunkenness she had caused the death of a child, would he appeal to the laws—would he in the former case sue for damages in Doctors' Commons, or petition Parliament for a divorce? No. He would give his wife a sound thrashing, and all the world would think it a very natural act, considering his condition and circumstances" (34). In "Marriage Relations, Money, and Domestic Violence in Working-Class Liverpool, 1919–1939," in *Labour and Love: Women's Experience of Home and Family, 1850–1940,* ed. Jane Lewis (London: Basil Blackwell, 1986), Pat Ayers and Jan Lambertz note an ongoing "pattern of male authority and female responsibility [that] could legitimize male violence within the home, whatever its cause" (197).

4. Tomes, "'Torrent of Abuse,'" 336, 339.

5. Frances Power Cobbe, "Wife-Torture in England," *Contemporary Review* 32 (April 1878): 72–73.

6. Ibid., 58.

7. Ibid., 64, 69.

8. Ibid., 82.

9. In "The Fixed Eye and the Rolling Eye: Surveillance and Discipline in *Hard Times,*" *Studies in the Novel* 21 (spring 1989), Cynthia Northcutt Malone comments that "Sissy's role as the reclaimer and rehabilitator of Louisa deserves close attention. By representing this watchdog of bourgeois morality as a child of the lower classes, *Hard Times* constructs a socially useful myth. Through Sissy Jupe, the novel seems to argue, with F. M. L. Thompson, that the working class did not need instruction in respectable behavior; indeed, *Hard Times* goes further, representing Rachael and Sissy as the moral giants of the novel. This strategy masks the novel's interest in propagating a program of middle-class reform" (22).

10. See Lisa Surridge's "Dogs' Bodies/Women's Bodies: Wives as Pets in Mid-Nineteenth-Century Narratives of Domestic Violence," *Victorian Review* 20 (summer 1994): 1–34, for an analysis of other Dickens novels in which mistreated dogs stand in for mistreated women. In "The Paradox of the Clown in Dickens," *Dickens Studies Annual* 5 (1976), Joseph Butwin sums up Senor Jupe as a clown who "drinks heavily, beats his dog, abandons his daughter, and weeps after every unsuccessful attempt to make people laugh" (116). Placing Jupe's character in the broader context of other clowns in Dickens as well as nineteenth-century art in general, Butwin argues that, far from representing an escape from industrial capitalism, the figure of the weeping clown epitomizes it (132).

11. On the positive side, in *The Great Tradition* (New York: New York University Press, 1960), F. R. Leavis finds Sissy "wholly convincing in the function Dickens assigns to her" (235), and Harsh calls Sissy the novel's "most active force . . . an indispensable influence for good" (*Subversive Heroines,* 86). Weighing in on the negative side, Jean Ferguson Carr argues that "[t]he opposition Sissy seems to represent—of imagination,

emotion, questioning of patriarchal discourses—stands like the circus-master's fancy, a fantastic dream that amuses children but does not displace Gradgrindian fact" (172). Her article, "Writing as a Woman: Dickens, *Hard Times,* and Feminine Discourses," *Dickens Studies Annual* 18 (1989), raises crucial questions about the paradox of Dickens's increasing preoccupation with women, especially oppressed and lower-class women, in his novels at the same time that they defend patriarchal ideology. Carr asks, "why his interest hovers at the edge of articulation, why it goes so far and then retreats, or goes so far and then is silent. Why is Dickens simultaneously empathetic with oppressed women and insistent on the constraints and stereotypes that restrict them? What does his practice suggest about how women are rendered silent in Victorian culture and novels, how their perspective is undermined or preempted?" (163). But about Sissy's function, in particular, Carr claims, "Sissy's discourse derives its power, not from any essential woman's knowledge that Louisa and [Mrs. Gradgrind] could share, but from her experience as a working-class child who knows counter examples and a different world than 'fact'" and that what Sissy represents "has no ability to construct a shared feminine discourse that can alter the rigid polarities of fact and fancy, meaning and no-meaning" (172). I find Sissy's working-class experiences heavily gendered, and I think her description of her life with her father reveals "woman's knowledge" and creates a "feminine discourse," although, because it deals with such shameful topics as domestic violence and abandonment, it may be questioned how openly this discourse can be "shared."

12. I am grateful to Katherine A. Retan's "Lower-Class Angels in the Middle-Class House: The Domestic Woman's 'Progress' in *Hard Times* and *Ruth,*" *Dickens Studies Annual* 23 (1994), for pointing out this reversal. Retan focuses on the issue of sexual taint contained in the paired images of angel and fallen woman, arguing that in earlier Dickens's novels, such as *Dombey and Son* and *Bleak House,* a "daughter's acceptance of shame establishes her identity as a middle-class angel and teaches her that regulatory capacity which, for Dickens and other domestic ideologists, ensures the quality of life associated with the middle-class home. Florence and Esther gain the power to foster those moral values which are seen as an antidote to the dis-ease associated with the public sphere through their encounters with that transgressive sexuality associated with class unrest" (185). In the later *Hard Times,* however, Dickens has become "less optimistic" about the ability of the middle class to reform itself, and this is reflected by the fact that "the middle-class daughter is directly associated with gender and class unrest" (189). It is at this point that Dickens reverses class relations and introduces a lower-class angel into the middle-class household.

13. The absence of such violence in *Hard Times* is made all the more significant when it is compared with other Dickens novels. *The Tale of Two Cities,* of course, directly represents revolution; *Barnaby Rudge* concludes with a riot. Murder is frequently represented. Even domestic violence is very muted in *Hard Times,* as can be seen in comparison to the melodramatic murder of Nancy in *Oliver Twist. Hard Times* also erases the violence of other predecessors. In Frances Trollope's *The Life and Times of Michael Armstrong, the Factory Boy* (1839), the factory owner, Sir Michael Dowling,

whose aggressive personality prefigures Bounderby's, takes sadistic pleasure in beating the factory boy he has adopted. Wilkie Collins was writing *Hide and Seek* while staying with Dickens in 1853. That novel introduces the plot of a circus girl adopted by a middle-class family. In *Hide and Seek*, however, the girl has been so abused by the circus ringmaster that she is now a deaf-mute.

14. David Sonstroem, "Fettered Fancy in *Hard Times*," *PMLA* 84 (May 1969): 523.

15. For discussions of the class and gender implications of metaphor and metonymy, see Stephen J. Spector, "Monsters of Metonymy: *Hard Times* and Knowing the Working Class," *English Literary History* 51 (summer 1984): 365–84; and my article, "*Hard Times* and the Structure of Industrialism: The Novel as Factory," *Studies in the Novel* 21 (summer 1989): 128–37.

16. D. A. Miller, *The Novel and the Police* (Berkeley: University of California Press, 1988), 103.

17. Gallagher, *Industrial Reformation of English Fiction*, 149, 159.

18. Malone, "Fixed Eye and the Rolling Eye" 15, 21.

19. Bodenheimer, *Politics of Story in Victorian Social Fiction*, 205.

20. Laurie Langbauer, *Women and Romance: The Consolations of Gender in the English Novel* (Ithaca, N.Y.: Cornell University Press, 1990), 136, 153–54.

21. Richard Fabrizio, "Wonderful No-Meaning: Language and the Psychopathology of the Family in Dickens' *Hard Times*," *Dickens Studies Annual* 16 (1987): 80.

22. As Fabrizio points out, Blackpool is already in a feminized position because Dickens reverses the roles of husband and wife. In this working-class marriage, it is the wife who stays out, comes home drunk, and is physically abusive: "Blackpool plays the female role—allows his wife to take his property, allows her to dominate him sexually and financially" ("Wonderful No-Meaning," 85). Also see Kristin Flieger Samuelian, "Being Rid of Women: Middle-Class Ideology in *Hard Times*," *The Victorian Newsletter* 82 (fall 1992): 58–61.

23. Baird, "Divorce and Matrimonial Causes," 408.

24. Tomes, "'Torrent of Abuse,'" 337.

25. Sigmund Freud, "A Child Is Being Beaten," in *Collected Papers*, vol. 2, trans. Joan Riviere (New York: Basic Books, 1959), 172–201.

26. Gallagher also points out the disturbing implications of Merrylegs' role, although she does not discuss his beating: "In this ending, exemplary family behavior and 'the wayth of the dogth' are indistinguishable" (*Industrial Reformation of English Fiction*, 158).

27. Michael Hiley, *Victorian Working Women: Portraits from Life* (Boston: David R. Godine, 1979), 48–60.

28. Frances Hodgson Burnett, *That Lass O' Lowries* (Woodbridge, Suffolk: Boydell Press, 1985), 1; further citations will appear in the text.

29. P. J. Keating, *The Working Classes in Victorian Fiction*, 87. Gill Davies' "Foreign Bodies: Images of the London Working Class at the End of the Nineteenth Century," *Literature and History* 14 (spring 1988): 64–80, contains a provocative analysis of monstrous working-class women characters in George Gissing's novels.

30. *Hansard,* Series 3, House of Commons, *Session: 5 February–14 August 1844,* 15 March 1844, vol. 10, cols. 1099–1100.

31. George Gissing, *The Nether World* (New York: Oxford University Press, 1992), 120; further citations will appear in the text.

32. Rudyard Kipling, "The Record of Badalia Herodsfoot," in *The Barwash Edition of the Complete Works in Prose and Verse of Rudyard Kipling,* vol. 5 (New York: Doubleday, 1941), 357; further citations will appear in the text.

33. Tomes, "'Torrent of Abuse,'" 342.

Epilogue

1. Gallagher, *Industrial Reformation of English Fiction,* 219–67.

2. Naomi Schor, *Breaking the Chain: Women, Theory, and French Realist Fiction* (New York: Columbia University Press, 1985).

3. In his examination of the role of servants in *Felix Holt,* Bruce Robbins sees the female servants, Denner and Lyddy, as playing somewhat disruptive roles, although he describes them as "choral rather than causal" (*Servant's Hand,* 95). He argues that male servants have a greater effect on the plot.

4. See Helen Blackburn's *Women's Suffrage: A Record of the Women's Suffrage Movement in the British Isles with Biographical Sketches of Miss Becker* (London: Williams & Norgate, 1902), 12–13, 61–78; and Susan Kingsley Kent's *Sex and Suffrage in Britain, 1860–1914* (Princeton: Princeton University Press, 1987), 187–88. See also Bonnie Zimmerman, "*Felix Holt* and the True Power of Womanhood," *English Literary History* 46 (fall 1979): 432–51, for a discussion of women and politics in the novel.

5. Carole Pateman, *The Disorder of Women: Democracy, Feminism, and Political Theory* (Palo Alto, Calif.: Stanford University Press, 1989), 4–5, 17–18.

6. Cited in Patricia Hollis's *Women in Public: The Women's Movement, 1850–1900: Documents of the Victorian Women's Movement* (London: George Allen & Unwin, 1979), 307–8.

7. Critics have traditionally found Mrs. Transome the most artistically compelling character in the novel, but there are contrasting assessments of her political meaning. William Myers calls her "the spirit of reaction" ("George Eliot: Politics and Personality," in *Literature and Politics in the Nineteenth Century,* ed. John Lucas [London: Methuen, 1971], 125), while Terry Eagleton finds her "a pathetically outdated feudalist" and comments that "the novel mourns in her the death of traditional society" (*Criticism and Ideology* [London: Redwood Burn, 1975], 117). By contrast, Judith Wilt describes Mrs. Transome as "dashingly liberated" in her younger days ("Felix Holt, the Killer: A Reconstruction," *Victorian Studies* 35 [autumn 1991]: 51). Alison Booth and Deirdre David come the closest to my own view in bringing together the conflicting elements in Mrs. Transome's political meaning. Connecting the novel's conservatism to its feminism, Booth argues that "Mrs. Transome's cold lust for power" is "a sign of the self-wounding that comes of angry confrontation with men, as well as a forerunner of hostile images of suffragettes and women's-libbers" ("Not All Men Are Selfish and Cruel: *Felix Holt* as a Feminist Novel," in *Gender and Discourse in Victorian Literature and Art,* ed. Antony H. Harrison and Beverly Taylor [Dekalb, Ill.: Northern Illinois

University Press, 1992], 151). In *Intellectual Women and Victorian Patriarchy: Harriet Martineau, Elizabeth Barrett Browning, George Eliot* (Ithaca, N.Y.: Cornell University Press, 1987), David calls Mrs. Transome "an emblem of a lost and ambiguously valued Toryism" (204) but also sees her as performing "a spectacular work of sabotage" (199), helping the novel to subvert the world of male political action.

8. See John Burnett, David Vincent, and David Mayall, eds., *The Autobiography of the Working Class: An Annotated Critical Bibliography,* vol. 1, 1790–1900 (New York: New York University Press, 1984), xviii. See also Rebecca O'Rourke, "Were There No Women? British Working-Class Writing in the Inter-War Period," *Literature and History* 14 (spring 1988): 48–63. Poetry, however, proves to be more open to working-class women writers than does prose. See, for example, Florence S. Boos's "Cauld Engle-Cheek: Working-Class Women Poets in Victorian Scotland," *Victorian Poetry* 33 (spring 1995): 53–74; and Susan Zlotnick's "Lowly Bards and Incomplete Lyres: Fanny Forrester and the Construction of a Working-Class Woman's Poetic Identity," *Victorian Poetry* 36 (spring 1998): 17–35, for discussions of Victorian poetry by working-class women.

9. William Dodd, *Narrative of the Experience and Sufferings of William Dodd, A Factory Cripple Written by Himself* (London: Cass, 1968).

10. Regenia Gagnier, *Subjectivities: A History of Self-Representation in Britain, 1832–1920* (New York: Oxford University Press, 1991), 143.

11. John Burnett, ed., *Annals of Labour: Autobiographies of British Working-Class People, 1820–1920* (Bloomington: Indiana University Press, 1974), 67–77.

12. Virginia Woolf, preface to *Life As We Have Known It,* ed. Margaret Llewelyn Davies (London: Hogarth Press, 1931), xxxvii.

13. Julia Swindells, *Victorian Writing and Working Women: The Other Side of Silence* (Minneapolis: University of Minnesota Press, 1985), 137–61.

14. Pamela Fox, *Class Fictions: Shame and Resistance in the British Working-Class Novel, 1890–1945* (Durham, N.C.: Duke University Press, 1994), 57, 100–02.

15. Ellen Johnston, "Autobiography of Ellen Johnston, the 'Factory Girl,'" in Zlotnick, *Women, Writing, and the Industrial Revolution,* 261, 260, 262. See Zlotnick's extensive discussion of Johnston's work in ibid., 216–22, and in her "'A Thousand Times I'd Be a Factory Girl.'" Also see Regenia Gagnier on Johnston as well as the other women autobiographers I include here, except for Luck (*Subjectivities,* 49–54, 144–45).

16. Johnston, "Autobiography of Ellen Johnston, the 'Factory Girl,'" 262, 265.

17. Emma Smith, *A Cornish Waif's Story* (New York: E. P. Dutton, 1956), 23, 74.

18. Ibid., 118, 129–30.

19. Annie Kenney, *Memories of a Militant* (London: Edward Arnold & Co., 1924), 12, 22, 15.

20. Ibid., 31, 30.

21. Mrs. Scott, J. P., "A Felt Hat Worker," in Davies, *Life As We Have Known It,* 87, 89, 87, 91.

22. Kathleen Woodward, *Jipping Street: Childhood in a London Slum* (New York: Harper & Brothers, 1928), 1; further citations will appear in the text.

Bibliography

Alexander, Sally. "Women, Class, and Sexual Difference." *History Workshop Journal* 17 (spring 1984): 130–49.

Anderson, Amanda. *Tainted Souls and Painted Faces: The Rhetoric of Fallenness in Victorian Culture.* Ithaca, N.Y.: Cornell University Press, 1993.

Armstrong, Nancy. *Desire and Domestic Fiction: A Political History of the Novel.* New York: Oxford University Press, 1987.

Auerbach, Nina. "Dickens and Dombey: A Daughter After All." *Dickens Studies Annual* 5 (1976): 95–114.

Ayers, Pat, and Jan Lambertz. "Marriage Relations, Money, and Domestic Violence in Working-Class Liverpool, 1919–39." In *Labour and Love: Women's Experience of Home and Family, 1850–1940,* edited by Jane Lewis, 195–219. London: Basil Blackwell, 1986.

Baird, John D. "'Divorce and Matrimonial Causes': An Aspect of *Hard Times.*" *Victorian Studies* 20 (summer 1977): 401–12.

Belkin, Roslyn. "Rejects of the Marketplace: Old Maids in Charlotte Brontë's *Shirley.*" *International Journal of Women's Studies* 4, no. 1 (1981): 50–66.

Bell's Penny Sunday Chronicle, 15 May–12 June 1842.

Belsey, Catherine. *Critical Practice.* London: Routledge, 1980.

Blackburn, Helen. *Women's Suffrage: A Record of the Women's Suffrage Movement in the British Isles with Biographical Sketches of Miss Becker.* London: Williams & Norgate, 1902.

Blake, Robert. *Disraeli.* New York: St. Martin's Press, 1967.

Bodenheimer, Rosemarie. *The Politics of Story in Victorian Social Fiction.* Ithaca, N.Y.: Cornell University Press, 1988.

———. "Private Grief and Public Acts in *Mary Barton.*" *Dickens Studies Annual* 9 (1981): 195–216.

Boos, Florence S. "Cauld Engle-Cheek: Working-Class Women Poets in Victorian Scotland." *Victorian Poetry* 33 (spring 1995): 53–74.

Booth, Alison. "Not All Men Are Selfish and Cruel: *Felix Holt* as a Feminist Novel." In *Gender and Discourse in Victorian Literature and Art,* edited by Antony H. Harrison and Beverly Taylor, 143–60. Dekalb, Ill.: Northern Illinois University Press, 1992.

Boumelha, Penny. *Charlotte Brontë.* Bloomington: Indiana University Press, 1990.

Brantlinger, Patrick. *The Spirit of Reform: British Literature and Politics, 1832–1867.* Cambridge: Harvard University Press, 1977.

Braun, Thom. *Disraeli the Novelist.* London: George Allen & Unwin, 1981.

Briggs, Asa. "Private and Social Themes in *Shirley.*" *Brontë Society Transactions* 13, no. 3 (1958): 203–19.

Brontë, Charlotte. *Shirley.* 1849. Harmondsworth: Penguin, 1974.

———. *Jane Eyre.* 1847. Harmondsworth: Penguin, 1968.

Burnett, Frances Hodgson. *That Lass O' Lowries.* 1877. Woodbridge, Suffolk: Boydell Press, 1985.

Burnett, John, ed. *Annals of Labour: Autobiographies of British Working-Class People, 1820–1920.* Bloomington: Indiana University Press, 1974.

Burnett, John, David Vincent, and David Mayall, eds. *The Autobiography of the Working Class: An Annotated Critical Bibliography.* Vol.1: *1790–1900.* New York: New York University Press, 1984.

Butler, Josephine. *An Autobiographical Memoir.* London: J. W. Arrowsmith, 1909.

Butwin, Joseph. "*Hard Times:* The News and the Novel." *Nineteenth-Century Fiction* 32 (September 1977): 166–87.

———. "The Paradox of the Clown in Dickens." *Dickens Studies Annual* 5 (1976): 115–32.

Carr, Jean Ferguson. "Writing as a Woman: Dickens, *Hard Times,* and Feminine Discourses." *Dickens Studies Annual* 18 (1989): 161–78.

Cazamian, Louis. *The Social Novel in England, 1830–1850.* Trans. Martin Fido. Boston: Routledge & Kegan Paul, 1973.

Clark, Anna. "The Politics of Seduction in English Popular Culture, 1748–1848." In *The Progress of Romance: The Politics of Popular Fiction,* edited by Jean Radford, 47–70. London: Routledge & Kegan Paul, 1986.

———. *The Struggle for the Breeches: Gender and the Making of the British Working Class.* Berkeley: University of California Press, 1995.

———. *Women's Silence, Men's Violence: Sexual Assault in England, 1770–1845.* London: Pandora, 1987.

Cobbe, Frances Power. "Wife-Torture in England." *Contemporary Review* 32 (April 1878): 55–87.

Collett, Clara. "Women's Work." In *Life and Labour of the People of London,* edited by Charles Booth, 256–327. New York: AMS Press, 1970.

Collins, Wilkie. *Hide and Seek.* 1854. New York: Dover, 1981.

Cunningham, Valentine. *Everywhere Spoken Against: Dissent in the Victorian Novel.* Oxford: Clarendon Press, 1975.

David, Deirdre. *Fictions of Resolution in Three Victorian Novels.* New York: Columbia University Press, 1981.

———. *Intellectual Women and Victorian Patriarchy: Harriet Martineau, Elizabeth Barrett Browning, George Eliot.* Ithaca, N.Y.: Cornell University Press, 1987.

Davidoff, Leonore. "The Separation of Home and Work? Landladies and Lodgers in Nineteenth- and Twentieth-Century England." In *Fit Work for Women,* edited by Sandra Burman, 64–97. London: Croom Helm, 1979.

Davies, Gill. "Foreign Bodies: Images of the London Working Class at the End of the Nineteenth Century." *Literature and History* 14 (spring 1988): 64–80.

Davies, Margaret Llewelyn, ed. *Life As We Have Known It.* London: Hogarth Press, 1931.

Dickens, Charles. *Hard Times.* 1854. Harmondsworth: Penguin, 1969.

Disraeli, Benjamin. *Novels and Tales.* Vol. 1. Bradenham ed., edited by Philip Guedalla. New York: Knopf, 1927.

———. *Sybil, or The Two Nations.* 1845. Harmondsworth: Penguin, 1980.

Dodd, William. *Narrative of the Experience and Sufferings of William Dodd, A Factory Cripple Written by Himself.* 1841. London: Cass, 1968.

Dutton, H. I., and J. E. King. *'Ten Per Cent and No Surrender': The Preston Strike: 1853–1854.* New York: Cambridge University Press, 1981.

Eagleton, Terry. *Criticism and Ideology.* London: Redwood Burn, 1975.

———. *Myths of Power: A Marxist Study of the Brontes.* New York: Barnes & Noble, 1975.

Editorial Collective of *Questions féministes.* "Variations on Common Themes." In *New French Feminisms: An Anthology,* edited by Elaine Marks and Isabelle de Courtivron, 212–30. New York: Schocken Books, 1981.

Eliot, George. *Felix Holt, the Radical.* 1866. Harmondsworth: Penguin, 1972.

Fabrizio, Richard. "Wonderful No-Meaning: Language and the Psychopathology of the Family in Dickens' *Hard Times.*" *Dickens Studies Annual* 16 (1987): 61–93.

Fox, Celina. "The Development of Social Reportage in English Periodical Illustration during the 1840s and Early 1850s." *Past and Present* 74, no. 74 (1977): 90–111.

Fox, Pamela. *Class Fictions: Shame and Resistance in the British Working-Class Novel, 1890–1945.* Durham, N.C.: Duke University Press, 1994.

Fraiman, Susan. *Unbecoming Women: British Women Writers and the Novel of Development.* New York: Columbia University Press, 1993.

Freud, Sigmund. "A Child Is Being Beaten." In *Collected Papers,* vol. 2. Translated by Joan Riviere, 172–201. New York: Basic Books, 1959.

Gagnier, Regenia. *Subjectivities: A History of Self-Representation in Britain, 1832–1920.* New York: Oxford University Press, 1991.

Gallagher, Catherine. *The Industrial Reformation of English Fiction: Social Discourse and Narrative Form, 1832–1867.* Chicago: University of Chicago Press, 1985.

Gaskell, Elizabeth. *Mary Barton.* 1848. Harmondsworth: Penguin, 1970.

———. *North and South.* 1854–55. Harmondsworth: Penguin, 1970.

Gaskell, Peter. *The Manufacturing Population of England: Its Moral, Social, and Physical Conditions, and the Changes Which Have Arisen from the Use of Steam Machinery.* London: Baldwin & Cradock, 1833.

Gezari, Janet. *Charlotte Brontë and Defensive Conduct: The Author and the Body at Risk.* Philadelphia: University of Pennsylvania Press, 1992.

Gilbert, Sandra M., and Susan Gubar. *The Madwoman in the Attic: The Woman Writer and the Nineteenth-Century Literary Imagination.* New Haven: Yale University Press, 1979.

Gissing, George. *The Nether World.* 1889. New York: Oxford University Press, 1992.

Greene, Sally. "Apocalypse When? *Shirley*'s Vision and the Politics of Reading." *Studies in the Novel* 26 (winter 1994): 350–71.

Greimas, A. J., and François Rastier. "The Interaction of Semiotic Constraints." *Yale French Studies* 41 (1968): 86–105.

Gubar, Susan. "'The Blank Page' and the Issues of Female Creativity." In *Writing and Sexual Difference*, edited by Elizabeth Abel, 73–93. Chicago: University of Chicago Press, 1982.

Hammerton, A. James. "The Targets of 'Rough Music': Respectability and Domestic Violence in Victorian England." *Gender and History* 3 (spring 1991): 23–44.

Hansard. Series 3. House of Commons. "First Report of the Commissioners on the Mines." *Session: 3 February–12 August 1842*, vols. 15–17.

———. Series 3. House of Commons. "First Report of the Factories Inquiry Commission." *Session: 5 February–10 August 1833*, vol. 20.

Harman, Barbara Leah. *The Feminine Political Novel in Victorian England*. Charlottesville: University Press of Virginia, 1998.

Harsh, Constance D. *Subversive Heroines: Feminist Resolutions of Social Crisis in the Condition-of-England Novel*. Ann Arbor: Michigan University Press, 1994.

Hewitt, Margaret. *Wives and Mothers in Victorian Industry*. London: Rockliff, 1958.

Hiley, Michael. *Victorian Working Women: Portraits from Life*. Boston: David R. Godine, 1979.

Hollis, Patricia. *Women in Public: The Women's Movement, 1850–1900: Documents of the Victorian Women's Movement*. London: George Allen & Unwin, 1979.

Ingham, Patricia. *The Language of Gender and Class: Transformation in the Victorian Novel*. London: Routledge, 1996.

Ives, Maura. "Housework, Mill Work, Women's Work: The Functions of Cloth in Charlotte Brontë's *Shirley*." In *Keeping the Victorian House: A Collection of Essays*, edited by Vanessa D. Dickerson, 259–89. New York: Garland Press, 1995.

Jameson, Anna. "Condition of the Women and the Female Children." *Athenaeum*, 18 Mar. 1843: 257–58.

Jameson, Fredric. *The Political Unconscious: Narrative as a Socially Symbolic Act*. Ithaca, N.Y.: Cornell University Press, 1981.

John, Angela V. *By the Sweat of Their Brow: Women Workers at Victorian Coal Mines*. London: Croom Helm. 1980.

———. *Coalmining Women: Victorian Lives and Campaigns*. Cambridge: Cambridge University Press, 1984.

———. "Colliery Legislation and Its Consequences: 1842 and the Women Miners of Lancashire." *Bulletin of the John Rylands University Library of Manchester* 61 (autumn 1978): 78–114.

Johnson, Patricia E. "*Hard Times* and the Structure of Industrialism: The Novel as Factory." *Studies in the Novel* 21 (summer 1989): 128–37.

Johnston, Ellen. "Autobiography of Ellen Johnston, the 'Factory Girl.'" In Susan Zlotnick's *Women, Writing, and the Industrial Revolution*, 257–66. Baltimore: Johns Hopkins University Press, 1998.

Kaplan, Cora. "'Like a Housemaid's Fancies': The Representation of Working-Class

Women in Nineteenth-Century Writing." In *Grafts: Feminist Cultural Criticism,* edited by Susan Sheridan, 55–75. London: Verso Press, 1988.

———. "Pandora's Box: Subjectivity, Class, and Sexuality in Socialist Feminist Criticism." In *Sea Changes: Essays on Culture and Feminism,* 147–76. London: Verso Press, 1986.

Kaplan, Deborah. "The Woman Worker in Charlotte Elizabeth Tonna's Fiction." *Mosaic* 18 (spring 1985): 51–63.

Keating, P. J. *The Working Classes in Victorian Fiction.* New York: Barnes & Noble, 1971.

Kenney, Annie. *Memories of a Militant.* London: Edward Arnold & Co., 1924.

Kent, Susan Kingsley. *Sex and Suffrage in Britain, 1860–1914.* Princeton: Princeton University Press, 1987.

Kestner, Joseph. *Protest and Reform: The British Social Narrative by Women, 1827–1867.* Madison: University of Wisconsin Press, 1985.

Kettle, Arnold. "The Early Victorian Social-Problem Novel." In *The Pelican Guide to English Literature,* vol. 6, edited by Boris Ford, 169–87. Baltimore: Penguin, 1958.

Kingsley, Charles. *Alton Locke, Tailor and Poet: An Autobiography.* 1850. New York: Oxford University Press, 1983.

Kipling, Rudyard. "The Record of Badalia Herodsfoot." In *The Barwash Edition of the Complete Works in Prose and Verse of Rudyard Kipling,* vol. 5, 357–83. New York: Doubleday, 1941.

Knies, Earl A. *The Art of Charlotte Brontë.* Athens, Ohio: Ohio University Press, 1969.

Korg, Jacob. "The Problem of Unity in *Shirley.*" *Nineteenth-Century Fiction* 12 (September 1957): 125–36.

Krueger, Christine L. *The Reader's Repentance: Women Preachers, Women Writers, and Nineteenth-Century Social Discourse.* Chicago: University of Chicago Press, 1992.

Lambertz, Jan. "Sexual Harassment in the Nineteenth-Century Cotton Industry." *History Workshop* 19 (1985): 29–61.

Langbauer, Laurie. *Women and Romance: The Consolations of Gender in the English Novel.* Ithaca, N.Y.: Cornell University Press, 1990.

Langland, Elizabeth. "Dialogue, Discourse, Theft, and Mimicry: Charlotte Brontë Rereads William Makepeace Thackeray." In *Understanding Narrative,* edited by James Phelan and Peter J. Rabinowitz, 246–71. Columbus: Ohio State University Press, 1994.

———. *Nobody's Angels: Middle-Class Women and Domestic Ideology in Victorian Culture.* Ithaca, N.Y.: Cornell University Press, 1995.

Larson, Janet L. "'Who Is Speaking?' Charlotte Brontë's Voices of Prophecy." In *Victorian Sages and Cultural Discourse: Renegotiating Gender and Power,* edited by Thais E. Morgan, 66–86. New Brunswick, N.J.: Rutgers University Press, 1990.

Lawson, Kate. "Imagining Eve: Charlotte Brontë, Kate Millett, Helene Cixous." *Women's Studies* 24, no. 5 (1995): 411–26.

Leavis, F. R. *The Great Tradition.* New York: New York University Press, 1960.

Levy, Anita. *Other Women: The Writing of Class, Race, and Gender, 1832–1898.* Princeton: Princeton University Press, 1991.

Lewes, George Henry. Unsigned review of *Shirley*. In *The Brontës: The Critical Heritage,* edited by Miriam Allott. London: Routledge & Kegan Paul, 1974.

Liddington, Jill, and Jill Norris. *One Hand Tied behind Us: The Rise of the Women's Suffrage Movement.* London: Virago, 1978.

Lucas, John. "Mrs. Gaskell and Brotherhood." In *Tradition and Tolerance in Nineteenth-Century Fiction,* edited by David Howard, John Lucas, and John Goode, 141–205. New York: Barnes & Noble, 1967.

Lukacs, Georg. *The Historical Novel.* Boston: Beacon Press, 1963.

Macherey, Pierre. *A Theory of Literary Production.* Translated by Geoffrey Wall. London: Routledge, 1978.

MacKinnon, Catharine A. *Sexual Harassment of Working Women: A Case of Sex Discrimination.* New Haven: Yale University Press, 1979.

Malone, Cynthia Northcutt. "The Fixed Eye and the Rolling Eye: Surveillance and Discipline in *Hard Times.*" *Studies in the Novel* 21 (spring 1989): 14–26.

Marxist-Feminist Literary Collective. "Women's Writing: *Jane Eyre, Shirley, Villette, Aurora Leigh.*" *Ideology and Consciousness* 1 (1978): 27–48.

Melada, Ivan. *The Captain of Industry in English Fiction, 1821–1871.* Albuquerque: University of New Mexico Press, 1970.

Michie, Elsie B. *Outside the Pale: Cultural Exclusion, Gender Difference, and the Victorian Woman Writer.* Ithaca, N.Y.: Cornell University Press, 1993.

Miller, D. A. *The Novel and the Police.* Berkeley: University of California Press, 1988.

Moglen, Helene. *Charlotte Brontë: The Self Conceived.* New York: Norton, 1976.

Morgan, Susan. *Sisters in Time: Imagining Gender in Nineteenth-Century British Fiction.* Oxford: Oxford University Press, 1989.

Mort, Frank. *Dangerous Sexualities: Medico-Moral Politics in England Since 1830.* 2d ed. London: Routledge & Kegan Paul, 1987.

Munich, Adrienne. *Queen Victoria's Secrets.* New York: Columbia University Press, 1996.

Myers, William. "George Eliot: Politics and Personality." In *Literature and Politics in the Nineteenth Century,* edited by John Lucas, 105–30. London: Methuen, 1971.

Nead, Lynda. *Myths of Sexuality: Representations of Women in Victorian Britain.* Oxford: Basil Blackwell, 1988.

Neff, Wanda Fraiken. *Victorian Working Women: An Historical and Literary Study of Women in British Industries and Professions, 1832–1850.* New York: Columbia University Press, 1929.

Nord, Deborah Epstein. *Walking the Victorian Streets: Women, Representation, and the City.* Ithaca, N.Y.: Cornell University Press, 1995.

Ohmann, Carol. "Charlotte Brontë: The Limits of Her Feminism." *Female Studies* 6 (1972): 152–63.

O'Kell, Robert. "Two Nations, or One? Disraeli's Allegorical Romance." *Victorian Studies* 30 (winter 1987): 211–34.

O'Rourke, Rebecca. "Were There No Women? British Working-Class Writing in the Inter-War Period." *Literature and History* 14 (spring 1988): 48–63.

Pateman, Carole. *The Disorder of Women: Democracy, Feminism, and Political Theory.* Palo Alto, Calif.: Stanford University Press, 1989.

Pinchbeck, Ivy. *Women Workers and the Industrial Revolution, 1750–1850.* London: Virago, 1981.

Poovey, Mary. *Uneven Developments: The Ideological Work of Gender in Mid-Victorian England.* Chicago: University of Chicago Press, 1988.

Rabine, Leslie. *Reading the Romantic Heroine: Text, History, Ideology.* Ann Arbor: University of Michigan Press, 1986.

Retan, Katherine A. "Lower-Class Angels in the Middle-Class House: The Domestic Woman's 'Progress' in *Hard Times* and *Ruth.*" *Dickens Studies Annual* 23 (1994): 183–204.

Robbins, Bruce. *The Servant's Hand: English Fiction from Below.* Durham, N.C.: Duke University Press, 1993.

Rose, Sonya O. *Limited Livelihoods: Gender and Class in Nineteenth-Century England.* Berkeley: University of California Press, 1992.

Ross, Ellen. "'Fierce Questions and Taunts': Married Life in Working-Class London, 1870–1914." *Feminist Studies* 8 (fall 1982): 575–602.

Sampson, Jennifer. "*Sybil,* or the Two Monarchs." *Studies in Philology* 95 (winter 1998): 97–119.

Samuelian, Kristin Flieger. "Being Rid of Women: Middle-Class Ideology in *Hard Times.*" *Victorian Newsletter* 82 (fall 1992): 58–61.

Schor, Naomi. *Breaking the Chain: Women, Theory, and French Realist Fiction.* New York: Columbia University Press, 1985.

Scott, Joan Wallach. *Gender and the Politics of History.* New York: Columbia University Press, 1988.

Seccombe, Wally. "Patriarchy Stabilized: The Construction of the Male Breadwinner Wage Norm in Nineteenth-Century Britain." *Social History* 11 (January 1986): 53–76.

Smith, Emma. *A Cornish Waif's Story.* New York: E. P. Dutton, 1956.

Smith, Sheila M. *The Other Nation: The Poor in English Novels of the 1840s and 1850s.* Oxford: Clarendon Press, 1980.

Sonstroem, David. "Fettered Fancy in *Hard Times.*" *PMLA* 84 (May 1969): 520–29.

Spector, Stephen J. "Monsters of Metonymy: *Hard Times* and Knowing the Working Class." *English Literary History* 51 (summer 1984): 365–84.

Stevenson, Catherine Barnes. "'What Must Not Be Said': *North and South* and the Problem of Women's Work." *Victorian Literature and Culture* 19 (1991): 67–84.

Stone, Donald. *The Romantic Impulse in Victorian Fiction.* Cambridge: Harvard University Press, 1980.

Surridge, Lisa. "Dogs' Bodies/Women's Bodies: Wives as Pets in Mid-Nineteenth-Century Narratives of Domestic Violence." *Victorian Review* 20 (summer 1994): 1–34.

Swindells, Julia. *Victorian Writing and Working Women: The Other Side of Silence.* Minneapolis: University of Minnesota Press, 1985.

Taylor, Barbara. *Eve and the New Jerusalem: Socialism and Feminism in the Nineteenth Century.* London: Virago Press, 1983.

Thomis, Malcolm I. *The Luddites: Machine-Breaking in Regency England.* Hamden, Conn.: Archon Books, 1970.

Thomis, Malcolm I., and Jennifer Grimmett. *Women in Protest: 1800–1850.* London: Croom Helm, 1982.

Thompson, Dorothy. "Women and Nineteenth-Century Radical Politics: A Lost Dimension." In *The Rights and Wrongs of Women,* edited by Juliet Mitchell and Ann Oakley, 112–38. Harmondsworth: Penguin, 1976.

Thompson, E. P. *The Making of the English Working Class.* New York: Vintage Books, 1966.

Tillotson, Kathleen. *Novels of the Eighteen-Forties.* New York: Oxford University Press, 1961.

Tomes, Nancy. "A 'Torrent of Abuse': Crimes of Violence between Working-Class Men and Women in London, 1840–1875." *Journal of Social History* 11 (spring 1978): 328–45.

Tonna, Charlotte Elizabeth. *Helen Fleetwood.* In *The Works of Charlotte Elizabeth,* vol. 2, 503–644. New York: M. W. Dodd, 1844.

———. *The Wrongs of Women.* New York: J. S. Taylor & Co., 1843.

Trollope, Anthony. *The Prime Minister.* 1876. Oxford: Oxford University Press, 1983.

Trollope, Frances. *The Life and Adventures of Michael Armstrong, the Factory Boy.* 1839. London: Frank Cass & Co., 1968.

Valenze, Deborah. *The First Industrial Woman.* New York: Oxford University Press, 1995.

Valverde, Marianna. "'Giving the Female a Domestic Turn': The Social, Legal, and Moral Regulation of Women's Work in British Cotton Mills, 1820–1850." *Journal of Social History* 21, no. 4 (1988): 619–34.

———. "The Love of Finery: Fashion and the Fallen Woman in Nineteenth-Century Social Discourse." *Victorian Studies* 32 (winter 1989): 169–88.

Vincent, David. *Bread, Knowledge, and Freedom: A Study of Nineteenth-Century Working-Class Autobiography.* London: Europa Publications, 1981.

Webb, Igor. *From Custom to Capital: The English Novel and the Industrial Revolution.* Ithaca, N.Y.: Cornell University Press, 1981.

Walkowitz, Judith R. *City of Dreadful Delight: Narratives of Sexual Danger in Late Victorian London.* Chicago: University of Chicago Press, 1992.

———. *Prostitution and Victorian Society: Women, Class, and the State.* Cambridge: Cambridge University Press, 1980.

Westminster Review. Article on the *First Report of the Children's Employment Commissioners: Mines and Collieries.* Vol. 38 (1842): 86–139.

Wheeler, Michael. "Two Tales of Manchester Life." *The Gaskell Society Journal* 3 (1989): 6–28.

Williams, Raymond. *Culture and Society, 1780–1950.* New York: Harper & Row, 1958.

Wilt, Judith. "Felix Holt, the Killer: A Reconstruction." *Victorian Studies* 35 (autumn 1991): 51–69.

Woodward, Kathleen. *Jipping Street: Childhood in a London Slum.* New York: Harper & Brothers, 1928.

Yeazell, Ruth Bernard. "Why Political Novels Have Heroines: *Sybil, Mary Barton,* and *Felix Holt.*" *Novel* 18 (winter 1985): 126–44.

Zimmerman, Bonnie. "*Felix Holt* and the True Power of Womanhood." *English Literary History* 46 (fall 1979): 432–51.

Zlotnick, Susan. "'A Thousand Times I'd Be a Factory Girl': Dialect, Domesticity, and Working-Class Women's Poetry in Victorian Britain." *Victorian Studies* 35 (autumn 1991): 7–27.

———. "Lowly Bards and Incomplete Lyres: Fanny Forrester and the Construction of a Working-Class Woman's Poetic Identity." *Victorian Poetry* 36 (spring 1998): 17–35.

———. "Luddism, Medievalism, and Women's History in *Shirley:* Charlotte Brontë's Revisionist Tactics." *Novel* 24 (spring 1991): 282–95.

———. *Women, Writing, and the Industrial Revolution.* Baltimore: Johns Hopkins University Press, 1998.

Index

XYZ